Creating excellence in the boardroom

THE HENLEY MANAGEMENT SERIES

Series Adviser: Professor Bernard Taylor

Also available in the McGraw-Hill Henley Management Series:

MANAGING INFORMATION
Information systems for today's general manager
A V Knight and D J Silk   ISBN 0-07-707086-0

THE NEW GENERAL MANAGER
Confronting the key challenge of today's organization
Paul Thorne   ISBN 0-07-707083-6

THE COMPETITIVE ORGANIZATION
Managing for organizational excellence
Gordon Pearson   ISBN 0-07-707480-7

TOTAL CAREER MANAGEMENT
Strategies for creating management careers
Frances A Clark   ISBN 0-07-707558-7

CREATING THE GLOBAL COMPANY
Successful internationalization
Dr Colin Coulson-Thomas   ISBN 0-07-707599-4

THE HANDBOOK OF PROJECT-BASED MANAGEMENT
Improving the Processes for Achieving Strategic Objectives
Rodney Turner   ISBN 0-07-707656-7

Details of these and other titles in the series are available from:

The Product Manager, Professional Books, McGraw-Hill Book Company
Europe, Shoppenhangers Road, Maidenhead, Berkshire SL6 2QL
Telephone 0628 23432   Fax 0628 770224

Creating excellence in the boardroom

A guide to shaping directorial competence and board effectiveness

Colin Coulson-Thomas

McGRAW-HILL BOOK COMPANY

London · New York · St Louis · San Francisco · Auckland
Bogotá · Caracas · Lisbon · Madrid · Mexico · Milan
Montreal · New Delhi · Panama · Paris · San Juan
São Paulo · Singapore · Sydney · Tokyo · Toronto

Published by
McGRAW-HILL Book Company Europe
Shoppenhangers Road, Maidenhead, Berkshire SL6 2QL, England
Telephone 0628 23432
Fax 0628 770224

British Library Cataloguing in Publication Data
Coulson-Thomas, Colin
  Creating Excellence in the Boardroom:
  Guide to Shaping Directorial Competence
  and Board Effectiveness. – (Henley
  Management Series)
  I. Title   II. Series
  658.4

  ISBN 0-07-707796-2

Library of Congress Cataloging-in-Publication Data
Coulson-Thomas, Colin.
    Creating excellence in the boardroom: a guide to shaping
  directorial competence and board effectiveness / Colin Coulson
  -Thomas.
      p.   cm. — (Henley management series.)
    Includes bibliographical references and index.
    ISBN 0-07-707796-2
    1. Directors of corporations. 2. Corporate governance.
  I. Title.   II. Series.
  HD2745.C65   1993
  658.4'22—dc20   93-892
                                                                   CIP

First published 1993

12345 CUP 96543

Typeset by BookEns Ltd, Baldock, Herts,
and printed and bound in Great Britain at the University Press, Cambridge.

For Tat and Père

Contents

Acknowledgements

I would like to thank my research collaborator Alan Wakelam of Exeter University, my Adaptation colleague Susan Coulson-Thomas, and John Harper and his team at the Centre for Director Development of the Institute of Directors for their encouragement, help and support.

My own interest in directors and boards stems from a period I spent at the Institute of Directors some years ago. The Institute has sustained a continuing and single-minded commitment to developing directors and raising directorial standards. It deserves the general thanks of all those who are concerned with excellence in the boardroom.

It is particularly pleasing to have this book published in the Henley Management Series. I have had the good fortune to work on other projects with Professors Bernard Taylor and Keith Macmillan of Henley. Both have a long-standing interest in directors and boards.

In order to cover a broad field, I have been very selective in my choice of what to include in this book. Any deficiencies are entirely my own responsibility. I hope this contribution does justice to the urgent need to raise understanding and performance in the boardroom, and encourage and develop fresh directorial talent.

1
Introduction

The board of directors is the mind and will of the company . . . the source of power and authority, the fount of inspiration and leadership. (RICHARD MASTERMAN, chairman, Key Organics Ltd and other companies.)

1.1 Directors and boards under scrutiny

If a company had a heart or a soul it would be found in the boardroom. Intelligence and strength might be discovered in greater measure elsewhere within the corporate organization, but whether or not the company will live and grow, or wither and die, will depend upon the purpose established by the board. It will depend upon the values, the sense of will to generate customer satisfaction, and the drive to achieve excellence and quality that emanates from the board.

Purpose, values, will and drive are the essential items that attract people to the company, whether as customers or as employees. Purpose, values, will and drive all find their expression in a compelling and shared vision that is distinctive and motivates. The vision, which is the essence of the purpose of the company, is articulated by the board. It is communicated by the directors, and will influence attitudes and behaviour to the extent that the board is visibly committed to its achievement.

Or is it? Does this view of the author represent what could be, or perhaps should be, rather than what is? What about the 'rubber stamp' board, or the supine board that is dominated by the chief executive officer (CEO)? What should the relationship be between board and management, and how can, and should, the board 'add value'?

1.2 The board: an enabler or a burden?

If commitment is lacking in the boardroom, or if there are divisions among the boardroom team, this is likely to be detected elsewhere. A company can be cramped and stunted by a lack of vision among members of the board. Divisions can encourage the 'office politicians' to play one director against another. Major changes are generally more difficult to introduce when the top team is not united.

In determining their own standards of behaviour and performance many managers take their cue from director role models. Concentric rings of negative and destructive influences can emanate from and spread out from the boardroom, corrupting and sapping the loyalty and commitment of those they reach. Inconsistencies between rhetoric and conduct, or the failure of actions to match words, can undermine trust and lead to cynicism and despair.

It is difficult for an ambitious executive to aspire to any vision when the directors are blinkered and inhibited. In such conditions, the full potential of people will not be harnessed and assets are likely to be underutilized. In spite of its strengths and its unfocused energy, the company may fail or be taken over by another boardroom team that may, or may not, perform more effectively.

In competitive markets, the very existence of a company may be under constant threat. Sustained corporate success cannot be assumed. A corporation requires 'lifespace', and the board has a crucial role to play in establishing, defending and renegotiating it.[1]

When failure occurs, directors come under the spotlight. Investors may have lost money. Customers may have been let down. Hard-working employees may feel betrayed by the members of their company's board. Some may feel they have been duped. There will be those who show resentment and anger.

An examination of companies in crisis has revealed a link between corporate decline and board inadequacy and ineffectiveness.[2] *The key to sustained corporate success is an effective board composed of a united team of competent directors.* This relatively simple statement is rarely contradicted, but is infrequently sought – and excellence in the boardroom can be difficult to achieve. In a great many companies no-one is consciously focusing upon board effectiveness or the competence of directors. No steps are being taken to enhance either of them.

1.3 Rationale for the book

At the start of the 1990s companies and their boards operate in a turbulent and demanding business environment. A growing burden of legal duties and responsibilities has been placed upon directors. Yet, in respect of the boardroom, confusions, myths and misunderstandings abound. What is or should be the role of the board? Given the differences between companies and their market contexts, can the competencies of a director be defined? Paradoxically, the more management is understood, the greater the risk of failing to think through the distinction between direction and management.

Because a crucial element of the distinction between direction and management lies in the legal duties and responsibilities of directors, much that is written about directors and boards can appear arid and inaccessible to other than lawyers and accountants. What directors actually do, and what characterizes the competent director and the effective board tends to be overlooked. Much is written in the specialist media about the requirements of the latest legislation, but other than the occasional academic study of strategy formulation, there is a relative dearth of material on directors and boards.

This book aims to go some way towards remedying this deficiency. Its focus is upon the role of the board, and the creation of an effective board that is able to complement, and add value to, management in the development and adaptation of a business to meet changing customer requirements.

The development of competent directors, and the establishment and maintenance of a coherent and productive boardroom team, is the subject of another book by the author on 'developing directors' which appears in the McGraw-Hill training series.[3] The 'companion' book examines preferences regarding sources of training as well as barriers to training, before attempting some conclusions and recommendations concerning how boardroom effectiveness might be improved by appropriate training. It also contains exercises that can be used both by directors as individuals, and by boardroom teams, to address most of the issues raised in this book. It therefore acts as a workbook to accompany the present volume.

1.4 The evidence

Both books draw upon a programme of questionnaire and interview surveys undertaken by the author which examine the function, size and composition of boards, as perceived by directors themselves (see Appendix 2). The surveys cover the frequency of board meetings, the criteria used in selecting board members, the contribution expected from board members, how the effectiveness of individual directors is assessed and how effectively they work as a team, the requirement to remain up to date, and professional development preferences.

Over 900 individual directors have participated in the research programme, and over two-thirds of these have positions as chairman, CEO or managing director of a company. As a consequence of the findings, nine distinct categories of services have been developed to improve the performance of both individual directors and boardroom teams. These are available from selected professional associations and other specialist organizations.

The boards covered by the surveys are representative of the total population of companies. The replies to most of the questions that were posed in the course of the surveys do not appear to be significantly influenced by company size or status. Hence, the findings are thought to be applicable to a wide range of boards. A project undertaken by the author for the UK's Department of Employment to develop an induction programme for new TEC directors, and a recent survey of NHS Authority members and Trust directors,[4] suggest that many of the findings are also applicable to the governance of a wide range of public sector organizations.

While the organizations participating in the survey programme are primarily UK based, they include a mix of companies with headquarters elsewhere in Europe, the US and Japan. As far as the role of the board, the attitudes of directors, and certain key boardroom issues are concerned, a degree of consensus was found across the participants, irrespective of 'corporate nationality'. A study by Demb and Neubauer[5] of 71 directors serving upon boards in eight countries has also found certain common features that appear to be broadly independent of the local legal framework.

The reader might feel that the conclusions need to be treated with some caution in view of the very small fraction of the total population of directors surveyed. However, the pattern and consistency of responses suggest that a significantly larger sample would not necessarily have led to different conclusions.

The participants have also stressed the extent to which each board comprises a particular combination of people who will need to think through the application of any suggested approaches or techniques to their own situation. If the book encourages the asking of collective questions in the boardroom concerning the operation and contribution of the board itself, it will serve a useful purpose.

1.5 Image and reality

Portraying the board and its members as the heart, soul and will of a company is a sobering thought to those outside the boardroom, and a humbling one for those within. Whatever members of boards may think, consider the following, which represents a small selection of the views of boards encountered in the course of writing this book:

> I don't know what they do. I am sure they are good people, but they have never communicated with me. We don't know what they are about.

Where were the directors of the various entities making up the Bank of Credit and Commerce International, or the members of the boards of the many companies constituting the portfolio of interests of the late Robert Maxwell in the months and years leading up to their demise?

Whatever happens the directors are OK. The future of the rest of us is on the line, but the directors have fixed their service contracts. They win whichever way it goes.

If I'm incompetent I get fired. A director that needs to be got rid of gets a golden handshake.

Being a director is a matter of status, it's an adjective and a label. It also means lots of perks. Status and greed is what it is all about.

At the end of the day the board was not really committed. They would sacrifice anything for short-term profit, the ratios that make them look good. The words they use with us are just that, words.

When the chairman and chief executive goes, the whole bunch of them will be out within no time. They are just bootlickers. Anyone new would clean them out.

It's a mystery to me how the company got into this situation. All the directors I've spoken to say they had doubts, yet when the resolution was put everyone on the board voted for it. Why didn't someone speak up?

How can the board know what is going on? They are busy and get filtered and summarized reports once a month. When did they last meet a customer? When will they give up a boardroom lunch to visit us?

They are nice people, but they did not see it. It now seems all so obvious but none of them saw it coming.

They are individuals. They go in and fight their corner. I get no sense of the board operating as a team.

I resigned and wish I had left the board earlier. I had no idea what I was letting myself in for. If I was offered a directorship tomorrow by someone I didn't know I would run a mile.

We all agreed, we had two board meetings on it. We went off to a hotel for a day on one occasion to talk about it. But, frankly, we are not doing it.

I've just said that in appointing new directors I look for those who are willing to learn. But we have done absolutely nothing in the last ten years to learn as a board from our experience as a board.

Surely all these comments represent myths and misunderstandings, and do great injustice to the competence of directors and the effectiveness of boards? Alas, not so. We shall encounter evidence during the course of

this book that suggests that few chairmen are satisfied with the performance of their boards, and that insufficient effort is devoted to creating
competent directors and effective boards.

1.6 Aims and scope

We shall establish during the course of the book that:

- Companies face a formidable range of challenges in the business environment. These challenges, and their impacts, need to be understood if
  a company is to adapt and respond accordingly.
- The board has a crucial role in the determination of the essence and
  purpose of a company, its vision and mission, and its strategy, policies
  and values. It also has a responsibility to the various stakeholders in a
  company to ensure that aspiration is translated into achievement.
- Yet few companies review on a regular basis the size, composition and
  effectiveness of their boards. There has traditionally been little experimentation with new ways of organizing and operating boards.
- Directors have onerous duties and responsibilities that are distinct
  from those of managers. The penalties can be severe for those who do
  not exercise due care, and retribution in the marketplace can be swift
  for those who are not competent.
- Directors also have training and development needs that are distinct
  from those of managers. Many corporate training and development
  programmes do not reach into the boardroom.
- While it might require some modification in the context of each company, it is possible in general terms to profile a competent director and
  an effective board. The knowledge and skills that are required in the
  boardroom can also be identified.
- There is some consensus concerning what makes a good director, and
  the criteria used in selecting directors. However, these criteria are rarely
  understood by managers, and in many companies they are not taken
  into account in career planning.
- Only a small minority of directors receive any formal preparation for
  their boardroom roles. A wide gulf exists between how directors are prepared for their boardroom roles, and how they could and should be prepared.
- Few chairmen are happy with the effectiveness of their boards, and few
  boards operate satisfactorily as a team. In many companies the board
  itself, and particularly in terms of its commitment, is a barrier to change
  rather than a facilitator of change.
- Inadequate attention is given to evaluating personal effectiveness in the

boardroom, and the performance of the board as a whole. In many companies there is an urgent need for action, the board representing 'the last training frontier'.

1.7 The issue of corporate governance

The research for this book has been undertaken against the background of an emerging debate concerning the adequacy of corporate governance. For example:

- Allegations have been made that the boards of major companies may no longer be subject to the checks and balances that enforce their accountability to shareholders. The result can be the abuse of directorial power.[6]
- *The Economist* has concluded that: 'The institutions that hold most shares are poorly equipped to act as proprietors; their skill lies in managing portfolios or dazzling trustees not in running companies.'[7]
- Contrary to the widespread view that directors have considerable power and influence, many individual board members feel inadequate and
- powerless in the face of a strong CEO. Lorsch and MacIver have raised the question of whether directors are pawns or potentates.[8]
- How independent and objective are non-executive directors, and can they effectively control a determined CEO and the management team of a major public company? Much will depend upon the calibre of the individuals concerned, but there is always the danger of a board becoming a 'cosy club'.[5]
- There have been criticisms of the levels of remuneration that directors have awarded themselves. The compensation of many US directors has also been described as excessive in relation to the performance of US companies.[9]
- During 1991 the performance of directors and boards, and the competence of lenders, were brought into question as a result of a succession of corporate failures as varied as the Roger Levitt Group, Polly Peck, the International Leisure Group, and various companies associated with the late Robert Maxwell. Codes of practice have been issued concerning the responsibilities of both directors and institutional shareholders.[10]
- The misuse of the assets of the Mirror Group pension fund by the late Robert Maxwell raises the question of the extent to which directors of companies who are also pension fund trustees are able to distinguish between distinct sets of responsibilities and act fairly between them.
- As if the incompetence of financial institutions in lending to companies

with inadequate boards were not enough, allegations of malpractice during 1991 touched such pillars of the financial services establishment as Nomura Securities of Japan and Salomon Brothers of the US. Accusations of negligence followed heavy losses sustained by Lloyd's of London.

- The collapse of the Bank of Credit and Commerce International (BCCI) revealed the existence of global networks of fraud and deception, and highlighted the problems of regulating the affairs of complex webs of international operations.

- The BCCI and other cases have also raised questions of how much faith should be put in audited accounts, and the extent to which company accounts can conceal or distort an underlying reality. Could changes to public accounting regulations make it more difficult for directors to 'window dress' their accounts in order to prevent shareholders, creditors, employees and other stakeholders from appreciating the true state of affairs?

- It is not clear that the performance of many boards is being appraised effectively on behalf of shareholders and other stakeholders. Nor is there an accepted consensus on the criteria to be used to assess directorial and board performance.

- Internationalization itself raises the question of how the international enterprise with resources, activities and operating companies in many nation states should be governed.[11] Few companies have an international board, with a mix of nationalities that matches the geographic spread of their interests.

- The desire of companies to transform themselves from functional bureaucracies to more flexible and responsive network organizations embracing customers, suppliers and business partners raises the question of the role of the board in facilitating the transition, and the issue of how the resulting network should be governed.[12]

- Demb and Neubauer emphasize the role of the major company in generating employment and economic growth, and bringing about change such as in eastern Europe. They conclude: 'At this point in history, existing mechanisms for governing corporations are no longer adequate. The scale, complexity, importance, and risks of corporate activity have overrun our institutions.'[5]

In the UK alone during 1990–91, over 1800 directors were convicted for offences of failing to file annual returns and accounts, and the Department of Trade and Industry accepted 178 requests for investigations into the affairs of companies.[13]

Prior to the excesses of 1991, the UK's Corporate Affairs Minister had concluded[14]:

The quality and style of Corporate Governance is now moving high up the agenda. A number of spectacular insolvencies, coupled with greater success by the authorities in tracking down cases of fraud, insider dealing, market manipulation and malpractice has triggered the debate.

Corporate cleanliness and deterrence of fraud, insider dealing, and market manipulation require strong detective work from the regulatory authorities and fearlessness in pursuing cases to court. Some of the dangers could be headed off if all companies had sensibly structured boards.

Against this background, it is not surprising that corporate governance has become a matter of inquiry and public debate on both sides of the Atlantic. In the UK, the 'Cadbury Committee', which has been reviewing the financial aspects of corporate governance, produced its first and draft report in May 1992.[15]

In the US, a more wide-ranging review is being undertaken by the subcouncil on 'Corporate Governance and Financial Markets' during the course of an examination of 'Competitiveness Policy' by a presidential council. The group concerned with corporate governance is investigating 'if, and to what extent [the] current system of corporate governance and the nature of financial markets constrain US corporations' ability to fully realize their strategic plans and to compete in world markets'.

Significant though these developments are, increasing external scrutiny is but one of the factors confronting the boards of many companies. In Chapter 2 we consider the challenges in the business environment that face companies and their boards of directors. The nature and diversity of both challenges and opportunities is forcing many companies to undergo a fundamental transformation, and in the process many boards are being confronted with their deficiencies and inadequacies.

1.8 Checklist

1. Do you consider the board of your company to be an enabler or a burden?
2. Is the board a united team?
3. How committed is it to the long-term future of the company?
4. Is the board 'in charge', or is it a 'rubber stamp'?
5. What do people within the company really think about the board?
6. If you are a director, what does membership of a board mean to you? How does it affect your 'self image'?
7. Do you enjoy being a director? What are your main frustrations?
8. What do you most gain from being a director? What would you lose if you ceased to be a director?

9. Does the board of your company 'add value' to the extent that you feel it could or should?
10. How would you and your colleagues be affected by company failure?
11. How much do you (or the directors) really care about the various stakeholders in the company?
12. When was the issue of corporate governance last raised within the boardroom, and what were the conclusions?
13. Has your board adopted a 'position' on such issues as the separation of the role of chairman from that of chief executive officer, the contribution of the non-executive or independent director, or the desirability of audit and remuneration committees?

Notes and references

1. Demb, A. and Neubauer, F.-F., 'The boards mandate mediating corporate lifespace', *European Management Journal*, **7** (3), 1989, 273–82; and 'How can the board add value?', *European Management Journal*, **8** (2), 1990, 156–60.
2. Slatter, S., *Corporate Recovery, Successful Turnaround Strategies and their Implementation*, Penguin Books, 1984 and 1987.
3. Coulson-Thomas, C., *Developing Directors: Building an effective boardroom team*, McGraw-Hill, 1993.
4. Coulson-Thomas, C., *Development Needs of NHS Authority and Board Members*. An Adaptation Ltd report prepared on behalf of the NHS Training Directorate, July 1992.
5. Demb, A. and Neubauer, F.-F., *The Corporate Board, Confronting the Paradoxes*, Oxford University Press, 1992.
6. Monks, R. and Minow, N., *Power and Responsibility*, Harper Business Books, 1991; Charkham, J. P., *Effective Boards*, The Institute of Chartered Accountants in England and Wales, 1986.
7. 'Redirecting directors', *The Economist*, 17 November 1990, pp. 19–20.
8. Lorsch, J. and MacIver, E., *Pawns or Potentates: The reality of America's corporate boards*, Harvard Business School Press, 1989.
9. Crystal, G. S., *In Search of Excess: The overcompensation of American executives*, Norton, 1992.
10. ISC, *The Role and Duties of Directors: A statement of best practice*, Institutional Shareholders Committee, 18 April 1991; and ABI, *The Responsibilities of Institutional Shareholders*, The Association of British Insurers, March 1991.
11. Coulson-Thomas, C., *Creating the Global Company: Successful internationalization*, McGraw-Hill, 1992.
12. Coulson-Thomas, C., *Transforming the Company: Bridging the gap between management myth and corporate reality*, Kogan Page, 1992.
13. Department of Trade and Industry, *Companies in 1990–91*, HMSO, 17 October 1991.
14. Redwood, J., MP, *Corporate Governance*, Department of Trade and Industry Press Notice P/90/722, 7 December 1990.
15. Committee on The Financial Aspects of Corporate Governance (chairman, Sir Adrian Cadbury), Draft Report issued for public comment, 27 May 1992, Committee on The Financial Aspects of Corporate Governance, 1992.

2
Challenges facing business and boards

Most boards concentrate on the urgent rather than the important mainly because the urgent is more easily understood. (DAVID THOMPSON, chairman, Rank Xerox (UK) Ltd.)

2.1 Essence and purpose

If the directors are the heart and soul of a company, the board should be the guardian of (a) the reason for a company's existence, and (b) the purpose that sustains its activities. Without a distinctive purpose or reason for existence a company will wither and die. There are progressively fewer corporate life-support machines in competitive markets as barriers to entry tumble and state aids are increasingly questioned within regional 'common markets'.

The will 'to go on' within a board is usually based upon, and draws its strength from, an underlying reality. The reason for continued existence, and the essence of what a company is 'all about', should derive from a distinctive capability to bring people together in order to satisfy needs and yield benefits that exceed the costs of maintaining relationships.

A board needs to understand the context in which a company operates. Key questions for the chairman are: To what extent do the individual members of the board, and the board as a whole, understand the nature of the business environment? Does it actively seek such an understanding, or sit back and wait for management reports?

A board that is not sensitive and aware of the business context within which a company operates is fatally flawed, regardless of its other attributes. The essence and purpose of a company must derive from opportunities, needs and requirements in the business environment. Ultimately it is the board's responsibility to determine the extent to which a company has a purpose. The following types of question need to be addressed by the board:

- Why does the company exist, and why should it continue to exist? What is its essence and purpose? What value does it add?
- Is there anything particularly distinctive or special about the company? Why should customers, potential employees and investors be interested in it? Who really cares whether the company continues to exist? What would be lost if it ceased to exist?

A board should provide a compelling rationale for sustaining relationships with external customers. Their interest should not be assumed. A distinctive essence and purpose may be needed to differentiate the company from competitors. The essence of the company should be rooted in the reality of conditions, circumstances and requirements in the marketplace.

If the directors do not agree and cannot articulate and share a distinct purpose for the company, its activities may well be based upon foundations of sand. It will become increasingly difficult to distinguish the company from alternative suppliers in competitive conditions.

2.2 The changed market environment

The British Institute of Management (BIM) report *Beyond Quality*[1] has suggested that the variety and fundamental nature of the many changes that have occurred, and which continue to occur, in the business environment are such as to suggest a transition has occurred to a new era. It is possible to list, albeit in simplistic form, the major differences between the 'old' and the 'new' (Table 2.1).

Table 2.1 Discontinuities in the business environment

Old	New
Confidence and rigidity	Insecurity and openness
Permanence and certainty	Turbulence and uncertainty
Incremental change	Revolutionary change
Facts and theories	Values
Logic	Intuition
Boundaries and disciplines	Interests, issues and problems
Organization	Adaptation
Attitudes	Feelings
Personalities and vested interests	Principles and business philosophy
Quantity	Quality and post-quality
Getting ahead	Achieving balance and harmony
Drives	Needs
Producer centred	Customer centred
Focus on activity	Focus on output
Conflict and rivalry	Cooperation and consensus

Old	*New*
Command and control	Two-way communication and sharing
Bureaucratic hierarchy	Horizontal relationships
Absolutes	Solutions relative to context
Simplicity	Diversity and relative complexity
One-dimension maximization	Multi-dimensional trade-offs
Answers	Questions
Solutions	Temporary accommodations
Authority	Consent
Sanctions	Encouragement
Departmentalism and procedures	Business processes
Discrete problems	Holistic issues
Uninformed customers	Demanding customers
Homogeneous customers	Diverse customers
Standard products and services	Tailored products and services
Local customers	International customers
Established relationships	Integration and fragmentation
Sales	Account management
Individuals	Teams
The self and the company	The group and the environment
The 'here and now'	The consequences and the future
Unsupported	Facilitating processes and technology
'Hoarding' by the few	Empowerment of the many
Single discipline	Multi-disciplinary
Diversification	Focus
Generalization	Segmentation
Knowledge	Competence
Teaching	Learning
Specialist teaching institutions	Integration of learning and working
Initial qualification	Continual updating
Lifetime practice	Functional mobility
Career ladders	Succession of projects
Standard employment	Various patterns of work
Commodity products	Search for differentiation
Limited competition	Open competition
Barriers to entry	Diversity of supply
Cartels and oligopolies	Competition and choice
Zero-sum relationships	Positive-sum collaboration
Independence and dependence	Interdependence and partnership

The number and fundamental nature of the many changes that are occurring in the business environment are such as to represent a profound challenge to companies and their boards. The directors of a company will need to re-assess continually the purpose and essence of the company in the light of such developments.

A board also needs to ensure that the people of the company are encouraged to question and challenge. A corporate culture should encourage debate and the ongoing re-assessment of shared paradigms if the corporation is to cope with revolutionary change.[2]

It may not be easy to persuade some boards to allocate time for such 'first principles' discussions. The following are the recorded comments of some directors who have taken a 'negative' view of a business environment review exercise:

> This sort of exercise is great for business school students. We have a company to run.

> What did all that do for any of our customers? We cannot change any of those things out there by talking about them.

> My priority is survival. I don't want to get an 'A' in current affairs and preside over a failing company.

On the other hand, some positive comments are more encouraging:

> We spend too much time on the immediate, and not enough looking ahead. We have always put off this sort of exercise. There is never a slack time, you just have to do it.

> At least we all now have a similar view of what is important. I also know my colleagues have views beyond their corporate roles. We need to make more use of this.

> I was worried that we might win the battle and lose the war. We need to widen our perspective.

> Survival is fine, but for what? That's the question that we have now started to address.

> I'll probably view events differently from now on, and so I should. We have to do more than observe. We have to think and we can't assume anyone else will be looking out for those things that will really impact upon us.

The time of directors is always likely to be at a premium, particularly in the case of those with executive responsibilities. Yet, understanding the changing and diverse challenges and opportunities that face the company is an essential foundation of the work of the board. When companies fail, beneath the immediate events that triggered the final demise, there is often a more fundamental underlying cause such as the failure to understand and anticipate the implications of a significant trend.

The changing nature of the business environment (Table 2.1) and the more onerous legal duties and responsibilities that have been placed upon directors (see Chapter 3) have had a very significant impact upon 'boardroom life'. The board should not be regarded as a 'safe haven', nor should a directorship be used to say 'thank you' for services rendered.

Few boards are presiding over a static state, and even fewer companies can take survival for granted. The business environment is turbulent and demanding and corporate strategies, policies and plans need to be sufficiently flexible to cope with continuous change.

It should not be assumed that directors are sensitive to, or monitor, developments in the external business environment. Many do not systematically consider fundamental developments. Their focus is almost exclusively upon board papers and the agenda for the next meeting, rather than upon what the agenda ought to be.

A chairman should ensure that members of the board are aware of and question the fundamental changes that are occurring in the marketplace, such as those in Table 2.1. Which of the developments in the business environment are of the greatest significance? Which can be considered a 'help' or positive factor, and which a 'hinder' or negative factor? What are the implications for the company and its stakeholders, particularly customers, employees and owners? In which areas is the company most vulnerable to external developments?

2.3 Issue monitoring and management

A board needs to establish patterns, links and relationships among and between the various challenges and opportunities in the business environment. How developments should be 'structured', and their impact and significance, will vary between companies. We shall see in the next chapter that one of the functions of the board is to understand the business environment in order to determine a distinct purpose for a company that lies in opportunities to add value for customers.

So how should this be done? Many companies have issue monitoring and management processes for:

- identifying and prioritizing developments in the business environment that are likely to have a significant impact upon 'the business';
- assessing and quantifying the nature of the impacts at local, national, regional or international levels;
- determining what action the company needs to take in response;
- ensuring that appropriate action is taken;
- monitoring the consequences; and
- taking remedial or further steps as required.

Such a process of review–action–review should occur in a continuous cycle. A degree of formality, perhaps a company-wide annual exercise, may be advisable to ensure a consistent and complete operation of the cycle. However, whatever the formal process, a board and its members should always be on the alert for significant developments that demand attention.

There is little point in identifying developments or issues if their impacts upon the company are not assessed. A director needs more than just an awareness of what is going on. He or she also needs the commitment and competence to relate developments to the situation a company is in. Once the impacts have been assessed it will be necessary to determine a response.

The board needs to ensure that an assessment of developments and impacts is communicated and shared among members of the management team. The directors must also ensure that appropriate resources of the company, supplemented if necessary by external expertise, are harnessed in the formulation and implementation of a response. The effective board ensures that understanding and intention is followed by appropriate action, then monitors the consequences.

The review process should not be rushed. An over-hasty identification of issues could lead to resources being devoted to matters that subsequently turn out to be of little significance. Similarly, the inadequate analysis of impacts could lead to the wrong problems being addressed.

Many boards unnecessarily constrain themselves to a 'standard format' board meeting, when certain activities such as a review of issues or the purpose, vision or strategy of the company may require a workshop format over several hours. More than one iteration of a workshop process may be necessary before a board is satisfied with the outputs it has obtained. The effective board should be judged by the quality of its output and not by 'input' factors such as time-keeping.

2.4 Understanding the market environment

A board should structure its identification of developments in the business environment so that logical connections can be perceived, and the significance of issues for the company can be more easily understood. Example 2.1 presents the conclusions of the initial deliberations of one board concerning developments in the external business environment. At a broad level of generalization, the board has identified some developments of particular importance to its international operations, their implications for relationships with customers, and a number of critical success factors.

The nature of many of the developments that are occurring in the business environment amount to a significant challenge to the continued viability of many corporate entities. Boards accustomed to 'steering' and

International markets are becoming more open

De-regulation and privatization global phenomena

More intense competition:
Strengthened bargaining position of consumers *vis-à-vis* suppliers
Pressure upon prices and margins

Decline in real cost and growth in performance and quality

Consumers now expect reliability and quality

Danger of 'commodity products trap'

Search for new forms of differentiation

These market conditions give an advantage to:
Companies that can act quickly
Companies that operate with slim overheads
Companies that move responsibilities closer to the customer
Companies that can implement and project manage

Size and past achievements do not guarantee future success

Example 2.1   The changed market environment[13]

'fine tuning' have had to come to terms with radical restructurings and corporate transformation programmes. We shall examine the changes occurring within corporate organizations later in this chapter.

The board as a whole should share a common understanding of relevant developments in the business environment. From time to time, this understanding should be tested and refined to ensure that it is up to date and that the perceptions of the board are consistent with external reality.

Care should be taken to avoid placing too much faith in 'rational approaches', projections and planning. An understanding of the past is often an imperfect and misleading guide to the future.[3]

Directors need to be aware, alert, sensitive, open-minded and flexible. What major changes are occurring in the marketplace? What is happening to customer expectations? What are the key requirements for success? What are the company's major deficiencies, and how might they be remedied?

2.5 Understanding the business sector

A board needs to understand the business sector in which the company is operating. For example:

– What is happening in the sector in terms of market trends, customer

and success requirements, segmentation and relationship opportunities, and supplier reactions?
– What changes are occurring in the structure of the sector, the dynamics of competition and the relationships between the 'key players'; and would additional collaborations and arrangements be desirable?

The 'key factors' in the business environment will vary between sectors. Those in Example 2.2, for instance, relate to 'IT' companies and have been identified by the board of an IT services company.

Technological innovation and rapid replication continues
Companies working harder to maintain a lead
Customers becoming more demanding and cynical
Customers demanding tailored solutions
Competition on implementation and project management
Increasing cost of developing technology
Companies are becoming more selective and focused
R&D moving closer to the customer
Products being developed with the customer

Example 2.2   The changed IT sector environment[13]

As a consequence of such developments as those in Example 2.2, methods of operating with which directors and boards have become familiar are having to be changed. This is why developments in the business environment are being considered in this chapter before we turn in the next to a review of the role and function of the board. In many companies these are having to be re-assessed.

Companies are entering into new forms of relationship with customers and suppliers. Boards are having to focus simultaneously on internal change and the building of external relationships. Internally and externally the key to success is increasingly the sustaining of relationships rather than the exercise of power. Many of the key groups, such as customers, employees and business partners, with whom a relationship of trust and mutual understanding needs to be built, will have alternatives to whom they could turn their attentions.

A board should continually re-address issues such as those in Example 2.2. The more specific impacts of change upon the IT sector, following further discussion, are summarized in Example 2.3.

As a consequence of such developments as those identified in Example 2.3, IT companies are entering into families of strategic partnerships and

Levels of profitability are falling
Suppliers are having to slim down to survive
Drive for more flexible and responsive organizations
Considerable market restructuring is occurring
New groupings of suppliers are emerging
Global coordination, planning and allocation of resources
Greater focus on account management
Greater commitment to open systems
Difficult for individual companies to supply total value to customers
European dependence upon Japanese technology is growing
Development costs of core technology becoming an increasing burden
Companies are having to focus on core activities

Example 2.3   The impact of change upon IT suppliers[13]

arrangements. Their negotiation and management is demanding new skills. Within a company employing many thousands of managers there may only be a few, if any, managers with experience of entering into joint ventures and managing within a joint-venture framework. A board may need to address a range of implementation issues that would not arise within a more traditional form of operation.

When items that are new to everyone appear on the boardroom agenda, there may be few experts or consultants to whom a board can turn for advice. All companies may be in the same boat together, at the same stage of the emergence of a particular challenge or opportunity. All may be struggling to adjust. There may be few 'role model' companies to benchmark against. In such circumstances the board must wrestle with the issue concerned.

2.6 Customers

Customers feature prominently in the examples we have seen of changes in the business environment that have been identified by particular boards as significant for their companies. A director should never forget that the external customer is the ultimate source of the meaning and purpose of the successful company. The company that loses sight of the need to add value for customers will not survive for long in a competitive marketplace.

This point appears to be well understood by company chairmen, according to a survey undertaken by Adaptation Ltd for the Institute of Directors (IOD).[4] The top two boardroom issues both concern customers, namely 'satisfying customers' and 'delivering quality'. Over nine out of ten respondents thought 'satisfying customers' and 'delivering quality' to be 'very important'.

The third most important issue in the IOD survey is 'differentiation' of the respondents' companies from their competitors. The need for clear differentiation is particularly important in competitive markets in which there is a trend towards the 'commoditization' of goods and services. There are clear advantages for those companies and products that are perceived as distinct or different, particularly when the source of the differentiation lies in a closer appreciation of what constitutes value for customers.

A board has to do more than pay 'lip service' to its customers. It needs to understand and deliver customer satisfaction, quality and what represents value to customers. The participants in the BIM *Beyond Quality* survey on 'managing the relationship with the customer'[1] ranked 'customer satisfaction' and 'quality' at the head of a list of 16 'customer issues'. Both are thought to be very important by nine out of ten respondents. They are followed by 'identifying what constitutes value to the customer', which three-quarters of the respondents thought to be very important.

Significantly the various 'Ps', such as price and place, so loved by those delivering management courses and writing marketing textbooks, appear at the bottom of the list of 'customer' issues. While these matters are important for the managers who are responsible for them, the perspective of the board needs to be focused firmly upon the customer.

Stressing the importance of the customer might appear to the reader to be an unnecessary concentration upon a 'motherhood' matter that should be taken for granted, so let us examine the outcomes of review sessions that the author conducted with various boards:

– While acknowledging the importance of the customer, the priority of most boards remains the company's 'internal' requirements for survival and performance, rather than the 'external' requirements of customers.
– Relatively few boards put customer satisfaction ahead of market share or financial measures, such as return on net assets when they establish business objectives. In reality, medium- and long-term market share and financial performance is a consequence of satisfied customers.
– Many boards do not use customer satisfaction surveys and other means of determining customer requirements and identifying sources of customer dissatisfaction. Hence they do not have a clear idea of what to do to either build satisfaction or remove the main causes of dissatisfaction.
– Few companies are organized around their customers, or determine and allocate roles and responsibilities according to what needs to be

done to build relationships with customers and deliver value to them. Individual employees and work groups do not understand what they can do to contribute towards improved customer satisfaction.

- Still fewer companies understand, or have documented and re-engineered, the key cross-functional business processes that deliver those few things that really generate value for customers. Even in 'slimmed down' companies, much effort is usually wasted on activities and tasks that add little to customer satisfaction.
- In most companies, few people are motivated or encouraged, in terms of reward and remuneration, to give priority to those activities and tasks that add value for customers. The rhetoric of the 'house journals' and promotional videos acknowledges the customer, but the realities of advancement depend upon serving the corporate machine.
- In many companies, even though some employees are tasked and motivated to concentrate upon activities that add value for customers, they are neither empowered to act nor provided with the approaches, tools and techniques, facilitating processes, and supporting technology to discharge their responsibilities. Telling people what they need to do is not enough; they must be equipped to 'make it happen'.

Customer perspective

In a further question in the same BIM survey,[1] the participants were asked to rank in importance a number of 'management issues'. 'Building longer term relationships with customers' emerges at the top of the list, followed by 'introducing a more customer-oriented culture'.

To build longer term relationships with customers it is necessary to adopt the customer perspective, and understand issues from a customer point of view. An awareness of issues in the business environment is of considerable value, as these also impact upon customer organizations Figure 2.1).

A board needs to understand not only the direct impact of external changes such as the evolution of a 'Single' European market, but also the indirect impact that results from the direct impact of the same, or related, changes upon customers, suppliers or business partners.

Understanding the impact of issues in the business environment upon customers can result in the identification of new business opportunities. For example:

- The desire of companies to slim down and focus upon core activities creates a facilities management opportunity. Alternatively, a 'self-contained' corporate activity could be encouraged to seek external sources of revenue.

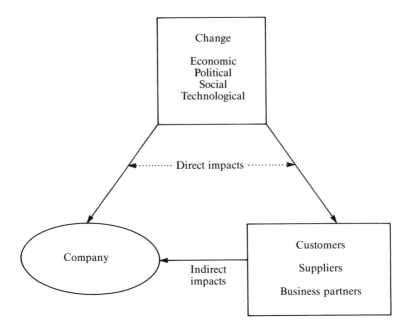

Figure 2.1 The impact of external changes

- Recognition that many other companies face a similar challenge could lead to the formation of a consortium, joint activity or other forms of collaboration. The pressure of adversity could encourage co-operation.
- The difficulties that companies are experiencing in the area of implementation could suggest there might be scope for introducing a range of training and consultancy services. The nature of the 'product' might be broadened to encompass a range of 'value added' services.

A focus upon the customer in the boardroom, and a customer perspective, should not be assumed. There are some key questions which the board should address. For example:

- Who represents the customer in the boardroom? How much time does the board spend discussing the customer, and how much time do individual members of the board spend with customers?
- How high does customer satisfaction rank among the company's business objectives? What are the 'vital few' things that need to be done to improve customer satisfaction significantly or to reduce customer dissatisfaction?

2.7 The organizational response

We have seen that profound challenges in the business environment are impacting upon companies and their boards. How are they responding? Some clues are suggested by recent surveys. Let us begin with the 'human resource' aspects, as the rationale of organization is to harness the talents of people in order to apply them to those activities that lead to satisfied customers. The priorities have remained relatively constant in recent years:

- 'Making the organization structure more flexible' was ranked first (in terms of 'very important' replies) of 14 human resource 'challenges' in the 1989 BIM report *The Responsive Organisation*.[5] The delegation and devolution of responsibilities, which ranked second in terms of 'very important' replies, was perceived by those interviewed as an important means of securing greater flexibility in the face of changing customer requirements.
- For the respondents in a 1990 survey undertaken by Adaptation Ltd for Surrey European Management School (SEMS),[6] concerning the importance of 12 human resource issues, the priority issue in terms of 'very important' replies was 'creating a more flexible and responsive organization'. Every respondent considered 'creating a more flexible and responsive organization' to be either 'very important' or 'important'.
- In a further survey undertaken in 1991 by Adaptation Ltd in conjunction with the Institute of Personnel Management (IPM) Research Group,[7] 'creating a more flexible and responsive organization' emerges as the number one of 13 'personnel issues'. 'Quality and teamwork', 'general management development', and 'changing the corporate culture' are key issues, as they were in both the 1989 and the 1990 surveys.

Discussions with participants in all three surveys[5-7] suggest that creating a more flexible and responsive organization is perceived as providing a basis for tackling a whole range of challenges and opportunities. In what Drucker has termed 'the age of discontinuity',[8] the search for flatter and more flexible organizations has become recognized as a global phenomenon.[9]

    In the surveys undertaken by the author,[5-7] a number of the other human resource issues were weighted in importance according to the extent to which they would facilitate the creation of a more flexible and responsive organization. For example, in the SEMS survey,[6] 'quality and teamwork' – which ranked second in terms of 'very important' replies – is thought to facilitate flexibility. 'Continuing updating and development of knowledge and skills', which is ranked third in terms of 'very important' replies, is also regarded as a key facilitator of ongoing learning, adaptation and change, the hallmark of the flexible organization.

    A question which inevitably emerges from consideration of the results of a longitudinal series of surveys is why 'creating a more flexible and responsive organization' should remain such a key boardroom issue for so long. Another BIM report, *The Flat Organisation*,[10] suggests that:

- There is widespread awareness among directors of the need to change. However, commitment to significant change in the boardroom is rarely matched by a confident understanding of how to bring it about.
- Simple and superficial change, such as shifting priorities or those involving the use of words, can and sometimes do occur overnight. However, the fundamental changes of attitudes, values, approach and perspective that are needed to cope with the range of challenges considered in this chapter usually take much longer to achieve.
- Boards in general are finding that 'corporate transformation' is taking longer to bring about than was first thought. A particular dilemma for boards is that the timescale to achieve fundamental change may extend beyond the lifetime of the change requirement.
- Often, there is a considerable gap between words and deeds. The short-term actions of many boards, in response to economic recession, are not always consistent with either a company's vision or the building of long-term relationships with its customers.
- While CEOs and members of boards stress the need for delegation and empowerment, and debate the importance of improving the quality of management, individual managers are not being equipped to handle the new demands that are being placed upon them.

Crafting an excellent strategy is not enough if it cannot be implemented. The achievement of corporate transformation has become a preoccupation of many boards, and forms the subject of a separate book by the author.[11]

2.8 Corporate transformation

So what are the characteristics of the new and flexible forms of organization that are emerging? What are the implications of these changes for boards of directors?

Corporate transformation is not sought for its own sake, but in order to respond to challenges and opportunities in the business environment. We have already encountered evidence of the importance attached by directors to satisfying customers. This requires responsiveness, and access to relevant resources and skills.

The participants in the BIM report *The Flat Organisation*[10] were asked to indicate the extent of their agreement with a number of statements concerning the business environment. The most strongly agreed with statement in order of 'strongly agree' replies, and supported by three-quarters of respondents, is that 'human resource is a critical success factor'. Second is the statement that 'customers are becoming more demanding', with which half of the respondents 'strongly agree'. When the 'strongly agree' and 'agree' replies are added together, all of the respondents consider 'human resource is a critical success factor'.

Central elements of BIM surveys in recent years have been the importance of the key 'internal' issue of motivating, developing and harnessing the talents of people[5] and the key 'external' issue of building closer relationships with customers.[1] These considerations weigh heavily in the design of new forms of organization.

Some aspects of the 'new organization' derive from the challenges faced by boards we have already examined. A selection of these from the perspective of one board are presented in Example 2.4.

Global marketplace/internationalization
Liberalization and competition
Regionalization, e.g. '1992'

Review vision
Establish global network
Internationalize perspective and board

Transitioning organizations
More demanding customers
Delivering beyond 'traditional' quality
Differentiation and focus

Focus on customer satisfaction
Relationship management
Facilitation of teamwork/learning/change

Information technology issues
Declining white-collar productivity

Focus on document management
Re-engineer management and business processes

Scarcity of human resource
Quality of management

Employee involvement and empowerment
Integration of learning and working
Introduce more cross-functional teamworking

Example 2.4   Challenges and requirements

Other characteristics of the more flexible and responsive forms of organization that are emerging derive from relevant trends in the marketplace and the resulting success requirements. Those considered particularly important by another board are set out in Example 2.5.

Clearer vision
Understand customer requirements
Enhanced 'capacity to act'
Achieve faster response
More tailoring to particular requirements
Lower cost of operation
Slimmer, flatter and tighter
Non-core activities hived off
Simplify business processes
Customer-focused roles and responsibilities
Delegation and devolution of responsibility
Demography: making maximum use of scarce skills
Involvement and empowerment
Flexibility: multi-functional teams
Internationalization: multi-location teams
Establish and re-engineer key management processes
Processes for learning and adaptation
Technology that can facilitate group and teamworking
Roles and responsibilities: specific tasks
Shift of focus from input to output
Assessment on output
Access to skills more important than employment

Example 2.5   Success requirements

In response to (a) an analysis of how best to respond to the challenges in the business environment and (b) the identification of the key requirements for success in the market context, certain elements of an 'organizational' solution may suggest themselves. Corporate transformation is not just being discussed in boardrooms; it is being actively sought. A considerable amount of 'change' appears to be occurring within the organizations participating in the survey undertaken for the BIM: *The Flat Organisation*.[10]

– Almost nine out of ten of the participating organizations are becoming slimmer and flatter; while, in some eight out of ten, more work is being undertaken in teams, and a more responsive network organization is being created (Table 2.2).

– Over two-thirds of participants acknowledge that functions are becoming more interdependent, and procedures and permanency are giving way to flexibility and temporary arrangements. Over a half consider that organizations are becoming more interdependent.

Table 2.2   What respondents' organizations are doing to better respond to challenges and opportunities within the business environment

Creating a slimmer and flatter organization	88%
More work is being undertaken in teams	79%
Creating a more responsive network organization	78%
Functions are becoming more interdependent	71%
Procedures and permanency are giving way to flexibility and temporary arrangements	67%
Organizations are becoming more interdependent	55%

Source: The Flat Organization. BIM. 1991.[10]

The BIM report reveals that there is a clear commitment to change, which is seen as a necessity rather than as a matter of choice. However, it goes on to endorse what has already been suggested in this chapter – namely, that in many companies achievement, or the results of corporate change programmes, are falling well short of corporate aspirations. Requirements are proving easier to state than to bring about.

The major characteristics of the form of responsive network organization that is emerging are set out in Example 2.6. Not all of these features will be found in every corporate transformation plan, but particular combinations of them are being sought by most major companies.

If a board has not already done so it should focus on its responsibilities for ensuring that the company's organization enables it to respond to challenges and opportunities in the external business environment, and particularly changing customer requirements. In particular, it should identify the major deficiencies or gaps between where the company is and where it needs to be to cope with external challenges and achieve marketplace success.

Figure 2.2 is a diagrammatic representation of the sort of network organization that is being sought by many boards.[1,5]

A central concern of many boards is to translate the 'transformation' vision that exists on paper into a marketplace reality. The following key questions should be addressed:

– Have the key corporate transformation tasks and requirements been defined in clear output terms?

Distinct and compelling mission
Focus on the customer
Negotiated and international network
Involves customers and suppliers
Blurred boundary with customers, suppliers and partners
Participating and empowered people
Shared commitment
Role model attitudes and behaviour
Multi-location and multi-functional teams
Multi-national teams
Integration of individuals into teams
Portfolio of projects
Facilitating processes and supporting technology
Need for flexibility and adaptability
Greater speed of response
Access international expertise
Facilitating networks, rather than bureaucracy
Processes, rather than procedures
Delegation, devolution and decentralization
Flatter, leaner, tighter
Processes for continuous change
Continuous process review and learning
Remuneration related to value added
Use of facilitating technology
Availability of relevant approaches, tools and techniques
Greater accountability and responsibility

Example 2.6 The emerging organization
Source: The Responsive Organisation.[5] *Beyond Quality*[1] *and Human Resource Development for International Operation.*[6]

- Has the board identified and addressed any overlaps or gaps in responsibilities, including responsibilities for the key management and business processes that will deliver the value that is sought by customers?
- Has an understanding of the transformation objectives, and the allocation of responsibilities for their achievement, been communicated and shared throughout the company?
- Has the board identified, and is it 'keeping its eye upon', those 'vital few' initiatives that will probably determine whether or not transformation is achieved?

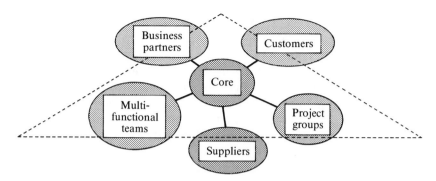

Figure 2.2   The network organization
Source: BIM reports: The Responsive Organisation [5] *and Beyond Quality* [2].

- Have all the people in the organization been encouraged, empowered and equipped to cope with the transformation tasks they are expected to perform?
- Are all members of the board united behind, and totally committed to, the achievement of corporate transformation?

2.9 People

What does all this mean for those who have an interest in companies, or people who work within or with companies, and the relationship of boards with these groups? Within the legalistic ambience of many boardrooms, directors may need to remind themselves of the importance of human relationships:

- Investors are people, and they will not necessarily 'understand' the company's point of view and situation if the board does not communicate with them.
- Customers, suppliers and business partners do not have relationships with a company's buildings, or its legal 'constitution', but with its people.
- Whether or not a corporate transformation programme succeeds will depend upon the quality and integrity of the relationship between the board and the people of the organization.
- Members of the board are people, and all directors should be 'role models' in all that they say and do.
- Ultimately, the survival of a company will depend upon the commitment of the board to understanding and satisfying the needs and requirements of people, and sharing the company's vision, mission, values, goals and objectives with them.

Firstly, it needs to be acknowledged that boards increasingly recognize the importance of people. We have already seen that in one 1991 survey[10] every respondent agreed that 'human resource is a critical success factor'.

A board should establish the qualities it is seeking in the people of the organization, and the standards of conduct it expects of them. The qualities that are sought will reflect the particular circumstances of each company. The human resource requirements of one board are presented in Example 2.7. People with these qualities are likely to expect a different relationship with a board than that traditionally found in many bureaucratic organizations.

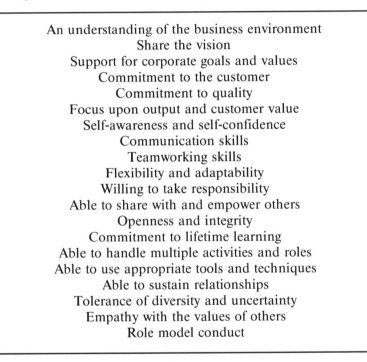

An understanding of the business environment
Share the vision
Support for corporate goals and values
Commitment to the customer
Commitment to quality
Focus upon output and customer value
Self-awareness and self-confidence
Communication skills
Teamworking skills
Flexibility and adaptability
Willing to take responsibility
Able to share with and empower others
Openness and integrity
Commitment to lifetime learning
Able to handle multiple activities and roles
Able to use appropriate tools and techniques
Able to sustain relationships
Tolerance of diversity and uncertainty
Empathy with the values of others
Role model conduct

Example 2.7   Human resource requirements

We shall return to the qualities sought in members of the management team in Chapter 5 on the distinction between direction and management. It is important to remember that the board has a significant role in relation to the people of a company:

– People, process, technology and organization issues are interdependent and come together in the boardroom. Directors tend to face holistic business issues rather than those which can be neatly pigeon-holed as 'people' or 'organization' issues.

- How people think and behave towards each other will reflect the 'tone' set by the board, and the corporate values, goals and standards of conduct established by the board.
- The extent to which people are motivated will depend significantly upon whether the board has communicated and shared a compelling vision, whether reward and remuneration is consistent with priority corporate objectives, and whether they have been equipped to cope.

Whether or not a company's personnel are able to perform will depend upon the extent to which: (a) they understand what is expected of them; (b) they are empowered and equipped with relevant approaches, tools and techniques; (c) they are supported by appropriate management and business processes; and (d) they have access to enabling technology.

As we shall see in the next chapter, it is the responsibility of the board to ensure that the necessary processes are in place to attract, motivate, and retain people of the required quality. One suggested people strategy process is shown diagrammatically in Figure 2.3.

The people strategy process in Figure 2.3 illustrates the extent to which: (a) both people and management and business process requirements derive from the vision and mission of a company, and from the needs of its customers; and (b) people and management and business processes are interdependent. The form of an organization, and the nature of relationships between people, also reflect the purpose of the company and the value it is seeking to generate for its customers.

There are certain key questions that need to be asked to determine the extent to which a board is committed to building relationships with people:

1. Has the board identified and established relationships with the key stakeholders in the company, and do all the directors understand their needs, interests, perspectives, attitudes and values?
2. Have roles and responsibilities relating to establishing and maintaining relationships with these groups of people been agreed by the board and allocated between individual directors?
3. Are communications with these groups two-way, i.e. does the board, and its individual members, listen; and are the relationships that have been established based upon mutual trust, respect and understanding?
4. Is the board able to deliver all that it has promised to each group of stakeholders, and do all directors act as role models when dealing with the various groups with an interest in the company?

2.10 Summary

In this chapter we have seen that the board is the heart and soul of a com-

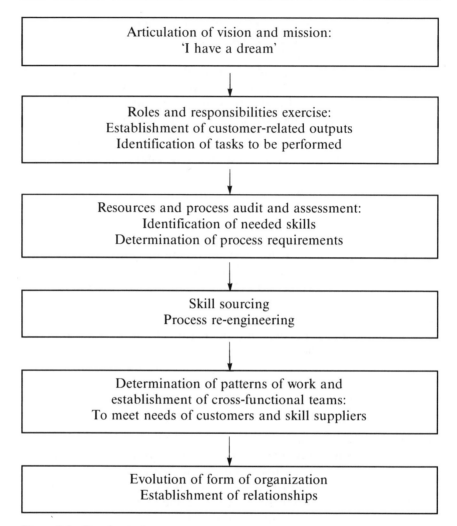

Figure 2.3 People strategy process

pany. However, there is often a gap between how directors and boards should behave, and how they perform in practice. The purpose of this book is to enable achievement and conduct to more closely match goals and aspirations.

The perspective of a director should encompass the company as a whole, its essence and purpose, the business, market and sector environment, its relationships with various stakeholders, and how it should be organized to add value for its customers. We have examined a number of issues and trends that represent challenges and opportunities in each of these areas, and how they might be monitored by a board.

Addressing the 'first principles' questions posed in this chapter might open up discussion of broader issues in the boardroom, and encourage directors to think about the key challenges facing businesses and boards. Further questions and exercises relevant to the issues raised in this and subsequent chapters are found in the author's companion book on the subject of developing directors.[12]

2.11 Checklist

1. How well does your company's board, and its individual members, understand the changing nature of the business environment?
2. Do the directors fully understand the magnitude of the challenges faced by the company, and their likely impacts upon it?
3. Is there a common understanding of the key challenges that has been openly discussed and is shared by all members of the board?
4. Does the board have a process for reviewing external challenges, issues and opportunities; assessing their impacts upon the company; and agreeing the action it should take in response?
5. Where such a review or issue monitoring process exists, are the directors committed to it, viewing it as of value and importance, or has it become a ritual?
6. Are the directors able to consider external developments in the context of the company as a whole, or do they monitor on a selective basis or with a 'departmental perspective', focusing mainly upon matters of concern to their particular responsibilities?
7. What has the company done, or what should it do, to learn from the customer?
8. Who in the company does, and should, add value for customers? Who is motivated, and encouraged in terms of reward and remuneration, to add value for customers?
9. Are the company's management and business processes, particularly those that cross departmental and functional boundaries, aligned and focused upon the priority requirements of customers?
10. Are roles and responsibilities allocated by the board on the basis of those things that need to be done to build customer satisfaction?
11. Are employees empowered to harness the resources of the company, independently of their location, in order to add value for individual customers?
12. Has the board articulated the values, and clearly formulated the rules of conduct, that should apply to relationships between people?

13. To what extent do stakeholders share the vision, mission, goals, values, and objectives of the company?
14. Do the directors regard their membership of the board itself as an exciting challenge, or are they bored and 'war weary'?
15. In the final analysis, do the directors really care where the company will be in ten years' time, and whether corporate transformation will be achieved?

Notes and references

1. Coulson-Thomas, C. and Brown, R., *Beyond Quality: Managing the relationship with the customer*, British Institute of Management, 1990.
2. Johnson, C., *Revolutionary Change*, Little, Brown & Company, 1966; and Pascale, R., *Managing On the Edge*, Simon & Schuster, 1990.
3. Popper, K., *The Poverty of Historicism*, 2nd edn, Routledge & Kegan Paul, 1960.
4. Coulson-Thomas, C., *Professional Development of and for the Board*, Institute of Directors, 1990.
5. Coulson-Thomas, C. and Brown, R., *The Responsive Organisation, People Management, the Challenge of the 1990s*, British Institute of Management, 1989.
6. Coulson-Thomas, C., *Human Resource Development for International Operation*. A survey undertaken by Adaptation Ltd for Surrey European Management School, 1990.
7. Coulson-Thomas, C., *The Role and Development of the Personnel Director*. An Adaptation Ltd interim survey undertaken in conjunction with the Institute of Personnel Management (IPM) Research Group, IPM, Wimbledon, 1991.
8. Drucker, P., *The Age of Discontinuity*, Heinemann, 1989.
9. Kanter, R. M., *When Giants Learn to Dance*, Simon & Schuster, 1989.
10. Coulson-Thomas, C. and Coe, T., *The Flat Organisation: Philosophy and practice*, British Institute of Management, 1991.
11. Coulson-Thomas, C., *Transforming the Company: Bridging the gap between management myth and corporate reality*, Kogan Page, 1992.
12. Coulson-Thomas, C., *Developing Directors: Building an effective boardroom team*, McGraw-Hill, 1993.
13. Examples 2.1–2.3 are taken from Coulson-Thomas, C., *Creating a Global Company: Successful internationalization*, McGraw-Hill, 1992. This book takes a more extensive look at issue monitoring and management, the role of the board, the determination of strategy, and a range of implementation considerations, in an international context.

3
Role and function of the board

To be successful, a board must first set its objectives; the most brilliant individual managers operating in the most buoyant economic circumstances and with access to unlimited finance will be totally ineffective unless it knows what it wants to do. In short, it must have a mission. (CHARLES LOWE, formerly deputy chairman of Blue Arrow Employment Group.)

What is the function of the board? In the last chapter we considered the business context in which directors are at work, and the need for a board to monitor developments in the business environment and ensure that appropriate changes occur in response to them. This chapter examines the individual and collective duties and responsibilities of directors, and the role and purpose of the board. We shall also consider how these are perceived by the chairmen of boards.

3.1 Corporate governance

The function of the board has been described by Lorsch and MacIver in terms of overseeing management, reviewing performance, and ensuring that the various activities of a company are socially responsible and in compliance with the law.[1]

Tricker's view of the board is more 'proactive'.[2] He has described its function in terms of establishing strategic direction and overseeing company strategy, assessing and monitoring performance, but also, and especially in the case of executive directors, becoming involved in action to ensure implementation.

There is little point in developing a strategy that remains 'words on paper'. The surveys upon which this book is based suggest that directors need to become more involved in identifying and overcoming obstacles and barriers to implementation. In too many companies, a considerable gap has appeared between aspiration and achievement. What is regarded as a lack of commitment, and what are perceived as gaps between 'what a board does and what it says', are undermining confidence and leading to internal conflicts.[3]

The term 'corporate governance' reflects the primary role of the board which is to govern. Governance, in the view of the author, involves:

1. Understanding the context within which a company operates, and the interests, attitudes, perspectives, needs and requirements of the various stakeholders.
2. Determining what needs to be done. An organization and its people require a purpose and vision, and there are broad goals and specific objectives to be established.
3. Creating the capability to do what needs to be done. People, finance and other resources are required, not for their own sake, but in order to achieve corporate goals and objectives.
4. Deciding how to do what needs to be done. Roles and responsibilities need to be agreed, and allocated within the board and among the people of the organization.
5. Ensuring that what needs to be done actually is done. Too often there is a gap between aspiration and achievement. Outcomes should meet expectations, and the highest standards of quality and excellence.
6. Ensuring that what is done, and how it is done, satisfies legal and other requirements.
7. Reporting to stakeholders upon what has been achieved. There are specific accountabilities to certain stakeholders.

The legal and formal accountabilities to stakeholders are established by the legislative and regulatory framework within which the company has incorporated. A group operating through companies incorporated in different countries may find that its accountabilities vary from place to place. For example, in the UK accountability is primarily to the owners, the shareholders, while in Germany the legal framework specifies greater responsibility to employees.

The focus of this book is upon the achievement of excellence, which demands more than the legal minimum. A board that concentrated solely upon a narrow legal interpretation of its responsibilities could fail in the marketplace as a result of not meeting the expectations and requirements of many groups that might consider themselves as having an interest in the company.

The elements of corporate governance

Let us look at each of the above elements of corporate governance in more detail:

DETERMINING WHAT NEEDS TO BE DONE

- Providing and maintaining a purpose for the company, a reason for its continued existence. This should be rooted in marketplace requirements.
- Determining, articulating, communicating and sharing a distinctive and compelling vision.
- Establishing, reviewing and communicating clear goals, values, and objectives derived from the vision. Objectives should be expressed in terms of measurable outcomes.
- Ensuring that the vision, any associated mission, and the goals, values and objectives of the company are consistent with the needs, interests and requirements of its various stakeholders.
- Formulating, reviewing and communicating realistic strategies for the achievement of the defined goals, values and objectives.

CREATING THE CAPABILITY TO DO WHAT NEEDS TO BE DONE

- Ensuring that the company has adequate finance, people, organization, supporting technology, and management and business processes to implement the agreed strategies and subsequent plans.
- In particular, appointing a management team and establishing the values, principles of conduct, and policies that define the framework within which management operates.
- Vancil[4] identifies the appointment of a new CEO as a key opportunity to influence the future direction and performance of a company.
- Establishing and maintaining partnership relationships with those people and organizations whose cooperation will be required if the vision, goals, values and objectives are to be achieved. Supply chain, network and joint-venture relationships could be involved.

DECIDING HOW TO DO WHAT NEEDS TO BE DONE

- Establishing and allocating clear roles and responsibilities within the boardroom team. Particular attention should be given to the roles of chairman and chief executive, and to allocating responsibilities for the key cross-functional and inter-organizational processes that deliver the value that is sought by customers.
- Delegating responsibilities as appropriate to the management team,

and ensuring that these, together with the operating framework and environment of the company, are understood by management.
- Ensuring that members of the management team are involved, empowered and equipped to do what is expected of them.

ENSURING THAT WHAT NEEDS TO BE DONE ACTUALLY IS DONE

- Examining proposals, and approving and reviewing various plans, submitted by the management team.
- Monitoring performance against agreed 'output' targets, taking corrective action where appropriate.
- In particular, identifying and initiating steps to overcome specific obstacles or barriers that hinder the achievement of corporate goals and objectives.

ENSURING THAT WHAT IS DONE, AND HOW IT IS DONE, SATISFIES LEGAL AND OTHER REQUIREMENTS

- Ensuring that the business of the company is conducted in an ethical and responsible way, even if this involves a conflict with economic objectives.[5]
- Ensuring that all the activities of the company observe the laws of those countries within which it operates, and are compatible wherever possible with local customs.
- In particular, ensuring the observance of those laws which particularly relate to companies and the duties and responsibilities of company directors.

REPORTING TO STAKEHOLDERS UPON WHAT HAS BEEN ACHIEVED

- Sustaining relationships with the stakeholders in the company. From time to time the needs, interests, requirements and priorities of stakeholders can change.
- Reporting performance to the stakeholders in the company, and particularly the company's owners.
- Maintaining a balance between the various stakeholders in the company, including a duty of care to the company itself.
- Maintaining a balance between short-, medium- and long-term pressures and requirements.
- Maintaining the capacity to care and cope in the face of adversity, uncertainty and surprise, and the will to confront what is new, daunting and unfamiliar.

The list of functions of the board is extensive. A board that picks and chooses which of them to perform runs many risks. Failing to discharge any of the above responsibilities could, in certain circumstances, severely prejudice the future of a company and the reputations of its directors. A key question should be: Is there a formal statement of the function of the board, and is it agreed, understood and periodically reviewed by the board and brought to the attention of all new directors?

The various accountabilities of a board are 'for real'. They are not 'interesting ideas' that might be applicable in an 'ideal world'. We shall see later in this chapter that a failure to discharge board accountabilities can result in legal penalties.

In order to discharge its various functions the board needs to examine its own operation and performance. This should involve the periodic review of board size, composition, structure and processes. The type, size and composition of boards will be examined in the next chapter.

3.2 Board review process

How can a board ensure that it addresses all its various functions and responsibilities? One method is to list them in the form of a checklist. At a minimum, an officer of the company, perhaps the company secretary, could produce such a checklist once a year for consideration by the board.

Most boards will recognize that their various functions differ in the demands they make upon directors. Some will require detailed consideration. A number are interdependent and difficult to tackle in isolation from one another. The main functions of the board could be linked together in the form of a board review process, such as that in Figure 3.1.

Most boards hold periodic meetings, but many do not operate conscious and formal review processes. The use of board processes that are understood and supported by all directors can significantly increase the value of board meetings.

The process of Figure 3.1 is given by way of illustration. Each company should develop a process that meets its own particular requirements. Whatever form of review process is used by a board, it is important that it should be:

- *comprehensive*: it should cover all the major accountabilities of the board, and address the key requirements of stakeholders;
- *understood* by all the members of the board, and, in particular, all the directors should understand their roles and responsibilities in relation to the process;

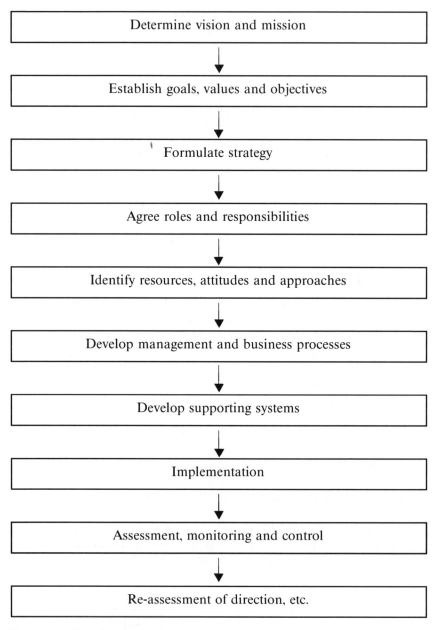

Figure 3.1 Board review process

- *regarded and treated as important*: all directors should be committed to its success;
- *'real', i.e. it should be used*: there should be no room for 'cosmetics' in the boardroom;
- *tough, and not rushed*: if the process is quick and easy, it is probably not being implemented with sufficient rigour;
- *sequential*: there is little point moving to the next stage if one is building upon 'foundations of sand' – a board should be convinced it has successfully tackled each step in the process before moving on;
- *focused*: at all times the board should keep in mind that ultimately the customer is the source of all value;
- *based upon fact rather than opinion*: wherever possible, discussion should be based upon evidence and informed comment rather than uninformed opinion;
- *supported by subprocesses and documents that assist understanding*: information that is not relevant, or does not contribute to understanding, should be avoided;
- *actionable*: outputs of the review process should be capable of implementation;
- *documented*: a record should be kept of process outputs and 'next steps' accountabilities.

3.3 Board accountability

To whom is the board accountable? The 'accountabilities' to stakeholders that were identified by one board are:

- the company itself
- shareholders
- parent company
- bankers
- employees
- social partners
- customers
- suppliers
- business partners
- government and public bodies
- financial advisers
- local communities
- the public at large.

This is not a complete listing of all the accountabilities that every board might have, but it does illustrate the range of interests that a board needs to understand and confront.

The number and nature of the varied responsibilities of directors and boards can sometimes be frustrating to those who seek a single rule such as 'the maximization of shareholder wealth' by which to guide their actions. Even within a single board it is not always easy to secure agreement on the nature, let alone priority, of the various accountabilities.

Stakeholders

Some of the stakeholders to whom the board is accountable include the shareholders, customers, suppliers, employees, the government and the general public (see list above). When drawing up such a list of accountabilities it is important to retain a sense of priority and proportion, and to remember that their relative importance can vary between countries.

In the UK and US, many directors are reluctant to be 'distracted' by accountabilities other than to shareholders. Elsewhere this may not be the case. For example:

- In many EC member states the interests of other stakeholders such as 'social partners' assume a higher priority.
- In Japanese companies the prime allegiance may be to a business philosophy that puts greater stress upon the drive for customers and quality.

Even in a country such as the UK, the reality of the situation, as Charkham has pointed out, is that many boards are relatively free of shareholder pressures.[6]

The board of a company that is operating in the international business environment should periodically consider the extent to which its ranking of 'stakeholder interest' priorities is helping or hindering its ability to compete. Many boards imprison themselves within a cage of their own creation. As a board extends its ambitions it should be prepared to challenge past assumptions.

Merely listing the interested parties or 'stakeholders' to whom a board is accountable is not enough. The directors must:

- understand the distinct interests, needs and requirements of each group of stakeholders;
- communicate and establish relationships with them;
- be sensitive to differences of view and perspective within particular groups where the stakeholders are not homogeneous;

- understand the minimum requirements of each group, in order to judge such factors as how far each can be pushed or to what extent each should be satisfied;
- appreciate the relative power of these groups in terms of the sanctions they could wield;
- where necessary, establish priorities and the basis for trading off the interests of one group of stakeholders against another;
- ensure that any review process used by the board, and the allocation of roles and responsibilities in the boardroom, are such that all accountabilities are covered;
- ensure that the resources and management and business processes are in place to 'deliver'.

Each of the major stakeholders in a company may be in a position to assist or hinder the achievement of corporate objectives. They will vary in their sources of power and the pressures they can bring to bear. A board needs to be sensitive to the various internal and external interests, and aware of the limits of what is acceptable to certain interests.

The extent to which a group of stakeholders are 'active' in the defence of their interests may grow or diminish over time. For example, within the US and UK there have been some suggestions that institutional shareholders should be more active in respect of the affairs and boards of those companies in which they invest, and there is some evidence of 'institutional' pressures causing changes within boardrooms.[7] An alert board identifies, monitors and reacts to such developments.

Trading off accountabilities in the boardroom

At times the requirements of different stakeholders may be in conflict. Perspectives may differ on such matters as timescale or a reasonable apportionment of the value added by the company. The board has to maintain a balance and at times arbitrate between the competing interests in a company. It should also be fair, particularly when some interests are more vocal than others.

The interests of shareholders may well be given a high priority, but directors of UK and US companies ignore other accountabilities at their peril. In practice, many UK and US boards give priority to increasing the value of the shareholders' investment in their companies while acting within ethical and legal constraints, and maintaining a balance between the interests of other stakeholders.

Companies that put a priority upon achieving financial results, perceiving this as being in the best interests of shareholders, may find that their preoccupation with financial performance makes it more difficult to achieve. The growth of shareholder wealth might be reduced, rather than increased, over time if the interests of customers are sacrificed to achieve short-term improvements in the ratios. The customers may take their business elsewhere. The boards of UK and US companies are more likely than their German and Japanese equivalents to make this mistake.

In recent years, more companies have begun to realize that the interests of their shareholders are best served by ensuring that the requirements of other groups, such as customers and employees, are met. Rank Xerox, for example, has put customer satisfaction and employee satisfaction ahead of return on net assets and market share objectives. The financial results are viewed as the consequence or result of having first satisfied customers and employees.

Accountabilities as constraints?

How restrictive in practice are regulatory and other constraints? Beyond what a company and its board are compelled to do there is a considerable area of discretion. Tricker[8] has taken the view that 'Independence in direction may be society's price for corporate scale and managerial power . . . The need is to find a formula which preserves enough managerial freedom to act with the required levels of accountability, oversight and control.'

The author has pointed out that: 'a very large company may be able to influence the very regulations to which it is subject. It is influenced by the environment or framework within which it operates and is itself able to modify this. The company's prosperity may be indistinguishable from that of the society within which it operates'.[9]

Accountabilities are regarded by some boards as a straitjacket. All the directors may moan about the 'tyranny' or burden of the 'obsession' of analysts with short-term financial ratios. Yet few of those who grumble develop programmes to tackle this constraint. There are usually options that could be explored. For example:

- Other sources of financing or different corporate structures could be explored. Complementary finance, additional listings, or new ownership could be sought, or the possibilities for a different place of incorporation investigated.
- New ventures could be put into a joint-venture framework involving partners with different timescales and accountability perspectives. Too many companies choose business partners that replicate and compound, rather than complement, their own deficiencies.
- A board could negotiate with key stakeholders in a company and other interested parties. Analysts may not be averse to longer term objectives

and aspirations that are shared by a board able to demonstrate that it has the commitment and competence to bring them about.

The board ignores 'special interests' at its peril. The support of those who have been overlooked may be needed when the going gets rough.

The board that takes the trouble to communicate with, and build a relationship with, particular groups of stakeholders may benefit from the understanding and goodwill that can be created. At times, for example in periods of difficult trading conditions, or when a company faces the prospect of a takeover, the support of certain stakeholders can be of decisive importance.

A board should identify and rank the various stakeholders in a company and set out what each group requires from the company. For each requirement, it could establish minimum and achievable standards of performance, and identify what steps could be taken to close any gaps that emerge between the current and a desired state. If necessary, trade-offs may have to be established. Roles and responsibilities relating to stakeholders could be allocated among the members of the board, and an implementation and monitoring process put in place to ensure that priority actions occur and that all key requirements of stakeholders are met.

3.4 Culture, attitudes and values

An aspect of the corporate framework which appears to have grown in importance in recent years is corporate culture. This embraces both attitudes and values. There are many sources of this increased concern. For example:

- Attempts are being made by many boards to define a culture that is unique, one that differentiates a company from competitors in the marketplace.
- Without a common vision, and shared goals and values, a network organization could fragment, as members of the network compete rather than cooperate.
- The board of an international company may be concerned that the culture and style of the enterprise is such as to harness the commitment and talents of those from a variety of national, religious, ethnic, and cultural backgrounds.[10]
- A board could be seeking to match the values of a company to those of particular groups, perhaps to attract certain types of potential employees, build closer relationships with customers, or to demonstrate to a local community that the company is concerned about their environment.

The 'climate of opinion' and 'tone' of a company can be set by the board. Values can also be an important differentiator:

- A business philosophy and corporate values can exist in a company as a pious resolution.
- In another company, lip service might be paid to values that are conveniently 'forgotten' when it is thought they could 'get in the way' of a profitable deal.
- There are other companies that do not allow trade-offs against what are regarded as core corporate values.

Corporate codes of conduct and statements of ethics are just words on paper without the visible commitment of the board behind them. Vision, mission and strategy are also merely documents until steps have been taken to implement them. Processes must be initiated to communicate and share them throughout the organization. This generally requires visible and sustained commitment.

3.5 Legal constraints

We have seen that in discharging its responsibilities a board may be subject to operational and moral constraints that are, to a degree, self-imposed. It is also subject to other constraints that are imposed and must be accepted as 'given'.

In carrying out its role the board is subject to certain legal, fiduciary, ethical and practical constraints which reflect its obligations to the various interests or 'stakeholders' in the company. For example, in the UK these constraints can be:

- internal and specific such as the Memorandum and Articles of Association; or
- external and general such as the Companies Act, Insolvency Act, Financial Services Act and other legislation placing specific duties and responsibilities upon directors and boards.

In the case of a public sector board, some constraints upon the freedom of the directors to act might be imposed by a contractual relationship with government, public accountability requirements, or guidance issued by a Minister or Secretary of State.

3.6 Duties and responsibilities of directors

The legal duties and responsibilities of directors are extensive, and are covered in some detail in other publications.[11] A board should periodically review its duties and responsibilities, preferably with a qualified lawyer in attendance.

The legal situation is liable to change, and general points made in this chapter should be regarded as illustrative of 'areas to watch' rather than as definitive. A director in doubt should seek advice from the company or corporate secretary.

The situation will vary from country to country, but in general terms, within the UK:

1. A director owes a fiduciary duty to the company. Hence the director should act in good faith, and in the best interests of the company.
2. The powers of the board should only be used for the purposes for which they were conferred.
3. A director is expected to act as an honest steward in respect of corporate property and confidential information.
4. A director should disclose any 'conflicts of interest' to board colleagues, and should not take personal advantage of corporate opportunities.
5. In particular, a director should seek to avoid *ultra vires* actions and activities that are outside the powers of the company, or his or her powers as a director of the company. The objects of a company, and its powers to carry out these objects, are set out in the objects clause of a company's Memorandum of Association.
6. Directors are under a duty of care not to be negligent in their directorial roles. The standard of skill expected will reflect the knowledge and experience of the individual director. It is recognized that a non-executive director may not be in a position to give continuous attention to a company's affairs.
7. A director is also expected to be financially prudent, and should avoid entering into commitments that cannot be honoured.
8. In particular, directors should avoid the risk of wrongful trading under the Insolvency Act 1986 (s. 214) which could result in personal liability. We shall examine this later.

A director is entitled to whatever information is necessary for the performance of his or her duties. Where there are no grounds for assuming that information supplied by management is wrong or misleading, the director is also entitled to rely upon it.

The extent of risk

The statutory responsibilities of directors are becoming progressively more extensive and demanding. The penalties for a failure to observe them can extend to fines, imprisonment and unlimited personal liability. For example, within the UK:

- Under the Insolvency Act 1986 (s. 213), directors who have acted to defraud creditors may be required to contribute to the assets of the company.
- Under the Company Directors Disqualification Act 1986 the court may disqualify a person from serving as a director for up to 5 or 15 years, according to circumstances.
- Conviction for failing to file an annual return and annual accounts can result in a fine and a criminal record.

We shall examine some particular areas of risk later in this chapter. The decision of whether or not to join a board is one that should not be taken lightly. In the US, some boards have found it difficult to attract potential directors of the desired calibre in view of the financial risks involved.

Minimizing risks

A competent director acts prudently and in good faith, and avoids conflicts of interest. An individual should investigate the affairs, conduct and financial standing of a company before agreeing to join a board. Thereafter a director should stay informed of changing circumstances, monitor up-to-date financial information, and seek professional advice as appropriate.

There are legal constraints on the avoidance of directorial responsibility. For example, within the UK the Companies Act 1985 (s. 310) makes void any contractual arrangements that provide for exemption from liability for negligence, default, breach of duty, or breach of trust.

A board, and its members, should seriously consider directors' and officers' liability insurance. A 'board' approach is normally taken, covering all directors and officers of the company, but individual cover can be obtained. The latter could be appropriate for a non-executive director serving upon a number of boards.

Shadow directors

Those who advise or influence directors and boards also need to take care. Certain duties and responsibilities of directors extend to 'shadow directors'.

A 'shadow director' is 'a person in accordance with whose directions or instructions the directors of the company are accustomed to act' (Companies Act 1985, s. 741(2)). However:

- those who give advice in a professional capacity such as lawyers and accountants are excluded;

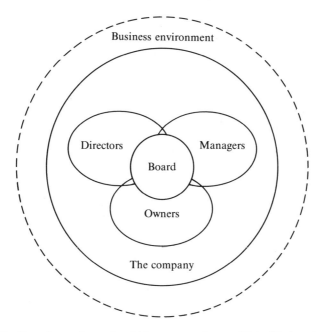

Figure 3.2   Board members should be aware of a conflict of interests

- those giving instructions within a holding company/subsidiary company relationship are not considered to be 'shadow directors'.

Conflicts of interest

It is particularly important that members of a board are able to distinguish between the roles of owners, directors and managers. There is often overlap between these categories. There are owner directors and owner managers as both directors and managers own shares in a company. It is possible for an owner executive director to be an owner, director and a manager.

An individual member of the board might have separate interests in, and obligations to, a company by virtue of being a director, an employee or manager, and an owner (Figure 3.2). When one or more of these roles are combined, the individuals concerned should be aware of the differences between them and take care to avoid conflicts of interest.

The disqualification of directors

The circumstances in which a director may be disqualified or removed from office varies from country to country, and reference should be made to the local situation. In the UK, directors who abuse the privilege of limited liability can find themselves under the close scrutiny of the Official Receiver. According to the Department of Trade and Industry,[12] 'His aim is to remove unfit directors from the corporate field as quickly as possible in order to protect the public from their dishonest activities.'

The Insolvency Act 1986 streamlined the procedures for handling bankruptcies and company liquidations, while the Company Directors Disqualification Act 1986 allows the Official Receiver to bring disqualification proceedings against incompetent, dishonest and negligent directors of insolvent companies.

According to the Department of Trade and Industry,[12]

a typical case for court action might involve:

– continuing to trade when insolvent with no reasonable prospect of payment of creditors' claims
– excessive remuneration and benefits to directors
– breaches of the Companies Act
– inadequate attention to the financial affairs of the company
– failure to keep proper accounts
– transactions which preferred the directors or close associates.

The courts, the DTI and the public expect a better standard of conduct than this. They expect one which demonstrates directors' willingness not only to adhere to their statutory obligations to file returns, prepare accounts, and maintain adequate records, but also to act competently in the best interests of the company, its creditors and its shareholders.

The Insolvency Service's network of Official Receivers, supported by insolvency practitioners, represent an important element of the regulatory framework which seeks to protect the public from delinquent directors. The Insolvency Service became an executive agency within the DTI on 21 March 1990.

The Official Receiver acts on the orders of the court who, when a company is compulsorily wound up, appoints the Official Receiver as liquidator. The Official Receiver has a duty under the Insolvency Act 1986 to investigate and report on the circumstances surrounding the collapse with a view to disqualification.

Section 6 of the Company Directors Disqualification Act 1986 allows the court to make a disqualification order of up to 15 years for unfit behaviour. Using this section, Official Receivers are now spending more time investigating the affairs of failed companies and proceeding against unfit directors. By the end of July 1991, The Insolvency Service had succeeded in obtaining over 1000 disqualification orders on incompetent, dishonest and negligent company directors.[12] At the end of June 1991 there were 699 applications under section 6 awaiting hearing by the courts.

The perils of insolvency

In demanding economic conditions, or when a company is experiencing financial difficulties, directors should take particular care not to trade wrongfully or fraudulently, or to enter into transactions at an 'undervalue' or which give a 'preference'. For example, in certain circumstances when a winding-up occurs in the UK a director can be required, under the Insolvency Act 1986, to make a financial contribution or repay monies, and transactions can be nullified:

- Section 212 applies in the course of a winding-up and covers any person who is or who has been an officer of a company, or a liquidator, or any person involved in the promotion, formation or management of the company, who misapplies, retains money or other property of the company or is in breach of any fiduciary or other duty owed to the company. On application by the liquidator or a creditor, the court may compel the repayment of money with interest or whatever other compensation it considers appropriate.
- Fraudulent trading is a criminal offence. Under section 213 where it appears in the course of a winding-up that the business of a company has been carried on with the intent to defraud creditors, any persons knowingly a party to this may be required by the court to make such contributions to the company's assets that it considers proper.
- Under section 214 the court has wide powers, on the application by the liquidator, to require a director or former director to make 'such contribution (if any) to the company's assets as the court thinks proper' where the person knew, or ought to have concluded, some time before the commencement of a winding-up and while a director, that there was no reasonable prospect that the company would avoid going into insolvent liquidation. Declarations will not be made under this section where the court is satisfied that a person took every step that ought to have been taken to minimize the potential loss of the creditors of the company.
- Section 238 is applicable where a company has entered into a transaction at an 'undervalue'. The court may make an order to restore the position to what would have been the situation had the transaction in question not occurred. Under sections 423 to 425 of the Act transactions at an 'undervalue' can be nullified.
- Section 239 applies in circumstances in which a 'preference' is given to a creditor or a guarantor of a company's debts who is thereby put in a

better position than would otherwise be the case when a company goes into insolvent liquidation. The court may make whatever order it considers would restore the situation to that which would have been the case had the 'preference' not been given.

It can sometimes be difficult to keep up to date with new developments, such as clauses 'buried' in new legislation, that place additional duties upon directors. A company secretary who keeps members of the board up to date with their responsibilities and refers to legal responsibilities as appropriate when various matters appear on the boardroom agenda can be invaluable.

3.7 Legal responsibilities of directors

All directors share common legal duties and responsibilities. There is no distinction in this regard between the executive and the non-executive director.

'Management' as such does not appear among the functions of the board. When acting as directors, the members of the board are concerned not with management but with the direction and governance of the company. Those members of the board who are executive directors are also likely to have management responsibilities relating to the implementation of particular plans and policies. In discharging these responsibilities such directors may find it necessary to liaise, coordinate and work with board colleagues responsible for other functions and aspects of the business. It is important that executive directors remain aware of their distinct responsibilities as directors and managers.

The responsibility of directors for ensuring the accuracy of financial information, and the adequacy of the financial recording and reporting system, requires them to have some understanding of the principles of accounts and financial reporting. In the case of a public company there will be Stock Exchange requirements to satisfy in addition to legal provisions that apply to all companies. There are certain questions that should be addressed:

- Are all members of the board aware of their legal and fiduciary duties and responsibilities; of the contents of the Memorandum and Articles of Association; and of the circumstances that can give rise to legal penalties and, in particular, wrongful or fraudulent trading?
- Are legal developments relevant to directors and boards brought to the attention of all the directors; and are the members of the board covered by an appropriate directors' professional liability insurance?
- Are all directors aware of the circumstances in which they might

experience a conflict of interest, are such conflicts of interest declared; and does the board make appropriate arrangements to avoid the conflicts of interest that can arise where one or more individuals may be a director, an employee and an owner?

- Has the board established and communicated a framework of corporate values, and is this observed; and do all members of the board themselves behave as role models in respect of all aspects of their conduct?

3.8 The role of the chairman

Whose responsibility is it for ensuring that, *inter alia*, the directors understand the purpose and function of the board and their legal duties and responsibilities? Should this be the responsibility of the chief executive, or of the chairman?

In the opinion of the author, the chairman has a special role in creating excellence within the boardroom.[13] When the same individual is both chairman and chief executive, it is important that the distinct responsibilities of the two roles are understood and addressed.

Aspects of the chairman's role of particular relevance to the theme of this book are listed in Example 3.1. In recent years, a number of chairmen have summarized their thoughts concerning the broader aspects of the role of the company chairman.[14]

Regular reviews of the function and purpose of the board, and of the individual and collective roles and responsibilities of its members, help to sharpen awareness of the distinct role of the director. They should be

---

Annually review the function and purpose of the board
Review individual and collective roles and responsibilities
Review the size, composition, operation and effectiveness of the board
Assess the effectiveness and contribution of all directors
Ensure that all new directors are aware of their legal duties and responsibilities
Ensure that all new directors are properly prepared for the boardroom
Ensure that the directorial skills of all directors remain current and relevant
Ensure that the business of the board is conducted effectively
Encourage an atmosphere of openness and trust
Encourage all members of the board to contribute
Build a united team embracing both executive and non-executive directors
Maintain a cohesive group without losing diversity and objectivity

---

Example 3.1   The role of the chairman

built into the board calendar and the corporate planning process to ensure that they do not take place in a vacuum. Similarly, reviews of board operation and effectiveness, and assessments of the contributions of individual directors should be related to the vision and mission of the company and the extent to which its goals and objectives are achieved.

The effective chairman ensures that all members of the board are encouraged to contribute.[15] To bring about fundamental change the board may need to act, and be seen to be operating, as a united team.[3] At the same time, as Demb and Neubauer warn,[16] familiarity should not be allowed to result in the board becoming a 'cosy club'.

Directors hold the fate of companies in their hands, and yet few receive any formal training either prior to, or subsequent to, their appointment to the board.[17, 18] Company chairmen need to assume responsibility for ensuring that all directors are properly prepared for their onerous responsibilities, and that their boards operate effectively as a team.

Evidence shows that, in the absence of formal preparation for appointment to the board, informal arrangements are being used by individual directors.[17] Chairmen should also ensure that full advantage is taken of informal learning and development opportunities. These issues will be addressed later in this book.

There has, in recent years, been much discussion of the need for greater investment in management education and development. In a growing number of companies such investment is now being made. However, most boards do not appear to be displaying the same commitment towards their own development.

The BIM report *Beyond Quality*[19] suggests that there is a danger of management education and development resulting in managers working smarter at the wrong things if an overall sense of direction is lacking and prioritization and focus do not occur. There is little point in an activity that is 'well done' but does not result in more satisfied customers. Initiatives to develop the competence of managers need to be matched by the development of competence in the boardroom.

3.9 Chairmen's perceptions of the function of the board

Having examined the formal accountabilities of directors and boards, and the special role of the chairman, let us turn to the chairman's perspective of the role of the board. In a 'chairman' survey undertaken by Coulson-Thomas and Wakelam,[13] questionnaire recipients were asked, not about the functions of boards in general, but about the functions of their particular board. Their responses in terms of the 'top ten' functions of the board are listed in Figure 3.3.

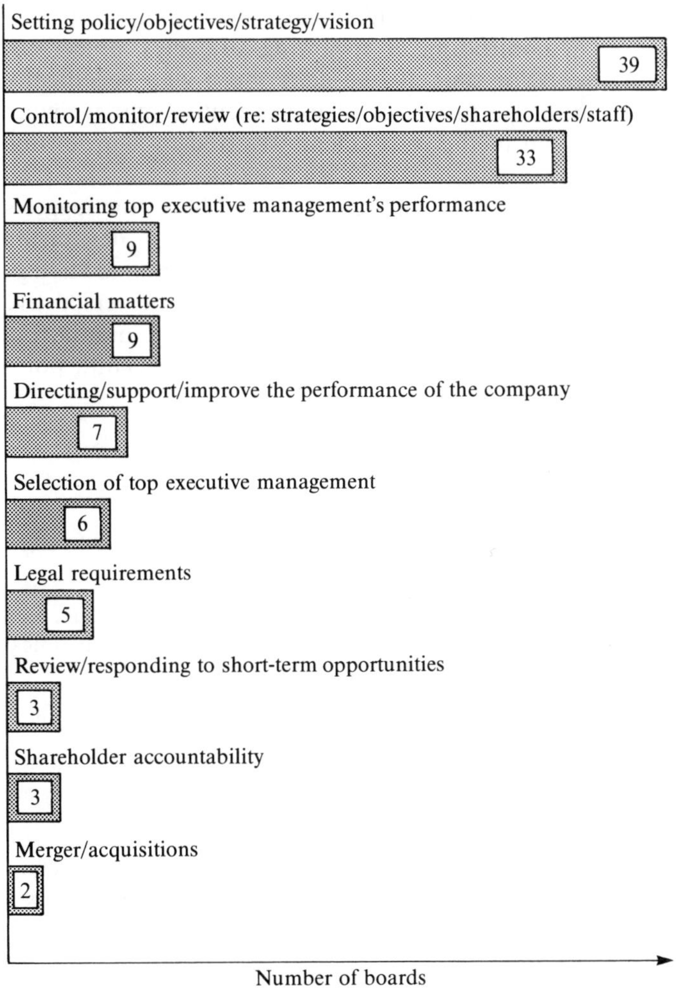

Setting policy/objectives/strategy/vision

| 39 |

Control/monitor/review (re: strategies/objectives/shareholders/staff)

| 33 |

Monitoring top executive management's performance

| 9 |

Financial matters

| 9 |

Directing/support/improve the performance of the company

| 7 |

Selection of top executive management

| 6 |

Legal requirements

| 5 |

Review/responding to short-term opportunities

| 3 |

Shareholder accountability

| 3 |

Merger/acquisitions

| 2 |

Number of boards

Figure 3.3   The 'top ten' functions of the board

Priority functions of the board

The largest single group of responses in the 'chairman' survey[13] could be categorized as setting the policy, objectives, strategy or vision of the company. If one includes the 'direction' of policy and strategy, then seven out of ten respondents described the function of their boards in proactive terms of establishing policy, objectives, strategy or vision.

The next largest group of replies could be categorized as a reactive or monitoring function of controlling or reviewing strategies, objectives, shareholder requirements, or staff. If one adds those who specifically referred to monitoring the performance of top executive management, then over seven out of ten of the respondents referred to a reviewing, monitoring and controlling role.

Another survey of boards within an area of the public sector suggests that many board members of public bodies share a similar view of the function of the board.[20] Establishing and reviewing objectives and strategy emerge clearly as the priority functions of the board from the perspective of the chairman. 'Establishing and setting' and 'reviewing, monitoring and controlling' are also related. Those interviewed felt there is little point in doing the former without the latter:

> The best strategy in the world is worthless if it cannot be implemented.

> The boards of plenty of dead companies knew the right answers.

> Every consultant we meet tells us what we ought to do. We are short of people who can help us to do it.

> You sweat blood on a strategy, and then you realize that all you have is a directors' minute. Nothing has happened yet. Nothing will happen unless you think through how to make it happen.

> The balance is changing. We are putting more effort into implementation.

> We used to give it to management, and they would get on with it. Not any more. We can't assume anyone knows what to do. We have to ensure they are motivated, and that they have the resources and the right tools.

> Delegation is one thing, abdication another. Concentrating on the 'big picture' isn't abdicating your responsibilities. The board has to stay with it and 'see it through'.

In practice, the involvement of many boards with strategy amounts to approving strategy proposals rather than strategy planning.[21] Evidence suggests that: (a) many boards are not effectively translating a strategic vision into a corporate reality; and (b) the development need relates to 'implementation' or 'making it happen' rather than the determination of strategy.[22]

To review the performance of top management effectively, executive directors need to be aware of their distinct roles as managers and directors, and when acting in the latter category they need to be objective and independent. In the case of those directly involved in the day-to-day conduct of business this will not be easy and will require detachment and self-discipline. Objectivity in the boardroom can be easier to achieve when separate individuals hold the appointments of chairman and chief executive.

Other functions of the board

Only one in three respondents in the 'chairman' survey[13] referred to a function that could be categorized as legal or financial. Over four out of ten respondents referred either to financial matters, or the monitoring or improvement of performance. Only one in seven referred to legal requirements or shareholder accountability. This is less than one might have expected given the number of those interviewed who referred to the pressures upon them to achieve financial results.

It would appear that responsibility towards the company itself, its survival and development, ranks ahead of that to shareholders. When considering the role of boards in general, one needs to bear in mind that only a small proportion of the total population of companies are public companies or 'plcs'.

Not a single respondent referred to understanding, assessing or interpreting the external business environment. The function of the board was largely described in terms of the company and its activities, rather than the business context within which it operates.

During interviews it emerged that directors, when prompted, acknowledge the importance of understanding the external business environment when establishing strategies, objectives and policies. Even in these areas, however, the main consideration appears to be the company's need for survival and development rather than how the company might respond to the nature of external challenges and opportunities.

The perspective of those surveyed, when they considered the function of the board, was largely that of the company as a whole. Less than one in ten described the function of their board in terms of specific activities or functional responsibilities.

In the 'chairman' survey,[13] about one in three respondents referred to the selection of top executive management and monitoring of their performance as a function of the board. This is a lower proportion than one might have expected. Those interviewed stressed the need to involve all employees, and not just senior managers, in the implementation of strategy. One respondent referred to 'lead by example' as a function of the board, but otherwise 'leadership' was not referred to. 'Leadership' *per se* did not emerge during the course of interviews as a particular concern of chairmen.

It appears that determining vision, mission and strategy may be perceived as 'direction' rather than as an aspect of 'leadership'. Those interviewed tend to apply 'leadership' to the process of motivating people to understand and achieve vision, mission and strategy once these have been defined by the board. In this sense 'leadership' is seen as a management rather than a boardroom competence. Other aspects of the distinction between direction and management will be considered in Chapter 5.

Customers and the board

Not one respondent in the 'chairman' survey[13] mentioned customers in the context of the function of the board. To put this into some perspective:

– We saw in Chapter 2 that in an Adaptation survey for the IOD[18] the top two business issues both concerned customers, namely 'satisfying customers' and 'delivering quality'. Over nine out of ten respondents thought these particular issues to be 'very important'.
– Similarly, we saw that in the BIM report, *Beyond Quality*,[19] 'building longer term relationships with customers' and 'introducing a more customer-oriented culture' ranked at the top of a number of management issues.
– Many of those interviewed in the 'chairman' survey[13] emphasized that a central purpose of determining strategy and setting objectives was to generate value for customers.
– Other interviewees drew a distinction between the company as a whole and the business of the board. Serving customers was seen as the core rationale for the continued existence of the company, and essentially everyone's responsibility.

Commitment to the customer should never be assumed. What is considered to be a priority business issue, and the essence or purpose of the company, may not always be uppermost in the minds of members of the board. One should also not underestimate the sustained effort needed to build satisfactory relationships with customers.[23]

According to Phillip Judkins,[24] a director of the Provincial Group plc, a mission statement or statement of 'basic beliefs' 'must focus on customers and what they are buying', and upon how people 'add value to the transactions between buyer and seller'. The board should ensure that the implementation of corporate visions, values, missions or goals does not focus upon 'internal' requirements at the expense of the customer.

3.10 Directorial commitment

Given the function and the many responsibilities of the board, how much time should be devoted to directorial duties? A Korn/Ferry survey of

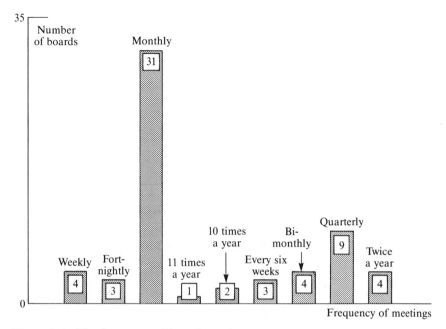

Figure 3.4   The frequency of board meetings

larger UK companies suggests that non-executive directors spend 10–12 days per annum on their directorial duties,[25] while an average of 14 days a year has been suggested for US directors.[1]

One indicator of commitment is the frequency with which the board meets. Those participating in *The Effective Board* survey,[13] were asked how often their boards met. The responses are summarized in Figure 3.4.

A majority of boards appear to meet on a monthly basis. Only one in eight of the boards meet on a weekly or fortnightly basis. About one in ten boards plan to meet on three or fewer occasions during the course of a year.

In all but one case board meetings are held on a regular or periodic basis. One respondent indicated his board met 'whenever there is statutory business to conduct', while other boards held additional meetings 'on an ad hoc basis as necessary'. The overwhelming majority of boards appear to do more than perform a minimum legal requirement.

The frequency of board meetings may depend upon the size and type of company. For example, in countries in which they are a requirement, the meetings of many supervisory boards are held on a quarterly basis.[16]

The commitment of very few directors should be limited to their attendance at formal board meetings. In the case of most companies, and even for non-executive directors, there will be board papers to read and digest, and other forms of preparation to be undertaken between board meetings.

According to an earlier survey that was undertaken by Alan Wakelam,[17] less than one in twenty directors devote over 80 per cent of their time to direction as opposed to management or other activities. Fewer than one in five directors devote over a half of their time to direction. Six out of ten directors appear to spend less than a third of their time on direction.

The directorial commitment of those who are members of boards – i.e. their duties as directors, as opposed to executives – appears to be intermittent. Many appear to perceive their commitment as largely related to formal board meetings. While executive directors are engaged, between meetings of the board, in 'managerial' tasks such as running a functional department, their non-executive colleagues may be preoccupied with matters unconnected with the company.

When board meetings occur on a bimonthly or quarterly basis, non-executive directors in particular can feel out of touch. In such cases informal or social contact outside of formal board meetings may be desirable. This can help to improve mutual understanding and relationships, and may enable board members to exchange information and remain more up-to-date with a company's situation.

3.11 Summary

In this chapter we have examined the role, function and accountabilities of the board, and the legal duties and responsibilities of directors. We have seen that the board has to arbitrate between, and build and sustain relationships with, various groups of stakeholders. To do this, and to discharge its various responsibilities, board processes are necessary. The chairman should assume responsibility for ensuring that the company has an effective board composed of competent directors.

3.12 Checklist

1. Does the board of your company understand its role and function?
2. To whom is the board accountable, and for what?
3. Has the board understood and prioritized the needs, interests and requirements of key stakeholders?
4. Which group of stakeholders is the most disgruntled, and why?
5. Do all the directors understand their legal duties and responsibilities?
6. What legal risks are the company, its board and its directors running?

7. If the company were a person, how would you describe it?
8. How 'moral' is the company?
9. Has the board formulated operational goals, values, objectives and policies, or are the aims just 'words on paper'?
10. How realistic is the strategy of the board?
11. Is the board as capable of implementing strategy as it is of formulating it?
12. Are the various resources of the company – i.e. finance, people, organization, technology, and processes – sufficient to enable it to meet its obligations and commitments to stakeholders, and to achieve its goals and objectives?
13. How adequate are the processes of the board itself? Does the board operate a review process that embraces its major accountabilities?
14. Do members of the board devote sufficient time to 'directorial' as opposed to 'managerial' duties?
15. Who is responsible for ensuring that the board is effective, and that its individual members are competent?
16. What do people in the company generally think of the board?
17. What would happen if the board ceased to meet? What would be missed the most?

Notes and references

1. Lorsch, J. and MacIver, E., *Pawns or Potentates: The reality of America's corporate boards*, Harvard Business School Press, 1989.
2. Tricker, R., *Corporate Governance: Practices, procedures and powers in British companies and their Boards of Directors*, Gower, 1984.
3. Coulson-Thomas, C., *Transforming the Company: Bridging the gap between management myth and corporate reality*, Kogan Page, 1992.
4. Vancil, R., *Passing the Baton: Managing the process of CEO succession*, Harvard Business School Press, 1987.
5. Carr, A. Z., 'Can an executive afford a conscience?', *Harvard Business Review*, July–August 1970, 58–74.
6. Charkham, J. P., *Effective Boards*, The Institute of Chartered Accountants in England and Wales, 1986.
7. ABI, *The Responsibilities of Institutional Shareholders – A Discussion Paper*, Association of British Insurers, 1991; and Walsh, F., 'Sweeping out the boardrooms', *The Sunday Times*, 16 June 1991, Section 4, p. 9.
8. Tricker, R. I., *The Independent Director: A study of the non-executive director and of the audit committee*, Tolley Publishing Company, 1978, p. 3.
9. Coulson-Thomas, C., *Public Relations is Your Business: A guide for every manager*, Business Books, 1981, p. 59.
10. Coulson-Thomas, C., *Creating the Global Company: Successful internationalization*, McGraw-Hill, 1992.
11. Institute of Directors, *Guidelines for Directors*, 4th edn, The Director Publications, May 1990; *The Penalties of Being in Business*, Federation of Small Businesses,

December 1990; and Wright, D., *Rights & Duties of Directors*, Butterworths, 1991.

12. Redwood, J., MP, *Over 1,000 Unfit Directors Disqualified*, Department of Trade and Industry Press Notice P/91/420, 31 July 1991.
13. Coulson-Thomas, C. and Wakelam, A., *The Effective Board: Current practice, myths and realities*. An IOD discussion document, 1991.
14. Cadbury, Sir A., *The Company Chairman*, Director Books, 1990; Iacocca, L., *Iacocca, An Autobiography*, Sidgwick & Jackson, 1988; and Harvey-Jones, Sir J., *Making it Happen*, 2nd edn, Fontana, 1989.
15. Belbin, R., *Management Teams*, Heinemann Educational Books, 1981; Coulson-Thomas, C., *Developing Directors: Building an effective boardroom team*, McGraw-Hill, 1993.
16. Demb, A. and Neubauer, F-F., *The Corporate Board: Confronting the paradoxes*, Oxford University Press, 1992.
17. Wakelam, A., *The Training & Development of Company Directors*. Report for the Training Agency, Centre for Management Studies, University of Exeter, October, 1989.
18. Coulson-Thomas, C., *Professional Development of and for the Board*. A questionnaire and interview survey undertaken by Adaptation Ltd of company chairmen. A summary has been published by the IOD, February 1990.
19. Coulson-Thomas, C. and Brown, R., *Beyond Quality: Managing the relationship with the customer*, BIM, 1990.
20. Coulson-Thomas, C., *Development Needs of NHS Authority and Board Members*. A report prepared by Adaptation Ltd on behalf of the NHS Training Directorate, July 1992.
21. Henke, J. W., 'Involving the board of directors in strategic planning', *Journal of Business Strategy*, **7** (2), 87–95.
22. Mace, M. L., *Directors: Myth and Reality*, Division of Research, Graduate School of Business Administration, Harvard University, 1971; and Coulson-Thomas, C., 'Strategic vision or strategic con?: Rhetoric or reality?', *Long Range Planning*, **25** (1), 1992, 81–9.
23. Schonberger, R., *Building a Chain of Customers*, The Free Press & Business Books, 1990.
24. Judkins, P., 'The personnel practitioner and the boardroom', paper presented at the Institute of Personnel Management 1991 National Conference, October 1991, p. 9.
25. Korn/Ferry, *Boards of Directors Study UK*, Korn/Ferry International, 1989.

4
Distinction between direction and management

Whilst the functions of direction and of management of a company are significantly different, they overlap and intertwine, and the quality of each is important to a business. (DR INGHAM LENTON, chairman of Compass Group plc.)

The effectiveness of many boards is reduced by the failure of their members to think through and understand the distinction between direction and management. This is particularly true of boards made up exclusively of executive directors. On occasion, meetings of directors can become little more than a management, or coordinating, committee to update information for those present and to allocate tasks.

This chapter examines what is 'different' about being a director, and in particular how being a corporate director differs from being a departmental manager. We shall consider not just the theoretical distinction derived from the role and function of the board as examined in Chapter 3, but also how working directors perceive and articulate the distinction.

Understanding of the distinction between direction and management is often confused by the fact that within the boardroom there are usually executive directors who are both managers and directors. Even on US boards, made up predominantly of non-executives, one is likely to find a CEO who leads the management team. In practice, directorial and managerial responsibilities can appear to overlap, and some people do not find it easy to keep the roles apart.

4.1 Directorial duties and responsibilities

We shall begin with the legal aspects of the distinction between direction and management. Directors have distinct legal duties and responsibilities that are not shared by managers. For example, they are appointed by, and are accountable to, shareholders.

It should not be thought, however, that managers are free of legal duties and responsibilities. For example, in the UK, under the Insolvency Act 1986, individuals who are not directors of a company, including officers or those who take part in its management, may be required in certain circumstances to restore money or other property to a company. However, the legal duties and responsibilities of directors are different from those of managers, and, taken as a whole, they are more onerous.

All directors should be made aware of their legal duties and responsibilities, and kept up to date with developments in the law relating to directors and boards. Their understanding should be tested periodically; it should never be taken for granted. Creating and maintaining awareness of directorial duties and responsibilities should form the initial plank or element of a director development programme.

4.2 The function of the board

The next step is to ensure that directors understand the function of the board. This can be done using the exercises suggested in the author's companion volume to this book on 'developing directors'.[1] This understanding provides them with a framework within which they can explore their own individual and collective accountabilities and responsibilities.

A shared understanding of the role of the board can also help to increase directors' awareness of the respective responsibilities of directors and managers. For example, directors could be responsible for strategy formulation, whereas managers might be responsible for the implementation of some aspect of strategy.

A single individual can be an owner or shareholder, a director, and a manager. Executive directors may need to distinguish between: (a) their rights and interests as shareholders; (b) their collective responsibility for the overall strategy and performance of the company; and (c) their individual responsibilities as heads of functions, divisions and business units for the delivery of certain aspects of the corporate plan.

4.3 Directorial qualities

When assessing the qualities, attitudes, approach and perspective of a particular board, or of the individual members of a boardroom team, it is usually desirable to test their understanding of the distinction between direction and management. How is this distinction perceived by directors in general?

In a survey based predominantly on company chairmen,[2] the qualities that were considered to distinguish 'direction', or the distinct role of the director, from 'management' are listed below. The survey was undertaken by Adaptation Ltd for the IOD. A wide range of qualities were identified by the participants, and only the 'top ten' are ranked.

1. Strategic awareness and planning
2. Objectivity – ability to see company as a whole
3. Long-term vision
4. Ultimate responsibility of company
5. Commanding respect/leadership
6. Decision/policy making
7. Anticipate changing trends
8. Delegation
9. Lateral thinking
10. Responsibility to shareholders.

For some two out of three respondents in the IOD survey the essence of the distinction between 'direction' and 'management' lies in a broad, longer term or strategic awareness and perspective. The quality to see a situation as a whole and look ahead is one that respondents clearly feel directors should have.

The position of 'responsibility to shareholders' at the bottom of the list is partly explained by the fact that the sample of companies used was selected to be representative of the total population of companies. It hence contained relatively few quoted companies.

It also emerged during interviews that while they were aware of their accountability to various stakeholders such as shareholders, directors tend to put a priority upon their responsibility to the company itself. In discharging this responsibility they emphasize the need for vision and strategy, and the importance of maintaining a balance between the interests of various stakeholders, while not excessively emphasizing the interests of one group at the expense of the others.

The qualities the IOD survey participants sought in new members of the board were overwhelmingly personal qualities and attributes. We shall examine these qualities in Chapter 8 on the criteria used in selecting directors.

The ranking of directorial qualities given above is consistent with the results of other surveys. For example, participants in a survey of personnel directors undertaken by Adaptation Ltd in conjunction with the Research Group of the IPM[3] also:

– identified strategic awareness and vision as the key distinguishing directorial qualities;

- emphasized the need for the perspective of directors to be that of the company as a whole, rather than that of a particular function;
- put a priority on responsibility to the company itself rather than responsibility to shareholders;
- stressed the need for business acumen and personal qualities rather than specialist or technical skills.

These findings have implications for director development. They suggest that:

- efforts to define and build management competences may not of themselves lead to the qualities considered desirable in company directors;
- experience derived from a track record in moving between managerial functions will not necessarily lead to the personal qualities and the perspective that are sought in new appointees to a board;
- whether or not a boardroom candidate possesses such qualities as 'strategic awareness' or 'the ability to see the company as a whole' may be the prime consideration, not the means or route by which these qualities have been acquired.

4.4 The essence of direction

So far we have focused on the role of the director, the function of the board, and the distinction between direction and management. Given this understanding, it ought now to be possible (a) to define the requirements for effective boards and competent directors; and (b) to consider what practical steps can be taken to promote excellence in the boardroom. However, before we move ahead it is necessary to ensure that the distinction between direction and management has been understood. If the essence of direction is not clear, any 'next steps' may be taken on insecure ground. A resulting programme could be based upon foundations of sand.

There are reasons for caution. For example, certain qualities that might be regarded as important by participants in a survey of directorial qualities might also be regarded as important qualities for managers to possess.

Senior management team qualities

What qualities are sought in members of a senior management team, and how do they compare with directorial qualities? The management qualities sought by major companies, according to a survey undertaken by Adaptation Ltd for SEMS[4], are summarized in Table 4.1. The

Table 4.1   Senior management team qualities ranked in order of 'very important' replies

Strategic awareness	76%
Customer focus	61%
Individual responsibility	59%
Communication skills	52%
Creativity	43%
Perspective	40%
Team player	35%
Objectivity	34%
Self-discipline	34%
International awareness and perspective	28%
Breadth	28%
Transnational confidence and effectiveness	21%
European awareness and perspective	18%
Language ability	1%

Source: Human Resource Development for International Operation, 1990

responses are presented in order of 'very important' replies. The most important quality sought is 'strategic awareness', followed by 'customer focus', 'individual responsibility' and 'communication skills'.

Some three-quarters of the respondents consider 'strategic awareness' to be a very important 'senior management' quality. 'Strategic awareness', 'customer focus' and 'individual responsibility' emerge as qualities that are important for both company directors and senior managers.[2, 4]

Some interviewees in the SEMS survey[4] compared and contrasted the qualities sought in senior managers and directors, respectively:

- The importance of particular 'management' qualities was thought to vary according to function and/or business unit. For example, qualities such as those relating to international and European operation were perceived as most relevant to managers within a company who were most concerned with international operations.
- In contrast, when these qualities were sought in directors they were considered to be relatively independent of function and important for the organization as a whole.
- Professionals ranked 'individual responsibility' relatively highly as a management quality. Although ranked third as a quality sought by all respondents (see Table 4.1), it was ranked first in terms of 'very important' replies by respondents from UK professional firms and associations.
- Interviewees made the point that, traditionally, both professionals and those holding a portfolio of directorships place considerable importance upon individual professional autonomy and responsibility. There are many individuals who might be attracted to the role of professional

director if more company chairmen could be persuaded to include more non-executive directors in their boardroom teams.

– A number of respondents stressed the importance of 'strategic awareness' as a senior management quality because of the need of senior managers to work closely with directors. In order to advise directors, senior managers needed to understand their perspective.

The qualities sought in both senior managers and directors may well reflect the national context. For example, in the SEMS survey:

– European and international respondents gave 'international awareness and perspective' a significantly higher importance rating than did respondents from UK companies.
– 'Language ability' was ranked significantly more highly by European and international companies. All but one of these respondents considered it to be either 'important' or 'very important'.
– 'Transnational confidence and effectiveness' was also ranked more highly by European and international companies than by UK companies.

The participants in the SEMS survey were also asked to state the 'other qualities' they sought in members of a senior management team. Their responses are listed in Table 4.2. The abilities to lead, motivate and develop others, both as individuals and in teams, emerge at the head of the list. Overall, personal qualities and attributes appear to rank ahead of technical expertise. Little importance is attached to 'qualifications', these being mentioned by only two respondents. These findings, relating to senior managers, are again consistent with survey evidence concerning the qualities sought in company directors.[2, 3, 5]

Another quality which is increasingly required by both directors and managers is the ability to communicate:

– Directors need to do more than just formulate and agree vision, goals, values and objectives. They have to communicate and share them with the management team and the external stakeholders in the company. This requires both political[6] and communication skills.[7]
– We shall see in Chapter 8 that 'communication skills' are among the top three qualities sought in new appointees to a board.[2] Other surveys have revealed the existence of a significant communication gap between directors and managers.[8-11]
– Many managers just pass on messages without seeking to understand or share them. A BIM report, *The Flat Organisation*,[9] has found that the 'ability to communicate' is regarded as the most important quality for managers to possess in the flatter and more flexible organizations that –

Table 4.2   Other qualities sought in members of the senior management teams

Qualities	No. of organizations
Leadership/motivational skills	16
Development of others/team building	10
Ability, intellect and 'other' personal qualities	9
Awareness and sensitivity	8
Financial understanding and awareness	7
Interpersonal skills	6
Flexibility	6
Communication/presentational skills	5
Ethics, values, trust	5
Strategy/planning	4
Technical expertise/qualifications	4

Source: Human Resource Development for International Operation, 1990

as we saw in Chapter 2 – are beginning to emerge. Over two-thirds of the respondents considered the 'ability to communicate' to be 'very important'.

The key questions that should be addressed are:

- Has the board articulated, agreed and communicated the qualities it is seeking in both its directors and its managers; and are the qualities that are sought periodically discussed and reviewed?
- Have guidelines been drawn up to assist assessment, review and career planning, and are they observed?
- Does the terminology that is used capture the subtleties of the distinction between directors and managers; and do definitions, guidelines, requirements and distinctions capture the essence of what it is to be a director?

If similar qualities are apparently being sought in both directors and managers, are any distinctions that exist between the two a question of kind or of degree? Is there a difference of focus, perspective or attitude between the two groups?

4.5 Directorial and managerial focus

Let us return to the survey undertaken for the IOD report, *Professional Development of and for the Board*.[2] This reveals that directors, when asked, are able to draw a clear distinction between managerial and directorial competences. In a 'follow-on' survey undertaken by the author and Alan Wakelam[5] the opportunity was taken, during the course of the interviews, to examine and compare certain aspects of the roles of directors and managers. A traditional view has been that there is a difference between the two roles. For example:

- Directors are typically focused on the external business environment within which the company operates, and are concerned with long-term questions of strategy and policy.
- In comparison, managers are thought to concentrate upon short-term questions of implementation. For many managers the principal focus has been internal. They have concentrated their energies on the administrative requirements of the bureaucratic corporate 'machine'.

Interview responses[5] suggest that certain developments have challenged this view. We examined in Chapter 2 how organizations are responding to the demands and opportunities of the business and market environment. Directors and managers now face pressures and requirements that may cause them to shift their focus and horizon (Figure 4.1). Directors and managers may respond differently to changing circumstances:

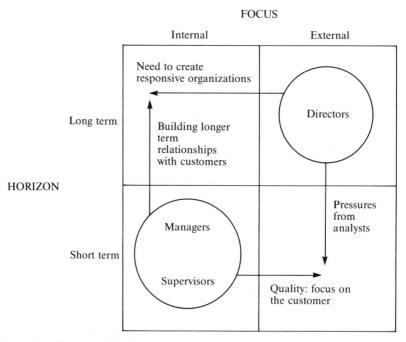

Figure 4.1 Focus and horizon

- Directors are realizing that, in order to cope with the changing business environment, their organizations need to be more flexible and responsive. Many are turning their attention to 'getting to grips' with their internal corporate bureaucracies. Corporate transformation, or creating a slimmer, flatter and more adaptable organization has become a high priority of many boards,[9] especially those of larger companies.
- At the same time, the boards of many public companies feel under increasing pressure from analysts and shareholders to improve short-term performance.[12] In response, many boards are having to give greater attention to short-term actions to improve ratios such as return on net assets, and the impact of their activities upon share price.
- Managers, in contrast, are being asked to devote more attention to customers and, in particular, to the improvement of longer term relationships with them.[11] They are being told how much more expensive it is to win a new customer than to keep an existing one, and are being sent to courses on 'relationship management'.
- Managers are also subject to other 'corporate culture change' initiatives. Quality programmes are encouraging them to shift their focus from the internal demands of the corporate machine to the external needs and requirements of customers.
- The priority given by some boards to 'customer satisfaction' and initiatives to link remuneration to customer satisfaction are designed to discourage managers from taking short-term actions that might help them to achieve internal objectives, but at the expense of the company's longer term relationships with its customers.

Similar findings have emerged from other surveys.[9, 10] The focus and horizons of both directors and managers do appear to be changing. There is some evidence that for many boards 'short-termism' could be a self imposed constraint, with fund managers and investment analysts taking a longer term view than chief executives and financial directors.[13]

The potential for conflict

A board needs to be aware of the consequences of the changing focus and horizons of both directors and managers. Tensions can arise between the two groups.[14] In some companies there is a lack of mutual trust and understanding between directors and managers.[9, 10]

Managers who have shared and 'internalized' a longer term vision, or who are concentrating upon building longer term and quality relationships with customers, can feel duped, tricked and betrayed by a board that is perceived as taking short-term and short-sighted decisions that appear to be in conflict with longer term requirements.[9, 10] As a consequence:

- A management team can become cynical and disillusioned.
- Tensions can grow between a head office and operating units, or between a holding company board and the boards of subsidiary companies.

When short-term decisions need to be taken that could be perceived by stakeholders as being in conflict with corporate vision, goals, values and objectives, a board should ensure that the reasoning behind the decisions or the rationale for them is explained. One chairman who was interviewed stated: 'Having encouraged our people to think, we shouldn't be surprised when they do think. We can't complain when we don't give them the facts to think about. If they live on rumour, and think the worst, whose fault is that?'

In an organization that positively encourages diversity and debate, there is always a potential for misunderstanding and conflict and differences should be expected rather than treated as a 'surprise' or 'challenge to directorial authority'.[8] Arenas of conflict should not be hidden or ignored; they should be assessed and tackled. Some pertinent questions should be asked:

- What action should the board take to improve communication and understanding in order to re-establish or build a relationship that is built upon mutual trust and support?
- Do the company's processes and procedures reduce or exacerbate the potential for misunderstanding and conflict, and should they be re-engineered?
- To what extent has the current allocation of roles and responsibilities contributed to misunderstanding and conflict, and should it be reviewed?

Myth and reality

The view that (a) the focus of directors is largely 'outside', or upon the business environment, while (b) the focus of managers is almost exclusively upon the internal requirements of the company, may no longer accord with reality (Figure 4.2). Increasingly, directors and managers concentrate upon the outside world and the company, and the interrelationship between the two.

It does not follow from this accumulation of evidence[5, 10] that the distinction between direction and management is no longer valid, but merely that certain aspects of it have become more subtle:

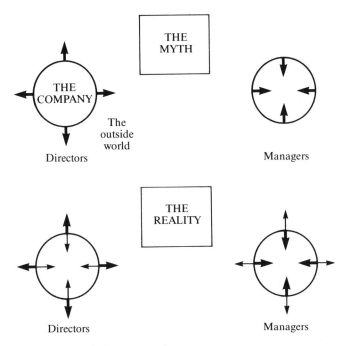

Figure 4.2   The roles of directors and managers

- The distinction between the focus of directors and that of managers is often one of emphasis.
- While directors and managers may both share the same vision, goals, values and objectives, and work on compatible tasks utilizing common processes, the board is likely to have taken the initiative in their formulation and establishment.
- Directors, on the whole, may well devote a higher proportion of their time to 'external' matters than is the case with most managers.
- The directors may also have direct accountabilities to, and have to sustain relationships with, a wider range of stakeholders.
- The perspective of directors is that of the company as a whole, whereas the perspective of most managers will be that of a particular function or business unit.
- The external vision and perspective of directors is particularly relevant to relationships with stakeholders and the establishment of 'corporate lifespace'.[15]
- While certain areas of activity may no longer be exclusively the prerogative

of the board, the legal duties and responsibilities of directors remain distinct from, and have if anything grown *vis-à-vis*, those of managers.

Involvement with the business environment

It is important that a board monitors trends over time in the allocation of roles and responsibilities between directors and managers. When changes occur, their implications need to be understood so that different roles are complementary and supportive rather than in conflict. Often responsibilities will need to be redefined and refocused. Let us consider an example. One trend that has been suggested[4, 5] is for an increasing number of employees, especially those in larger companies, to become involved with the business and market environment (Figure 4.3):

- In some companies it would seem that contact with the 'external world' was once the province of the chairman. In other cases it was primarily the responsibility of the board to relate the company to the environmental context within which it operated.
- Over time senior management, and subsequently middle and junior management, have become more involved with 'external' issues, as their variety and complexity have resulted in the delegation and devolution of responsibilities. In order to deliver 'customer satisfaction' it is necessary for 'everyone to be involved'. 'Understanding the business environment' has become an important management requirement.[9]

As a consequence of these developments it is even more important that the respective roles and responsibilities of directors and managers are clearly defined and understood. For example:

- The chairman may still have an important external role, but it might now be focused upon specific areas such as relationships with government, investors and business partners.
- The board also needs to be aware that managerial involvement with the 'external world' may be limited to its impact upon a particular function or business unit, whereas their own perspective needs to be that of the company as a whole.

Relationship between directors and managers

The successful management of change requires the interrelationship of strategic and operational factors.[16] An effective board is one that works harmoniously with the management team. Satisfactory relationships will require mutual understanding, trust and respect, and the commitment of all directors and managers. However, it needs to be remembered that the

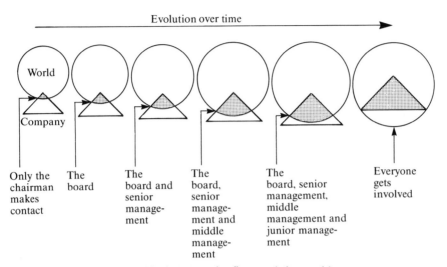

Figure 4.3 The relationship between the firm and the world

authority of managers derives from the board. This different basis or source of authority influences the qualities sought in both groups:

- Directorial accountabilities and qualities, and the function of the board derive from: (a) company law and other items of legislation; and (b) the company's Memorandum and Articles of Association.
- The qualities required by senior managers will depend upon the roles and responsibilities, and the authority, delegated by the board. Major roles and important tasks may be established by the board.

The board will also (as we saw in Chapter 3) establish the framework of values, policies, processes and procedures within which the management team operates. These will define such limits of authority as expenditures and other matters that require board approval. If the board is to operate effectively it is important that senior managers have the judgement to determine when a matter ought to be brought to the attention of the board.

Certain key management appointments may be made by the board itself. Changes in the composition and structure of the board may precipitate a review of the wider management structure of the organization and reporting arrangements.

Active and effective board involvement in the determination of strategy should not be assumed and may need to be encouraged.[17] According to Sir Adrian Cadbury: 'The chairman has a particular part to play in stimulating the board to reflect creatively on the company's strategy.'[18]

The understanding gap

In many companies there is an overlapping of, and a failure to distinguish between, the qualities that are sought in directors and those thought desirable in senior managers:

- In smaller and owner-managed companies the allocation of responsibilities between the board and the management team is often blurred and confused. Tasks are allocated according to such factors as personality, availability, or relevance of skill, rather than according to whether they are 'directorial' or 'managerial'.
- The directors of legally incorporated subsidiaries sometimes behave as managers rather than directors. Holding company executives at the US head office of a multi-national company may regard the managing director of the French national operating company as the equivalent of a manager of the Milwaukee branch.

The subsidiary boards of many global companies have been described as an underexploited resource.[19] At the operating company level there may be little discretion to decide what is sold, at what price, and how it is sold. Such a subsidiary board may operate as a management committee concerned with local implementation, rather than contributing to the review of threats and opportunities, and the policy-making process.

If an understanding gap persists in spite of a clear explanation of the respective accountabilities, roles and responsibilities of directors and managers, it may be necessary to explore whether there are differences of perspectives and attitudes between directors and managers. The questions to be answered are: I understand the legal side, and I have seen the organization chart and the allocation of roles, but how should I think and feel? What perspective should I have? What should my attitudes, hopes and fears be? How will becoming a director affect the 'inner me'?

Differing perspectives of directors and managers

Improving board effectiveness and becoming more competent as a director requires sensitivity to the differences that can occur between the perspectives of directors and those of managers. Some are more subtle than others, but recognizing them, and making them explicit, enables aspects of the directorial perspective to be developed.

Let us examine a few of the areas in which the manager and the director may have a different perspective. The following viewpoints have all emerged in discussion sessions facilitated by the author:

ACCOUNTABILITY

The accountability of the director is to the company as a whole, and to the various stakeholders and other parties with an interest in the company. As a result, the 'world' of the director tends to be one of trade-offs between competing interests, and of balance and harmony between conflicting objectives, between objectives and resources, and between achievement and motivation.

The 'world' of the manager can be more straightforward and focused. It is often one of single-minded maximization or optimization. The aim in negotiating situations may be to win, and to achieve specific rather than general outcomes. Often, the manager will be judged not on the performance of the company as a whole, but on the extent to which individual targets have been achieved.

THE DECISION FRAMEWORK

The manager tends to be concerned with incremental improvements within a framework of policies established by the board. The managerial perspective is essentially one of 'small steps' within the context of given rules, values, goals and processes.

The directorial perspective is broader, and embraces the framework itself. The culture established by the board should encourage continuing restlessness and challenge. At the same time, the board should look beyond incremental change, at 'step changes', and 'strategic options'. From time to time the board should be prepared to change the framework or 'rules of the game'.

DECISION MAKING

A director needs to be level-headed and dispassionate. Even when he or she is 'closely involved', the director has to remain detached and impartial. On occasion, it can be difficult for executive directors to be objective when judging matters with which they have been directly concerned. A non-executive director without emotional involvement will sometimes find it easier to retain a balanced perspective.

A manager has to exude enthusiasm and commitment. These energies may need to be harnessed or challenged. The manager may have a team to motivate. Others may expect the manager to stand up and fight for 'departmental' interests. They might also expect a manager to be a passionate advocate or champion of a project, perhaps, to be submitted to the board for approval.

EXPERTISE

Many managers may owe their positions in the corporate hierarchy to the possession of specialist skills. Expertise that is scarce can become a source of standing and power within the company, and also outside, when the individual concerned is asked to speak at professional and specialist conferences and seminars. There may be a temptation to 'hoard' a distinctive expertise, and not to share it with colleagues.

Within the boardroom, the individual who is 'drawn' from a specialist background is likely to encounter a more collective form of responsibility. Rather than give a 'right' answer in response to requests, the newly appointed director is expected to contribute to debate and discussion. Colleagues will expect any relevant insights and knowledge to be pooled and shared, so that by operating as a group the board can reach a collective decision.

Some find it possible to play the role of manager by acquiring relevant knowledge and skills. To add value to the boardroom team it is usually necessary to draw upon the 'whole person' to a greater extent. As one interviewee put it: 'Being a director is being a director, not playing the role of director.'

COMMITMENT OF SELF

Directors require a combination of personal qualities, and business and ethical awareness – in addition to relevant knowledge, skills and experience – to be effective in the boardroom. Such a range of attributes, albeit with a different focus and emphasis, could also be said to be desirable in managers. Often, however, the manager, who operates within a strategy, policy and value framework established by the board, is able to work effectively by drawing upon a narrower range of qualities.

Some find it possible to play the role of manager by acquiring relevant knowledge and skills. The manager may conceal much of his or her 'true self' in order to 'fit in'. A director has to relate to, and work with, other members of the boardroom team. In the boardroom context the commitment of the 'whole person' is required.

THE INDIVIDUAL AND THE TEAM

'Internal competition' between teams of managers, operating companies and business units may be actively encouraged by a board. In competing with colleagues, and in seeking to get ahead, the manager may 'play games'. Organizational politics abound within many corporate bureaucracies. Changes may be introduced merely to attract attention, whether or not they benefit customers. When accountabilities are blurred or shared, and frequent reorganizations occur, it is often difficult to apportion blame to particular individuals or groups when things go wrong.

Externally, competition between the interests of different stakeholders is discouraged. Within the boardroom there is clear and collective accountability. Generally there is also greater continuity. The board does not come into and go out of existence from time to time according to the 'whim' of corporate reorganization. It is always there and visibly responsible for total corporate performance. Furthermore, the 'bottom line' performance of the company is by law publicly available to stakeholders and others who are interested in the company.

APPEARANCE AND REALITY

In many companies, a person can progress a long way in a managerial career on the basis of appearing to be committed or the 'right stuff', and 'saying the right things'. Appearance can 'count for a lot' in companies whose boards have not cascaded or delegated clear output objectives down to the level of the individual manager.

Inevitably some boards will engage in 'creative accounting'. Others will try to put the best 'gloss' on corporate performance. However, in the longer term, satisfactory relationships with stakeholders and other interested parties are built upon openness and trust. Directors have to pay attention to the underlying realities. Ultimately, it is upon these realities that they will be judged.

REVIEWING AND OPERATING PROCESSES

Managers operate within processes, and their concern is likely to be with particular aspects or elements of a process. The board has to assume responsibility for the establishment and review of the total process. It has also to ensure that the key processes are in place, particularly those that cross functions and deliver the value that is sought by customers.

A company that is interested in building closer or 'above the line' relationships with customers could use a checklist such as that in Figure 4.4 to explore the differing perspectives of directors and managers. Rather than 'jump' straight to the supply of goods and services (below the dotted line) the company might wish to share the customer's vision, aspirations, etc., in order to identify ways in which customer and supplier could work together to generate greater value or improved satisfaction.[11]

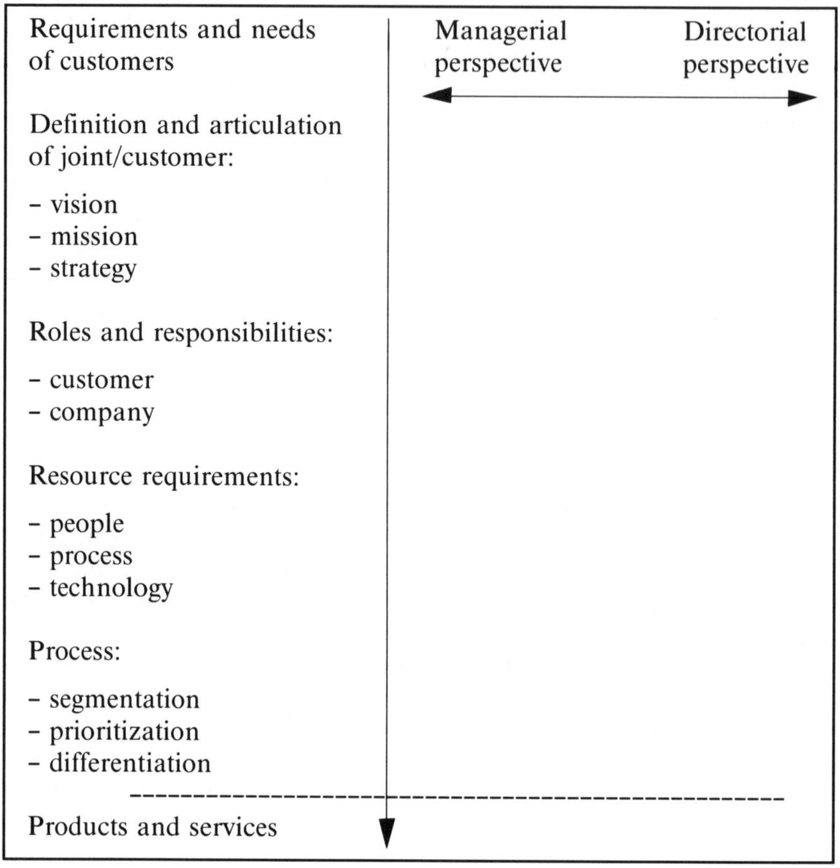

Requirements and needs of customers	Managerial perspective	Directorial perspective
	◄─────────────────────────►	
Definition and articulation of joint/customer:		
– vision – mission – strategy		
Roles and responsibilities:		
– customer – company		
Resource requirements:		
– people – process – technology		
Process:		
– segmentation – prioritization – differentiation		
-----------------------------	----------------------------	
Products and services ▼		

Figure 4.4 Customer relationship perspectives

A related exercise could be repeated with appropriate staff in the customer organization. By understanding each others' perspectives, people can find it easier to work together in generating a solution.

Managerial and directorial attitudes

Another possible area of distinction between direction and management might lie in the beliefs, attitudes and values of directors and managers. These could vary (a) as a consequence of their differing accountabilities, roles and responsibilities, and perspectives, or (b) because a board has failed to share corporate values and encourage appropriate attitudes.

Let us consider attitudes, as they are often easier to determine than values and beliefs. Managers and directors can have different attitudes on matters of concern to the board. Some attitudes can be supportive of corporate vision, goals, values and objectives, while other attitudes may be in conflict with them. Success in such areas as corporate transformation and quality can depend very much upon the extent to which attitudes and expectations can be changed.[8]

It is advisable to identify and understand attitudes and expectations before attempting to change them. They should also be monitored and tracked, in order to assess the impact of various programmes and activities upon them. A growing number of companies appear to undertake customer and employee attitude surveys, but relatively few specifically explore managerial or employee attitudes towards, and expectations of, the board. Surveys of directorial attitudes are also uncommon.

The overall pattern of results from attitude surveys can yield clues about the overall operation and impact of a board and the extent to which its members display 'role model' conduct. At the same time, the responses of individual directors might suggest that one or more directors do not share the attitudes of the rest of the board. This could indicate that they are out-of-step with colleagues or are not fully integrated into the boardroom team.

As a minimum, the chairman should take a view on the attitudes that are desirable in members of the board. The chairman could also initiate a discussion of the collective attitudes of the boardroom team. Such a discussion can be far from an academic exercise; for example:

– members of the board might not be working effectively as a team
– a change of attitudes might be necessary to cope with a significant change of circumstances
– a restructuring of the board might have occurred
– the board itself might need to be 'quality trained'
– conflicts of interest, attitudes or perspective may have arisen *vis-à-vis* certain groups
– the board might wish to establish the 'ground rules' for director 'role model' attitudes and behaviour.

Moving from manager to director

A key feature of the perspective of the director, and that of the company as a whole, derives from directorial accountability. The 'world' of the director can be more subtle and complex than that of the manager. For example:

– Directors can have more varied accountabilities. 'Zero sum' situations may be less common in situations of mutual dependency. More relationships could be 'positive sum', the director having to be aware of other people's interests in order to ensure that they are satisfied.

– Directors are also expected to assume responsibility for the enterprise as a whole, in addition to whatever functional or departmental responsibilities they might have as managers. It needs to be remembered that executive directors are both directors and managers.

The manager who becomes an executive director will continue to have management responsibilities in addition to the newly acquired responsibilities as a director. Certain individuals find it difficult to relinquish their managerial commitments, priorities and focus when they are appointed to a board. Some are encouraged by their 'elevation' to put more effort into achieving their managerial targets at a time when they should be delegating in order to concentrate upon their new directorial responsibilities.

In making the transition from director to manager the Institute of Directors recommends: 'Recognition of the significant difference between the role of director and that of manager, and the vital necessity of training in the particular responsibilities involved in being a director.'[20]

According to Bob Garratt, former chairman of AMED: 'There is a huge difference between managing and directing. Wise companies are beginning to recognize this, and are finding that good managers do not necessarily make good directors.'[21]

Those who associate their past success with long hours of work and 'being busy' may be tempted to remain 'energetic and active', without realizing that being a director usually involves (a) different kinds of activities and priorities and (b) a changed perspective. A newly appointed director may need to be reminded that:

– the director is 'energetic and active' in ways that do not involve attending endless meetings, juggling telephone calls or making 'instant decisions' throughout the day;

– in the directorial role there may be fewer but more important decisions to reflect upon;

– such decisions may need to satisfy many criteria, derived from the vision of a company, and its goals, values and objectives;

– many items that are on the boardroom agenda may be 'new', the result of changed conditions and circumstances, and past practice and understanding may not be relevant;

– there are legal duties and responsibilities, and accountabilities to stakeholders, to reflect upon;

– the quality of reflection, the 'quiet hours' spent considering an issue from a number of different perspectives, may distinguish the effective director.

Managers need time to think, but it may be even more important that executive directors do not allow pressing issues that demand their attention to drive out the time that is needed to reflect on more important matters.

As well as developing themselves, newly appointed directors need to develop those with whom they work to support them in their directorial roles. Some of those who surround the newly appointed director may be disappointed that they themselves have not yet obtained a seat in the boardroom. In time they may come to realize that they, too, might benefit from having the opportunity to work with and redefine their role in relation to the newly appointed director.

4.6 Summary

In this chapter we have examined the distinction between the roles, qualities, perceptions and attitudes of directors and managers. The qualities sought in directors derive from their duties and responsibilities and the function of the board. In practice, the differences in the qualities sought in directors and managers respectively can be subtle, and may not be immediately apparent.

The focus and horizon of both directors and managers is changing. We have seen that misunderstandings and conflicts can arise between the two, and a clear allocation of roles and responsibilities is required.

4.7 Checklist

1. Is the distinction between direction and management understood by members of your company's board and its senior management team?
2. Do all the members of the board share a similar understanding of the distinction between direction and management?
3. In what ways do senior managers have a different understanding from directors of the distinction between direction and management?
4. Are there occasions when certain directors behave as functional managers rather than as directors in the boardroom?
5. What needs to be done to develop more of a directorial perspective?
6. How might directorial attitudes be improved?
7. Do the qualities of the senior management team match and complement those of the board?
8. Is there an inherent conflict between the focus, perspective and horizon of directors and those of the senior management team?
9. What action needs to be taken to bridge any gap in approach, understanding or perspective that emerges?
10. Is there an integrated management programme that extends from initial induction to developing directorial attitudes, perspective and qualities?

11. How do the qualities that are sought in directors and managers compare with those identified in benchmark companies, and in companies in general?

Notes and references

1. Coulson-Thomas, C., *Developing Directors: Building an effective boardroom team*, McGraw-Hill, 1993.
2. Coulson-Thomas, C., *Professional Development of and for the Board*. A questionnaire and interview survey undertaken by Adaptation Ltd of company chairmen. A summary has been published by the IOD, February 1990.
3. Coulson-Thomas, C., *The Role and Function of the Personnel Director*. An interim Adaptation survey carried out in conjunction with the Research Group of the Institute of Personnel Management, 1991.
4. Coulson-Thomas, C., *Human Resource Development for International Operation*. A survey sponsored by Surrey European Management School. Adaptation Ltd, 1990.
5. Coulson-Thomas, C. and Wakelam, A., *The Effective Board, Current Practice, Myths and Realities*. An IOD discussion document, 1991.
6. Brunsson, N., *The Organisation of Hypocrisy*, John Wiley, 1991.
7. Bartram, P. and Coulson-Thomas, C., *The Complete Spokesperson: A workbook for managers who meet the media*, Kogan Page, 1991; and Coulson-Thomas, C., *Public Relations is Your Business: A guide for every manager*, Business Books, 1981.
8. Coulson-Thomas, C., *Transforming the Company: Bridging the gap between management myth and corporate reality*, Kogan Page, 1992.
9. Coulson-Thomas, C. and Coe, T., *The Flat Organisation: Philosophy and practice*, BIM, 1991.
10. Coulson-Thomas, C. and Coulson-Thomas, S., *Quality: The Next Steps*. An Adaptation Ltd survey for ODI, 1991. An executive summary has been published by ODI Europe, 1991.
11. Coulson-Thomas, C. and Brown, R., *Beyond Quality: Managing the relationship with the customer*, BIM, 1990.
12. 3i's, 'The FD and corporate governance; 3i's seventh plc UK survey', *Financial Director*, April 1992, 23–4.
13. MORI, *Shareholder Value Analysis Survey*, Coopers & Lybrand Deloitte, 1991.
14. Coulson-Thomas, C., 'Strategic vision or strategic con?: Rhetoric or reality?', *Long Range Planning*, **25** (1), 1992, 81–9.
15. Demb, A. and Neubauer, F-F., 'How can a board add value?', *European Management Journal*, **8** (2), 1990, 156–60.
16. Pettigrew, A. M. and Whipp, R., *Managing Change for Competitive Success*, Blackwell, 1991.
17. Zahra, S. and Pearce, J., 'Determinants of board directors, strategic involvement', *European Management Journal*, **8** (2), 1990, 164–73; and Zahra, S., 'Increasing the board's involvement in strategy', *Long Range Planning*, **23** (6), 1990, 109–17.
18. Cadbury, Sir A., *The Company Chairman*, Director Books, 1990.
19. Demb, A. and Neubauer, F-F., 'Subsidiary company boards reconsidered', *European Management Journal*, **8** (4), 1990, 480–7.

20. Jenkins, B., 'Companies in need of a code', *Boardroom Agenda*, **1**, February 1992, 18–19.
21. Garratt, R., 'The good manager is not necessarily a good director', Letter to the Editor, *Financial Times*, 8 April 1992.

5
Type, size and composition of boards

Non-executive directors should be willing to ask the questions in the boardroom no-one else is prepared to ask. (SIR BRIAN WOLFSON, chairman, Wembly plc.)

There is no such thing as a standard board. Each board is unique, its composition and operation reflecting the interplay of company situation, people and their personalities, and a market context. A board comprises a particular group of people, and how they behave and interact will depend upon circumstances and context. The behaviour of a team of directors, and the operation of a board, can, and often should, change as conditions, threats and opportunities change.

A 'live' board should be a dynamic and changing entity, adapting to circumstances. The board itself should periodically review its nature, size, composition and operation. It was suggested in Chapter 3 that the chairman is generally the most appropriate person to initiate such a review.

5.1 Varieties of board

There are many different types of board. Some areas of difference can be seen in Example 5.1. While these differences can be very significant, it should be borne in mind that directors who are members of a wide variety of boards carry many common legal duties and responsibilities. In practice, how different types of board operate, and the attitudes of their members, may be more similar than formal differences of structure and membership might suggest.[1]

The impact of company size upon the nature and operation of a board, and the subject-matter with which it is concerned, will vary. Market sector, the complexity of a process or technology, whether there are international

---

Large and small companies
Public and private companies
Domestic and foreign companies
Holding and subsidiary boards
Executive and non-executive directors
Functional and facilitating directors
Supervisory boards and representative directors
Nominee directors
Foreign or 'overseas' directors
Owner-directors

All the above may have common legal duties and responsibilities
Within the company there may also be managers with 'director' titles

---

Example 5.1   Types of board and director

operations, company structure and many other considerations will influence these factors.

The ultimate or main board of a foreign company may be subject to a different framework of company law to that which concerns a domestic company. Attitudes towards boards, and how they operate, can also reflect nationality and culture:

– Within the EC a number of distinct approaches to corporate governance coexist. Employee representatives may have seats on 'the board'. The precise legal situation should be checked, and mandatory requirements observed.
– In certain member states – for example, Germany and the Netherlands – two-tier structures and supervisory boards are relatively widespread.
– In the UK, companies are 'governed' by a single-tier board, typically composed wholly of executive directors or a mix of executives and non-executives.
– The US also adopts the single-tier approach, but, apart from the one or two people occupying the roles of chairman and CEO, the board of a major corporation may be composed wholly of non-executive directors.
– In Japan, the key stakeholders tend to share a consensus view on key issues and a relatively long-term perspective. There are extensive interlocking shareholdings, and a distinctive Japanese set of attitudes towards corporate governance leads to patterns of corporate behaviour in such fields as takeovers that are different from those of US and UK companies.[2]

A company with extensive international operations may face a choice of where to incorporate subsidiary companies, and of which models of corporate governance to adopt. Subsidiaries can exist in a purely domestic context, and the relationship between the directors of holding and subsidiary company boards can give rise to misunderstandings and particular operational problems. Some holding company directors – especially those who treat the members of subsidiary boards as if they were branch managers – may need to be politely reminded of the distinct and onerous legal responsibilities these individuals have. From the perspective of the subsidiary company director, it needs to be borne in mind that 'being in receipt of an order' can be a weak defence when illegal acts have occurred.

The point has already been made in Chapter 3 that all directors, regardless of the nature of the board upon which they sit, need to be informed of their legal duties and responsibilities. They should also be regularly reminded of them, and be kept informed of legal developments relating to directors and boards.

The most visible boards are often those of the larger 'plcs', but are they typical? The overwhelming majority of corporate entities are private companies. The composition, in terms of job titles, and the operation, of their boards are not so easy to determine. One option is to undertake questionnaire or interview surveys. In the case of those cited in this book,[3, 4] the companies in the categories covered are thought to be broadly representative of the population of companies as a whole.

Small and medium-sized companies can be significant from a national point of view. They play an important role in job and wealth creation in many countries. As the countries of eastern Europe, and what was formerly the Soviet Union, have sought transition from command to market economies they have discovered the value of those who can direct and assume responsibility for the affairs of an enterprise.

Even within established market economies, many enterprises and their boards experience problems in making the transition from small to medium, and subsequently, from medium to large. A number may also be at risk in the more competitive circumstances of the national, regional and global marketplace, as they face challenges such as the emerging single European market. While it is important that all companies are led by competent boards, in the case of many small and medium-sized companies that may lack in-depth management resources, the contributions made by directors can be decisive.

5.2 The evolution of a board

The nature of many boards will undergo an evolution as the business of the company expands and develops. The board and its directors need to grow and adapt with the business. Table 5.1 represents a highly simplified summary of how a board and its concerns might change as a business evolves from a 'start-up' to a public company that operates internationally.

Table 5.1   The process of corporate evolution

Stage of evolution	Board	Concerns
Start-up	Owner-directors	Survival and growth
Small business	New appointments to complement skills of founder directors	Succession; maintain independence
Medium-sized business	Appointment of functional directors	Balance the team; build relationships
Large business	Establishment of subsidiary boards	Reorganization and transformation; 'cover' main elements of organization and key activities; arrangements and joint ventures
Public company	Appointment of non-executive directors; creation of audit and remuneration committees	Strategy, planning and issue monitoring; image and reputation; accountability and protection of interests of widely scattered investors
International expansion	Establishment of foreign subsidiaries; appointment of non-nationals to the board	Internationalization; global alliances

Initially the membership of a board may be limited to a small group of founders of a business, or the founder and one or more friends or members of the family. Their meetings may be informal, consisting of little more than chats.

Some companies are formed for convenience or for reasons of lifestyle to create a particular form of entity with which others may contract, or to provide a framework within which one or more individuals may pursue their lifestyle ambitions. A company may prefer to contract with other companies rather than with private individuals. Certain activities of an individual may be carried on through the vehicle of a company for a variety of reasons.

Owner-directors need to be kept aware of the fact that an incorporated business is a legal entity in its own right. In return for the privilege of limited liability certain legal obligations must be assumed. The company's assets are not the private property of the directors. Members of the board have a fiduciary relationship towards the company.

As a business expands, more individuals may be invited to join the board. Some of these may be employees. Others may be non-executive directors. We shall see in Chapter 8 that many chairmen do not find it easy to identify candidates for the boardroom.

A larger company may employ a management team composed of managers grouped into functions or departments. Those heading particular functions may, because of the perceived importance of the function and the personal qualities of the individuals concerned, be asked to join the board.

There are dangers in appointing to a board 'functional heads' who lack directorial qualities. According to Charles Lowe, while deputy chairman of the Blue Arrow Employment Group: 'A board comprising of specialists is likely to lack direction even though its individual management expertise may be first class. Although a board needs a variety of talent, to be effective as directors its members must go beyond their own disciplines and use them as servants not masters.'

Membership of a board need not, and should not, be limited to the heads of 'traditional' functions. Where the route to a board is perceived as being via the management of a corporate function or department, unrealistic expectations may be created in individuals who do not have directorial qualities. An undesirable practice may arise of giving 'director' job titles to certain individuals who do not have seats upon a legally constituted board.

In time, a company may establish a network of operating units or divisions. Some of these may be incorporated as legal entities in their own right and become subsidiary companies. Business units and subsidiaries with local boards could be established abroad. Expatriate directors might sit on overseas boards, and one or more foreign directors might join the board of a main or holding company.

As a company expands, the board may need to seek additional sources of finance. This search for corporate funding can also have an impact upon the membership of the board:

– Some investors or providers of finance negotiate the right to nominate a representative nominee director to the board of a borrowing company. Such a nominee director may have the role of 'looking after their interests'.
– A board that is seeking a public quotation may seek additional members

of the board with relevant experience. Professional advisers might suggest that the 'appeal' to the investment community would be strengthened by the addition to the board of some respected directors with 'plc' experience.

In some parts of the world the use of nominee directors is relatively common.[5] In Germany the number of 'nominee' seats on supervisory boards held by the Deutsche Bank alone comfortably exceeds 100. Many nominee directors have similar, or the same, duties and responsibilities as other members of the board.

Such a view of corporate evolution is simplistic. Corporate histories can be very diverse. They can also be complex. A global enterprise may consist of a group comprising hundreds, and in some cases thousands, of legal entities in various parts of the world.[6]

Whatever the evolution of a company, it is likely to be unique. Certain stages of the process may represent a development challenge for the directors. Facilitating directors could be brought onto a board to help it cope with the challenge of corporate transformation. However, the form of board in a company should not be taken for granted and, periodically, the following types of question should be asked:

- Why is the board the way it is?
- When did the last significant change in the nature of the board occur, and why?
- Does the nature of the board reflect the type of company and the nature of the circumstances the company is in?
- What other models of corporate governance and boards might be appropriate, and what are their advantages and disadvantages?

In the case of a group, a holding company might wish to reflect upon how it interacts with subsidiary boards, and whether the division of responsibilities and allocation of accountabilities within the group should be reviewed. The key issues are whether the structure of corporate governance that has evolved within a group enables a company to meet its various obligations and commitments, and whether the allocation of accountabilities and responsibilities are both clear and operationally sound.

5.3 The size of the board

One relatively obvious way in which boards differ is in terms of their size. How many directors should a company have? Apart from legal requirements, is there an optimal number from the point of view of the efficient operation of a board? A general response to these questions on board size is that 'it all depends'. Whether or not a board of a certain size is effective will depend upon a number of factors such as its composition and dynamics, the personalities of its members, its priorities, the quality of board chairmanship, and how the business of the board is managed. When assessing the impact of board size upon its effectiveness, these other influences and considerations will need to be taken into account.

Board size in practice

Let us turn to the actual size of the boards of 'real world' companies. The 'distribution' of the size of the boards, according to respondents to a UK survey by Coulson-Thomas and Alan Wakelam,[3] is illustrated in Figure 5.1. There is little evidence from the responses received that there is an ideal or 'standard best' size for a board. A majority of respondents have an even number of directors on their boards, which suggests decisions by consensus rather than by majority voting.

Surveys of larger US companies suggest 13[7] and 14[8] as an average size of board. Such boards would be composed primarily of non-executive directors, and there are sufficient members to constitute working audit and other committees of the board.

One conclusion of the UK survey[3] is that larger companies, in terms of financial turnover and/or staff numbers, tend to have larger boards. In these 'larger' companies, there is some evidence that respondents felt there are certain 'portfolios' or 'slots' on the board such as 'financial director' that ought to be filled. In the great majority of cases, however, there was no such view.

Particularly in the case of the smaller companies there was little, if any, feeling of being under obligation, or it being the 'norm', to have a board of a certain size. Considerable variation was found in the size and composition of the boards of companies in this category. Changes in board size would often result from encounters with individuals who, it was thought, would make a 'good' director of that particular company.

The majority of boards, particularly of small and medium-sized companies, appear to be composed of a relatively small, tightly knit group of people[3]:

- Four out of ten of the boards of respondents' companies had five or fewer members.
- Six was the size of board mentioned by a quarter of the respondents.
- Four out of ten respondents were on a board of five or six members.
- At the other end of the size spectrum, only one in seven of the respondents served on a board with ten or more members.

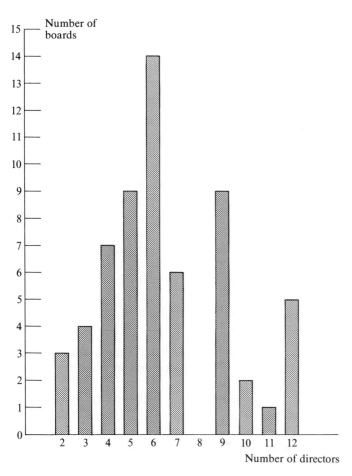

Figure 5.1   The size of the board

In an earlier survey, undertaken by Alan Wakelam,[9] again of a broad sample of UK companies, about half of the boards covered had three or fewer executive directors, together with three or fewer non-executive directors.

In the later survey,[3] companies with non-executive directors had larger boards than companies whose boards were composed entirely of executive directors. The responses suggest that, comparing companies of a similar financial turnover, the appointment of non-executive directors tends, other things being equal, to increase the size of a board.

The appointment of non-executive directors is by no means limited to large companies. Non-executive directors were perceived as of value across the full range of company sizes in the sample. Their contribution will be considered later in this chapter.

Determining the size of a board

The survey findings we have examined[3, 9] suggest that board size should not be taken for granted. Selected examples of the various forms of board that can result from the development of a UK business are shown in Figure 5.2. Each of the board types illustrated is based upon that of an actual company. In certain other EC member states, a supervisory board might, or would, need to be established once a company has reached a certain threshold of size.

The chairman should periodically reflect upon board size, and the advantages and disadvantages of having more, or fewer, directors in the context of (a) a company's particular situation and (b) the existing membership of the board. Similarly, there should be a review from time to time of the composition of the board. The following types of question could be posed in the context of such a review:

– How appropriate is the size of the board in the context of the current situation and circumstances of the company; and in what ways might additional members benefit the board?
– How does the size of the board compare with that of 'benchmark' companies; and does it help or hinder discussion and decision making?
– What impact do, might or could non-executive directors have upon the size of the board; and what would be the advantages and disadvantages of a smaller or larger number of directors?

The optimum size of the board depends, as has been suggested, upon the circumstances of the company, the qualities of the directors and how the business of the board is conducted. A board that is 'too small' may be deficient in certain areas of expertise, and might lack breadth and balance. One that is 'too big' may inhibit individual directors from making an effective contribution, and as a consequence they may 'feel less responsible'. A board, however, should not be so small as to be limited in capability, or provide insufficient people to staff board committees. At the same time, it should not be so large as to prevent the directors from working together effectively as a team.

Within limits, a company that is larger and more complex may benefit from a bigger board. With fewer than five directors, some of the normal dynamics of the boardroom may be lost. More than 12 to 15 directors,

Entrepreneurial small business

Small company

Medium-sized company
CEO and 'functional' directors

Large company
CEO and mix of 'functional' directors
and subsidiary company
managing directors

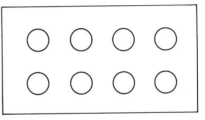

Public company

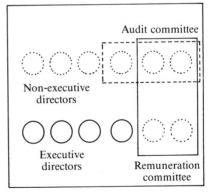

Figure 5.2   Varieties of board

and main meetings of the board may run the danger of taking on the qualities of a seminar. A strong CEO may also feel more inclined to view the board as an 'audience'.

5.4 The composition of the board

The impact of a strong CEO, such as Lee Iacocca at Chrysler, David Kearns at Xerox, Colin Marshall at British Airways, or Jack Welch at General Electric, can lead people to overlook the importance of a competent, perceptive and supportive board. When major changes need to occur it may be vital that a company is seen to be led by a united board[10] and an effective top management team.[11]

As the reader will probably by now expect, it is not possible to formulate or design a 'model board' that would represent the 'best solution' for even a small proportion of companies. So much depends upon circumstances, and the qualities and contributions of the existing members of the boardroom team. This is why exercises such as those in the author's 'companion' book on developing directors,[12] encouraging boards to examine and relate their composition to their own situation and aspirations, can be so important.

Much can be learned from the views, attitudes, opinions and perspective of the existing members of a board. These can act as either a facilitator of change, or a constraint upon it.

From the responses to the survey undertaken by Coulson-Thomas and Wakelam[3] there is little evidence of a consensus view concerning an 'ideal' or 'standard' model of a board. The composition of individual boards appears to be led by circumstances. There are almost as many different compositions of boards as there were respondents. However, some relationship appears to exist between company size and board composition:

- In the case of the smaller companies there tends to be an allocation of roles and responsibilities among members of the boardroom team according to inclination and availability of time. Often there are fewer 'vacancies', as there is less pressure to have a certain number of people on the board. Owner-directors of many smaller companies are inhibited by the cost of bringing extra people onto a board.
- As a company increases in size, there is a greater tendency to take the view that certain directors ought to have particular and exclusive responsibilities. Only in such larger companies is there clear evidence of a conscious search to appoint a director to a functional portfolio because of a 'vacancy'. The cost of remunerating the members of the board may amount to a small proportion of the total 'people cost' of the company.

Board appointments

The composition of a particular board might reflect the 'attractions of the appointment'. The membership of a board could be avoided, or much sought after, according to the circumstances. One directorship might be demanding; another a sinecure. The rewards available to the members of a board could be a factor in encouraging or inhibiting suitable candidates from coming forward.

The 'turnover' of directors is greater for some boards than for others. Some chairmen and boards are ruthless in their treatment of colleagues. In the case of other boards, directors have tended to be periodically and continually re-elected to office until they reach the official age of retirement. Adversity, such as the appointment of a 'new broom' chief executive officer, or a hostile takeover, can disrupt normal practice and trigger the wholescale reconstitution of a board.

The optimum term of office for a director will depend upon circumstances and the individuals concerned. A director who is new to the board, or one who is well past retirement age, might be given a shorter term than a 'tried and tested' director at the height of his or her powers. A degree of continuity on the board may be welcome, while at the same time people can become stale, and familiarity can lead to a loss of objectivity.

The chairman

Are there particular positions that tend to be found on most boards? In the survey undertaken by Coulson-Thomas and Wakelam[3] the role of chairman was the position that was mentioned most often:

- The chairman appears to be a common element of most company boards.
- Although all companies are required by law to have a company secretary, only about one in six of the respondents specifically mentioned their company secretary as an element in the composition of their board.
- Less than one in three respondents referred to a chief executive or managing director. Yet on many business school courses the role of chief executive is assumed to be the peak of business achievement, with the role of chairman mentioned much less often in this respect.

The chairman, or whoever fulfils the role of chairman, should assume responsibility for reviewing the composition of the board.[3] It is important that this is kept under review, particularly when a company is undergoing a significant change. A competent chairman ought to be familiar with the subject-matter of this book.

According to Sir John Harvey-Jones, only the chairman 'can develop the board as a collective organization, handle, select and motivate its members, and manage its work. . . . The actual way in which it works depends entirely on the chairman.'[13]

In practice, few chairmen appear to review systematically the composition and performance of their boards with any degree of success. According to a recent survey[3]:

- Review criteria are rarely explicit. For example, chairmen do not appear to proactively seek out 'candidates' with certain qualities or characteristics.
- Review criteria tend to be informal and subjective. Membership of the boards covered by the survey largely results from the display of personal qualities. These personal qualities are considered in more detail in Chapter 8 concerning the criteria used in selecting board members.
- The results of many reviews do not necessarily lead to appropriate action being taken. For example, it might not be possible to fill vacancies that are established. In interviews, some chairmen referred to being 'supply constrained', in that the size of their boards was limited by the availability of 'good people'.

When reviewing a board, account needs to be taken of any legal and regulatory requirements, and of any provisions relating to directors and boards in the constitution of the company. Account also needs to be taken of what mix of qualities and capability is necessary to turn the vision, goals, values, objectives and policies of the company into a reality.

A chairman should also consider whether there are situations that are imminent, likely or probable that would justify a substantial reconstitution of the board, and whether any contingency plans for coping with such an eventuality exist.

Chairmen and chief executives

When reviewing the composition of a board there are certain views and opinions that ought to be considered. For example, although contrary arguments have been put, there is a general trend of opinion in favour of the theoretical benefits of a separation of the role of chairman from that of chief executive.[3, 14]

The 'Cadbury Committee' has concluded that the chairman's role should in principle be separated from that of the CEO:

> If the two roles are combined in one person, it represents a considerable concentration of power. We recommend, therefore, that there should be a clearly accepted division of responsibilities at the head of a company, which

will ensure a balance of power and authority, such that no one individual has unfettered powers of decision. Where the chairman is also the chief executive, it is essential that there should be a strong, independent element on the board.[15]

However, in practice the two roles of chairman and CEO are often combined. When the latter is the case, it is advisable (a) to remember the distinct aspects of the dual role and (b) not to concentrate upon one at the expense of the other. Sir Adrian Cadbury has pointed out that, 'If the chairman is also the chief executive, he has to be scrupulously clear in his own mind when he is acting as one and when the other.'[16] Let us briefly examine the roles of the chairman and the CEO.

The chairman typically, and *inter alia*:
- presides at meetings of the board
- reviews the composition and performance of the board and appoints the directors
- takes responsibility for ensuring that the board formulates a longer term strategy
- ensures that the external accountabilities of the board are addressed
- acts as an external or public 'figure-head'
- plays a key role in liaison with government.

The chief executive typically, and *inter alia*:
- conducts internal 'management team' meetings
- reviews the composition and performance of the management team
- takes responsibility for delivery or implementation of the agreed strategy
- coordinates on a day-to-day basis the activities of the executive directors and members of the management team
- ensures that the internal accountabilities of managers are addressed
- acts as an internal or corporate 'figure-head'
- plays a key role in liaison with customers and business partners.

Demb and Neubauer suggest that while the chairman may preside over meetings of the board, in practice the CEO often has the greatest influence upon the boardroom agenda.[1] The chairman, in consultation with the company secretary, should ensure that in the course of a 'financial year' the agendas of the various board meetings dictate that the board focuses upon and discharges its legal obligations and other accountabilities to various stakeholders.

In many companies, the respective roles of chairman and chief executive will be very different from those suggested here. The activities listed are given purely by way of illustration, and to help make the point that the two roles can be both distinct and complementary. They are most likely to be in harmony rather than in conflict when overlap and confusion is avoided, personalities are compatible, and vision, values, goals and objectives are shared.

Non-executive directors

Another question that attracts strong views and opinions is whether or not the membership of a board should include non-executive directors. Again, views on the 'theoretical position' are not always reflected in corporate practice. In the US, one survey found some three-quarters of directors to be non-executives.[7] In the UK, survey findings[3, 9] suggest that non-executive or 'independent' directors are in a very different position. Only a minority of board members are non-executive directors. In only one out of ten boards are the non-executive directors in a majority.

Why is this the case, when non-executive directors can theoretically offer a higher degree of independence and objectivity in comparison with executive directors whose daily life, career prospects, and, in many cases, total remuneration package, is tied to the prospects of a single company? Among many chairmen of boards there is some reluctance to appoint non-executive directors, for various reasons:

- There is a perception that it is not easy to locate good candidates, particularly 'up and coming highfliers', with the right motivation. Chairmen are reluctant to appoint 'grandees who are full of themselves' or 'has beens looking for pocket money'.
- Larger companies have a tendency to 'hoard' good candidates, and are often reluctant to release their own senior executives to sit upon the boards of smaller companies, even though this would benefit their personal development.
- The timing may not be right. A chairman may be reluctant to bring a new person onto a board at a 'time of recession when redundancies have to be made' for fear of discouraging them. However, it is when times are hard that a board may benefit from the intellectual and emotional independence and objectivity of one or more new appointees.
- For many chairmen, the non-executive director has been 'sold' as a 'watch-dog of the shareholders' in the boardroom. Some chairmen are reluctant to bring into the boardroom team someone whom they feel is there 'to check on them'.

Given the caution and reluctance of many chairmen, advocates of non-executive directors would be advised to put more emphasis upon the benefits to the chairman and existing directors. Examples of such benefits include 'rubbing shoulders' with, and learning from the insights and approaches of people with particular kinds of experience.

We shall return to the question of non-executive directors during our consideration of the effective board in Chapter 7.

Is there a role for a dedicated functional director on the board?

In many companies there are expectations and ambitions that the heads of certain departments and functions, or those with particular specialist expertise, should be 'represented' in the boardroom. Often, those concerned have not thought through the distinction between direction and management, the subject of the next chapter. Whether or not the head of a functional department, such as personnel or information technology, should be given a seat on a board depends upon the individual and the context. The general consensus is that an individual lacking in directorial qualities should not be given a position on a board just to 'fill a particular slot'.[17, 18]

In the case of UK companies, the function that is most commonly represented on the board is finance. One survey of the boards of UK public companies found that: 'In nine out of ten companies, finance is the sole responsibility of an individual board director. Apart from board representation for heads of major subsidiaries, finance is the only function assigned to be the sole responsibility of a board member in most companies.'[19]

The case for the personnel director

Let us consider an example of a function in which many of those holding 'director' job titles do not have a seat on a legally constituted board. Of personal interest to many of those concerned with director development is the question of whether a board should normally include a dedicated personnel director.

During the 1970s in the UK it was felt that 'industrial relations' ought to be 'represented' in the boardrooms of many larger companies.[18] Subsequently, this view has fallen out of favour, in particular because of the conflicts of interest and loyalties that could, and on some occasions did, result from such board appointments.

Few dispute the importance of people to a company, and 'people issues' abound on many boardroom agendas.[20] However, does it follow that the boardroom team should include a personnel director? Not necessarily, appears to be the consensus response.[17, 18, 20] Viewpoints that could be reasonably held, or might be applicable according to the situation or context of a particular company[17, 18] include:

- People are a vital corporate resource and line management is becoming increasingly involved in personnel issues. People are too important to be 'left' to just one director; they are the responsibility of the whole board.
- The chairman and/or chief executive must give a lead in personnel matters. The 'top' person in the company must be visibly seen to be committed to the importance of people.
- A distinction needs to be drawn between appearance and reality.[10] The important thing is being respected, and having the 'ear' of the chairman, whether or not this is linked with a seat on the board.
- The important thing is not to be satisfied with sops, but to be where the power, influence and 'action' is. Being on the board can be largely 'cosmetic', what really counts is being among the 'inner circle' of directors who 'call the shots'.
- Visible recognition is better than words. Unless there is a dedicated personnel director on the board people issues will not get the attention they deserve.
- Good people will either leave or will not be attracted to the personnel department if it is not perceived to be a 'boardroom function'. The prospect of a boardroom seat can motivate a whole function.
- The whole board must debate people issues, but 'implementation' is helped when there is a dedicated personnel director on the board. Someone has to take responsibility within the board for making it happen.

Many chairmen are not satisfied that their senior personnel professionals have the personal and other qualities to 'hold down' or 'justify' a seat on the main board.[18, 20] They sometimes view personnel specialists as 'nice staff people' who are largely concerned with administrative and legal matters, and who lack business acumen and overall or strategic business and financial awareness. Very often there would be a seat on the board for those who could demonstrate that they (a) possess the necessary personal qualities and (b) could 'contribute'.

Being an expert, or being perceived as a professional specialist, does not usually help an individual to obtain a directorship.[3, 20] It is not necessary to appoint someone to the board to obtain the benefit of their expertise. A specialist can be hired to give advice as and when required.

We have looked in some detail at the case of the personnel specialist, but how typical is it? Evidence suggests the situation of certain other professions is similar. For example, as far as the consideration of those 'in' IT,[21–23] marketing,[24] R&D,[25] etc., for a boardroom appointment is concerned, ability in a functional role is generally considered in terms of the extent to which directorial qualities are displayed. Specialist and technical IT or marketing expertise is not sought *per se*, and we shall see later in this chapter that expert opinion tends to be treated with some caution and scepticism in the boardroom.[3]

Facilitating directors

We saw in Chapter 3 that boards are becoming more concerned about their ability to 'implement' or 'make it happen'. This raises the question of the boardroom role of facilitating directors. As more boards become involved in corporate transformation, further appointments of facilitating directors may be made to supplement or replace 'traditional' functional directors in order to enhance the ability of boards to cope with change.[10]

Rank Xerox (UK) is an example of a company that has faced a significant 'culture, structure, attitude and process' change problem. In response, two facilitating directors were appointed to the board to supplement and complement members of the existing team who were largely concerned with 'delivering the current business'. The additional directors were given longer term responsibilities relating to:

- reshaping the organization to meet strategic business development opportunities; and
- establishing and supporting its business systems requirements. A conscious attempt was made to bring about longer term change without losing a grip on the need to achieve shorter term business objectives.

Change, within the business and market environment we considered in Chapter 2, has become 'the norm'. It is no longer regarded by many companies as something 'abnormal' that requires special treatment, and directors should be catalysts in the establishment and maintenance of effective processes for ongoing implementation, learning, adaptation and change. Such processes are increasingly replacing standard procedures. The board will also need to monitor the operation of management and business processes to ensure that (a) balance is maintained, (b) inconsistencies do not arise and (c) growth and development can be sustained.

In the case of Rank Xerox (UK) three complementary processes, all initiated in the boardroom, were cascaded through the organization (Figure 5.3):

1. The first process, 'Business development planning', asked the question: 'What are we going to do?' The output of this first process consisted of

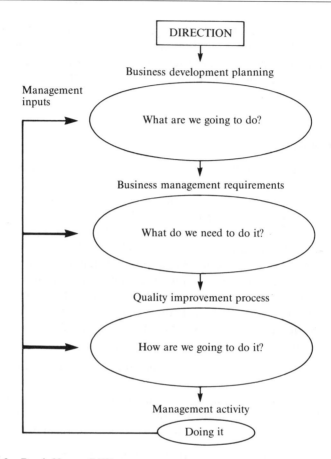

Figure 5.3 Rank Xerox (UK) processes

a mission, goals and strategy, roles and responsibilities, objectives and an organizational framework.
2. The second process, 'Business management requirements', concerned the resources that would be required, and asked the question: 'What do we need to do it?' Outputs from this second process consisted of the management process, rules and policies, business processes and systems, and skill and resource requirements.
3. The third process, the 'Quality improvement process', asked the question: 'How are we going to do it?' The outputs of this third process included business process changes, team commitment and issues requiring direction or resource re-evaluation.

The use of the first three-stage processes ensured that people within the company did not 'rush off into activity' or 'the doing' until they had first thought through (a) whether or not they should be doing the activities in question in the first place and (b) whether they had the resources to do them.

What has been the result of using these processes? The operation of the family of integrated processes within Rank Xerox (UK) has resulted in significant delegation of responsibility in respect of a range of individual decisions:

- The role, contribution and focus of the board in the areas of mission, goal, strategy and objectives has been enhanced.
- Refining mission, improving the understanding of a goal, clarifying strategy or amending an objective in the light of the results of management activities, have become a more important aspect of the ongoing work of the board.
- Members of the board appear more confident in their understanding of the distinction between direction and management, their roles as directors, and the function of the board.

The company has also made significant longer term investments, won quality and other awards, and increased its market share during a period of economic adversity that has had a severe impact upon its business sector.

5.5 Facilitating processes and corporate transformation

As management and business processes are introduced through a corporate organization, a key role of the board is to monitor progress. Barriers may well be encountered and there is some evidence[19] that these occur at the level of the 'office politician' found in the senior ranks of the organizational bureaucracy.[10] For such individuals, change can represent a threat to an existing status and standing. Yet it is from this, at times cynical, group that appointments are traditionally made to the board.

In many companies, few appointments to boards are made from such groups as members of the sales or service force who are in direct day-to-day contact with customers. The need for change is often better understood at lower levels in an organization:[26]

- Here there is likely to be greater contact with customers, and quality programmes may well have resulted in a clearer focus upon meeting their requirements.
- At this level, the standing of individuals may be more related to an effective response to particular customer requirements, and less dependent upon rank or position in the bureaucracy.

To ensure that processes for learning, adaptation and change reach all parts of an organization it may be necessary to 'attack' organizational barriers that resist change from both above and below. To achieve the latter, the chief executive and board colleagues may need to appeal directly to employees as a whole in order that they understand, accept and support the implications of ongoing change.

Board members need to be aware of 'office politics' and resistance to change, and ensure that barriers to change are identified and overcome. We shall return to this theme in later chapters of the book, but the achievement of fundamental corporate change, or 'transformation', is the subject of another book by the author.[10]

5.6 New boardroom roles

In spite of the formidable challenges they face, few boards have experimented with new forms of operation, and even fewer have been innovative in the establishment and allocation of boardroom roles and responsibilities.[3] The following are examples of particular boardroom roles that could be occupied by facilitating directors:

- a 'director of learning, creativity or thinking' to ensure that within the company there are the attitudes, processes and supporting technology so that both individuals and the company as a whole are able to learn from its experience[10]
- a 'director of quality or excellence' with a brief to ensure that the attitudes, values, processes, activities and techniques of the company are focused upon the achievement of excellence and quality
- a 'director of change or transformation' with the brief to facilitate the achievement of significant change[10]
- a 'director of internationalization' whose purpose is to 'internationalize' the company[6]
- a 'director of design' with a particular brief to audit or monitor the quality of design throughout the company
- a 'director of ethics' to ensure that appropriate codes of conduct are developed, understood and enforced
- a 'director of relationships' to facilitate and support the building and sustaining of relationships – built upon mutual understanding and respect – with all significant stakeholders.

There are many other possibilities, and those listed are given for the purposes of illustration only. These facilitating directors would work with other members of the boardroom team. Their presence on the board might help to ensure that certain issues are not overlooked. Once a year each could be asked to report and introduce an appropriate debate in the area of his or her brief.

In certain cases, where a significant change of attitudes takes some time to achieve, the appointment of a facilitating director might run for years. A succession of incumbents could occupy a particular post. In other circumstances the appointment could be for a shorter period that coincides with the time taken to achieve the sought-after change of focus.

5.7 Assessment of expert opinion

We have seen that it is not necessary to enrol someone to the board in order to secure a specialist or expert contribution. In the performance of their duties, individual directors, and boards as a whole, will draw upon professional advice. How are experts viewed and assessed in the boardroom?

In a survey undertaken by Coulson-Thomas and Wakelam,[3] the 'top ten' methods cited by respondents of assessing expert opinion are given in Figure 5.4. The findings suggest that a board should periodically review its use of expert advice and opinion as some areas of uncertainty emerged:

- Many professional advisers and consultants, claiming to be working at board level, are in the main providing specialized input to particular executive directors rather than working with a board as a whole.
- It is unlikely that this situation will substantially change as there is little, if any, evidence that directors consider themselves to be short of expert opinion on general matters that concern them as a board. Yet many directors do find themselves short of practical advice on 'implementation' or 'making it happen'.
- Some of those interviewed questioned what 'expert opinion' meant in the context of the deliberations and operation of a board. It was assumed that those preparing matters to be brought to the board would seek specialist advice as appropriate. It is not thought to be a function of the board to question or second guess the technical quality of such advice.
- The relevance of advice is regarded as another matter. It is thought to be the responsibility of the board to question the extent to which matters on which expert advice has been sought are consistent with the mission, strategy and objectives of the company. It is not clear to those interviewed how expert advice might help the directors in this respect.

In the main any assessment of expert opinion that does occur appears to

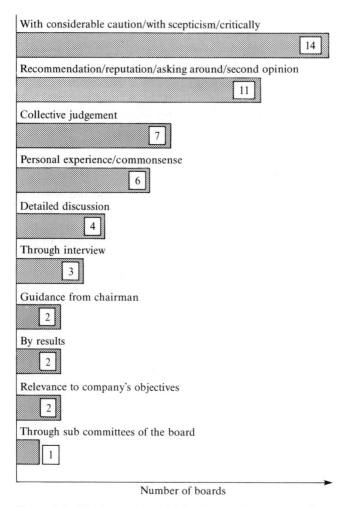

With considerable caution/with scepticism/critically

14

Recommendation/reputation/asking around/second opinion

11

Collective judgement

7

Personal experience/commonsense

6

Detailed discussion

4

Through interview

3

Guidance from chairman

2

By results

2

Relevance to company's objectives

2

Through sub committees of the board

1

Number of boards

Figure 5.4   The 'top ten' methods of assessing expert opinion

be informal or intuitive.[3] 'Experience', the 'track-record' of the expert, 'common sense' and 'trial and error' were all cited. Chairmen appear to attach some caution and scepticism to the label of 'expert'. About a quarter of the respondents used the terms 'carefully', 'with caution', 'warily' and 'critically' in connection with the assessment of expert opinion.

The challenge for management generally is to harness and manage relevant expertise by means of teams, task forces and project groups so that it contributes to the achievement of business objectives. According to Martin Bartholomew, director, Mercury Communications Mobile Services:

'Some teams have clones, some arguing misfits. They should be constructively varied. . . . Teams that value a variety of personality type are better at finding and analysing opportunities or problems, developing practical solutions, developing themselves.'[27]

In the board context, complementary skills and experiences are particularly valuable. Hambrick[28] has stressed the need for the skills and knowledge of the board and senior executives to match the business development needs of a company and the competitive context within which it operates.

Within the board, roles and responsibilities could be allocated according to interest, preference, or on the basis of relevance of expertise, function, cross-functional process, individual task, team or project accountability. A board might periodically review those areas of specialist expertise that ought to be available via a member of the board, rather than through an adviser or consultant to the board. It could also consider the innovative or facilitating roles, and further areas of facilitating expertise, that are desirable in the boardroom.

5.8 Summary

In this chapter we have examined the type, size and composition of boards. We have seen that there is no such thing as a standard board. The nature, size and composition of a board should reflect its aspirations, situation and context. A person with a specialist or functional background should only obtain a seat on the board if he or she displays the appropriate personal and directorial qualities.

In practice boards vary greatly, even among companies in similar circumstances. Many boards do not appreciate the extent to which they have opportunities to innovate and be creative in their operation and composition. The eyes of many directors need to be opened to the possibilities.

5.9 Checklist

1. Does the board of your company regularly review its size and composition?
2. Who is responsible for the review process, and is it adequate given the board's circumstances?
3. Does the board of your company benchmark itself against the boards of equivalent companies and best practice in order to identify areas for improvement?
4. What is the nature of the board in terms of category, form and type;

and how has the current form of the board evolved or come about?

5. Is the type of board operated by your company appropriate in the context of its size, ownership and operations, and the context of the business which it operates?

6. What steps could or should be taken to produce a more balanced and representative board?

7. What would be the advantages and disadvantages of a smaller or larger number of directors?

8. Given the current size of the board, what factors might result in a significant improvement in the effectiveness of the board?

9. Does the board as a whole, and its individual members, understand their roles and responsibilities?

10. In particular, is the distinction between the role of the chairman and that of the chief executive understood?

11. Are there gaps or overlaps in the responsibilities of members of the board?

12. Is there an appropriate mix of executive and non-executive directors, and of functional and facilitating directors, given the business of the board and its accountabilities?

13. Is there mutual trust, respect and understanding between the executive and non-executive members of the board?

14. What new or facilitating roles should be introduced into the boardroom?

15. What is the next most likely step in the evolution of the board?

Notes and references

1. Demb, A. and Neubauer, F-F., *The Corporate Board: Confronting the paradoxes*, Oxford University Press, 1992.
2. Kester, C., *Japanese Takeovers: The global contest for corporate control*, Harvard Business School Press, 1991.
3. Coulson-Thomas, C. and Wakelam, A., *The Effective Board: Current practice, myths and realities*. An IOD discussion document, 1991.
4. Coulson-Thomas, C., *Professional Development of and for the Board*. An Adaptation Ltd survey undertaken for the IOD. A summary was published by the IOD, 1990.
5. Gupta, L. C., *Corporate Boards and Nominee Directors*, Oxford University Press, 1989.
6. Coulson-Thomas, C., *Creating the Global Company: Successful internationalization*, McGraw-Hill, 1992.
7. Heidrick & Struggles Inc., *The Changing Board*, Heidrick & Struggles, 1987.
8. Bacon, J., *Membership and the Organization of Corporate Boards*, Research Report No. 886, Conference Board, 1986.
9. Wakelam, A., *The Training & Development of Company Directors*. A report on a

questionnaire survey undertaken by the Centre for Management Studies, University of Exeter for the Training Agency, December 1989.

10. Coulson-Thomas, C., *Transforming the Company: Bridging the gap between management myth and corporate reality*, Kogan Page, 1992.
11. Kakabadse, A., *The Wealth Creators: Top people, top teams and executive best practice*, Kogan Page, 1992.
12. Coulson-Thomas, C., *Developing Directors: Building an effective boardroom team*, McGraw-Hill, 1993.
13. Harvey-Jones, Sir J., *Making it Happen* (2nd edn), Fontana, 1989.
14. Bickerstaffe, G., 'Are two corporate heads really better than one?', *The Times*, Appointments page, 3 October 1991; and Morrison, R., 'Two views on a split personality', *Financial Times*, 4 October 1991, p.17.
15. Committee on the Financial Aspects of Corporate Governance (chairman: Sir Adrian Cadbury), Draft Report issued for public comment, Committee on the Financial Aspects of Corporate Governance, 27 May 1992, p. 13.
16. Cadbury, Sir A., *The Company Chairman*, Director Books, 1990, p. 102.
17. Coulson-Thomas, C., *The Role and Function of the Personnel Director*. An interim Adaptation Ltd survey carried out in conjunction with the Research Group of the Institute of Personnel Management, 1991.
18. Coulson-Thomas, C., 'What the personnel director can bring to the boardroom table', *Personnel Management*, October 1991, 36–9.
19. 3i's, 'Corporate strategies and the FD: 3i's sixth plc UK survey', *Financial Director*, February 1992, 24–5.
20. Coulson-Thomas, C. and Brown, R., *The Responsive Organisation*, BIM, 1989.
21. Coulson-Thomas, C., *Developing IT Directors*. An Adaptation Ltd report to the Department of Computing Science, Surrey University, 1990.
22. Coulson-Thomas, C., 'Directors and IT, and IT directors', *European Journal of Information Systems*, **1** (1), 45–53, 1991; and 'IT directors and IT strategy', *Journal of Information Technology*, **6**, 1991, 192–203.
23. Kelly, J., 'Baptism of apathy', *Infomatics*, March 1989, 55, 56, 58 and 60.
24. Coulson-Thomas, C., 'Customers, marketing and the network organisation', *Journal of Marketing Management*, **7**, 1991, 237–55.
25. Kenward, M., 'Should the boffins come on board?', *Director*, July 1991, 56–9.
26. Coulson-Thomas, C. and Coe, T., *The Flat Organisation: Philosophy and practice*, BIM, 1991.
27. Bartholomew, M., quoted in Coulson-Thomas, C. and Coe, T., *The Flat Organisation: Philosophy and practice*, BIM, 1991, p. 11.
28. Hambrick, D. C., 'The top management team: Key to strategic success', *California Management Review*, **30**, 1987, 88–108.

6
The competent director

Background discipline is immaterial. You can buy in corporate advice on anything from tax to computers. ('STEVE' SHIRLEY, Founder Director of FI Group plc.)

Chairmen and directors do not always find it easy to articulate and agree the qualities of 'good directors' beyond relatively predictable attributes such as wisdom and judgement. We have seen already that:

– they may also find it difficult to agree the main functions of the board (Chapters 2 and 3), let alone match particular directorial qualities to them; while
– many are not able to distinguish clearly between direction and management (Chapter 4), prior to moving on to the question of what constitutes a competent director.

In some companies the development of programmes to improve the effectiveness of the board and the contributions of individual directors is frustrated by a reluctance to define the qualities of the competent director.

For presentational purposes we shall deal in this chapter with the competence of directors and, in the next chapter, with the effectiveness of boards. In practice, the two are generally interrelated, and an integrated development programme should recognize this and address them both:

– The competence requirements of individual directors can derive from what is needed to improve the effectiveness of the board.
– The effectiveness of the board can reflect the individual competences of its members, and the extent to which these are complementary when they are brought together in the context of the boardroom.

6.1 Getting the competence review process right

The board ought to be, but may not always be, the best judge of its own competence requirements. The job of defining directorial competences is normally best done by the board, assisted by one or more facilitators, as appropriate. Where internal facilitators are inhibited, or ruled out, as a result of their own lack of direct board experience, the services of an external facilitator could be used.

It is important that director competences are defined by a process that is itself sound and authoritative, and is seen to be so. If this is not the case, the board may lack confidence in the outcome. At worst, effort may be devoted to developing qualities or attributes that are irrelevant in the context of a particular board.

Whoever is given the task of developing, or coordinating the development of, directorial competences, should be chosen with care. Experience of developing management competences may actually be a disadvantage. Many trainers, and a number of institutions, that have well-deserved and good reputations for their management programmes do director development a disservice by 're-treading' elements of these programmes as 'director' courses without addressing the distinct development requirements of directors.

6.2 The competent director

Survey and anecdotal evidence suggests that the competence of a director should not be assumed. For example:

- Studies of boards and directors in Canada,[1] the US[2], and the UK[3] suggest that many board members are not properly equipped in terms of background or approach to undertake their directorial duties.
- The 'long experience' of Philip Sadler, formerly chief executive of Ashridge Management College, has 'led inescapably to the conclusion that a significant proportion of company directors are *not* competent – they lack essential knowledge outside the functional area in which they have worked for most of their careers'.[4]
- Many directors lack the information and time to be effective, even if they had the capability to make good use of relevant information and available time.[5] These problems are also faced by public sector directors.[6]

So what constitutes a competent director? We have already established that:

- as a minimum, all directors should understand their legal duties and responsibilities;
- the qualities of the competent director and the effective board derive from the role and function of the board;
- competence needs to be related to such factors as the situation, circum-

stances, context, vision, purpose, composition, dynamics, etc., of the individual board;
- survey evidence[7, 8] suggests that directors themselves identify perspective, strategic awareness and personal qualities as key attributes of the competent director.

We have also seen that a board collectively should be capable of providing a company with a will to win, and a vision, values, goals, drive and purpose. According to one interviewee: 'Without a sense of purpose a company is rudderless. Without a clear and distinctive vision it is aimless. There is no future in a competitive marketplace for corporate zombies.'

Many directors are suspicious of suggestions and moves to define, formally, detailed directorial competences. Consider the following views, which have been expressed by experienced directors:

> I genuinely believe that good directors are born and not made. Direction is all about personal qualities. Many of these defy development. It is sad but true that we cannot alter our real selves.

> Good directors arise out of experience in the boardroom. They learn from it and build on it. You cannot become a good director by ticking off the requirements of a checklist drawn up by someone who is remote from the realities of the boardroom.

> The dynamics of a board thrives on the creative interplay of diverse but complementary qualities and personalities. I would hate to spend money on developing 'clone' or 'identikit' directors and driving all variety and balance out of the boardroom.

> I worry that a massive list of management competences may end up in the boardroom. Everyone looking at the list will think of an extra one or two to add. We will end up with everything under the sun as a director competence, and miss the essence of what being a director is all about.

In practice, the membership of the boards of large companies is predominantly composed of males in late middle age.[9, 10] Many boards comprise people of very similar backgrounds, and drawn from a narrow and small section of the community. Most non-executive directors appear to serve upon more than one board.[10] When in doubt, people appear to recruit in their own image.

Deriving director competences

A more detailed breakdown of the distinguishing attributes and qualities of the competent director is required if: (a) criteria are to be established against which individual directors can be assessed; and (b) deficiencies are to be addressed, and desired qualities are to be consciously encouraged and built, by means of formal director development activity.

A good place to begin is by examining the director competences that can be derived from the function of the board that we examined in Chapter 3. The relative significance of these may well vary from board to board, and might change over time. However, the following selection identifies some of the more general competences that suggest themselves:

- To determine a distinct purpose for, or the essence of, a company requires sensitivity, awareness, realism, an understanding of the business and market environment, and a practical grasp of current capabilities and particular strengths.
- To formulate and agree a corporate vision requires an understanding of the company as a whole in the context of customer requirements, a sense of balance and perspective, a degree of personal vision, and the ability to work with other directors in a team.
- In order to understand the company 'as a whole' it helps to have perception, intellect, experience, and an awareness of more than one function. Cross-functional experience may be of greater value than in-depth exposure to different facets of one particular function.
- As well as understanding the particular business of the company, a wider appreciation of business as a whole is an advantage in a turbulent and changing market environment. Common sense and business acumen or commercial instincts are also desirable qualities.
- Working with a team of fellow directors requires tact, sensitivity, the ability to engender trust and respect, and awareness of the perspectives, interests and values of others. These are also the qualities that directors need to establish and sustain relationships with stakeholders and other groups with an interest in the company.
- Members of the board have a direct accountability to certain groups. Balancing the interests of the various stakeholders in a company requires empathy with their requirements, a willingness to make choices, and, on occasion, considerable diplomacy in the face of what might amount to hostility.
- The establishment of clear objectives requires wisdom, independence and objectivity, a willingness to see the company as it is, and a degree of realism. According to Dr Ingram Lenton, chairman of Compass Group plc, the 'key qualities are . . . independence of thought and the ability and willingness to think the unfashionable'.
- An independent and objective director should be prepared to challenge, and pursue a challenge through obfuscation. A secure and perceptive director may be able to persist with a line of questioning without ruffling feathers.

- When establishing strategy, judgement is needed to distinguish between alternative options. The ability to see connections and establish relationships is of value when thinking through implications for consistency and claims upon resources. To understand the various factors influencing policy requires both insight and balance.
- The vision, goals, values, objectives and strategy of a company will all remain as just 'words on paper' unless members of the board have the communication skills to share them and motivate others to contribute to their achievement. Roger Graham, chairman, The BIS Group plc, emphasizes that: 'An executive director requires an ability to communicate in a relevant way to the top team.'
- The appointment of a management team requires judgement of people, and particularly of their capabilities, aspirations, motivation and limits. Directors need to understand how best to harness the talents of people, how to involve them, empower them and 'turn them on'.
- Delegation, devolution and the allocation of roles and responsibilities requires a preparedness to share, the ability to trust and secure commitment, and a willingness to take sensible and calculated risks.
- While recognizing the importance of trust and some tolerance of failure if people are to give of their best, the director should not be naive. A director who, in the course of a boardroom career, does not encounter individuals who 'sail close to the wind', if not fraud, is lucky indeed. The board must ensure that adequate processes exist to protect the company and its assets.
- A director must be prepared to assume responsibility. The buck stops in the boardroom. The responsibilities of the director are various and onerous, and moral and ethical as well as legal.
- A strong sense of personal morality is needed in the boardroom. There is the fiduciary and legal duty to provide information, both to those with the right to know and those who ought to know. Matters that are material and significant and could be concealed may have to be reported.
- The allocation and sharing of roles and responsibilities with boardroom colleagues, and their delegation elsewhere in the corporate organization, demands a degree of self-awareness, and also awareness of, and sensitivity to, the vested interests of others. The director needs to be prepared to put the interests of the company, and those of its stakeholders, above self-interest.
- The director needs to be able to distinguish between individual and corporate objectives, between the explicit and the hidden. Obstacles and barriers need to be identified and overcome. A more effective board spots them earlier, and while 'keeping things in proportion' and not acting prematurely moves quickly to tackle them.

- Directors need a sense of proportion, and the rigour to identify and prioritize what really constitutes value for customers and the core interests and requirements of other stakeholders.
- Members of the board also need to be able to think through and across a corporate organization in order to identify those processes, many of which may be cross-functional, that deliver value and satisfaction.
- Directors do not need to be experts in information technology, or be aware of every new management process that becomes available, but they should focus on uses and applications of whatever empowers people to do better and best enables them to satisfy customer requirements.
- To monitor and control ongoing activities and the implementation of specific programmes effectively, it helps to be alert, sensitive and shrewd. A director should know how to question, probe and see beyond numbers and the 'right words'.
- When difficult challenges arise, the director needs to be decisive, and, on occasion, courageous. A person who is averse to uncertainty, risk and the assumption of responsibility for consequences should avoid the boardroom.
- The achievement of fundamental change requires consistency, tenacity and persistence. A director may need constancy of purpose in the face of backsliding and doubt when 'the going gets tough'.
- At the same time, as circumstances change, the director needs to be flexible and adaptable. Getting it right for the company should be more important than being right. A willingness to amend and change when it is appropriate to do so is a strength. A tendency to flit, or to be fixated by every new twist and turn, can be a weakness.
- A director needs to be able to distinguish between appearance and reality. Is change desirable, or is it change for the sake of change? Will it cost more, and take longer, than the estimates? What is motivated by a managerial desire to become more visible may not add value for the external customers.
- Reference has already been made to a turbulent and demanding business environment in which openness and flexibility are desirable qualities. A genuine desire and willingness to learn is particularly important in a director. Those whose views are 'fully formed', or who believe that they know all the answers, can be very dangerous in the boardroom.

This long list consists primarily of a range of personal characteristics and qualities, and it is these personal attributes that are sought in new members of the board.[7, 8] Jonathan Charkham, formerly head of PRO NED and with long experience of non-executive director selection and appointment, has concluded: 'In the appointment of a non-executive director, it is the person who counts, with his qualities, experience and character.'[11]

Selecting and grouping competences

The above list of 'derived competences' is a long one, and it could have been continued. Its purpose is to illustrate the diversity of competence requirements that can arise, rather than provide a definitive or standard list of directorial competences. An individual board needs to think through the competence requirements that derive from its own situation and context if any development activity that might be undertaken is to be focused.

The rationale for the inclusion of particular requirements in a list of directorial competences needs to be kept in mind lest they be considered as 'nice to have' or 'motherhood' qualities. This context, and its implications, can also breathe 'life' and meaning into what might otherwise remain as 'words'.

Competences that have been identified can be grouped, categorized and prioritized. For example, the attributes or qualities of the competent director could be grouped as follows:

1. Personal qualities such as wisdom, courage, judgement, tact and diplomacy.
2. Awareness of the business environment, and of what constitutes value to customers. Awareness of developments in the business environment should include ethical and environmental considerations.
3. A sense of accountability to stakeholders, and a willingness to put responsibility to the company above self-interest.
4. Vision, and a strategic perspective that should embrace the totality of the company's operations, situation and context.
5. Business acumen and sound commercial judgement.
6. Knowledge of relevant legal and financial issues and requirements. Particular knowledge is required of the role of the board, and of the legal duties and responsibilities of directors.
7. Understanding of the structure and operation of the board, effective boardroom practice, and boardroom matters such as the succession, assessment and remuneration of directors.
8. Skills in such areas as decision making and teamwork in a boardroom context, strategy determination, formulating and achieving objectives, organizing and motivating people, and the monitoring of performance.
9. Experience of relevance to the particular corporate context.
10. Ethical awareness and sensitivity to the attitudes and values of others.

Such a list of categories of competence could be the basis of a checklist for use in the assessment or self-assessment of the competences of individual

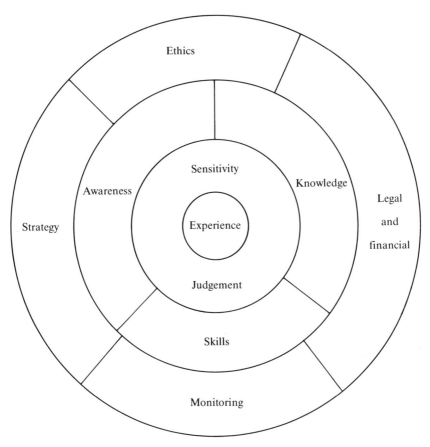

Figure 6.1   The competent director

directors. Figure 6.1 is a schematic representation of the areas that need to be addressed by those concerned with developing more competent directors.

Assessing and prioritizing competences

Assessing the current competences of the individual members of the board against a priority list could enable the key competence deficiencies of each director to be identified.[12] Key questions to consider are:

- Has account been taken of the competences deriving from (a) the purpose of the company; (b) the function of the board; (c) the duties, responsibilities and accountabilities of directors; and (d) the key requirements of stakeholders?

– Are there additional and specific competence requirements that derive from (a) the particular 'make-up' or membership of the boardroom team, or (b) the perceived deficiencies of individual directors?

The ranking of deficiencies could depend upon the extent to which they hinder the individual director's contribution to the achievement of corporate vision, goals, values or objectives. The results could be used as a basis for drawing up director competence development plans for each member of the board.

The nature of the deficiencies might suggest whether formal or informal learning would be more appropriate.[12] Many directors naturally learn from each other, or from one or more individuals whom they can trust and to whom they may turn from time to time to test their reaction to a proposed development. 'Natural learning such as this should be encouraged'.[13]

The boardroom itself represents a potentially rich learning environment. The board as a team could review and assess particular decisions or developments to see what can be learned from what happened. Individual directors could adopt a similar approach towards situations they encounter.

6.3 Knowledge and information

Obtaining relevant knowledge requires more than the accumulation of information. In many companies this is an area that needs urgent attention, and some form of document audit may be desirable:

– Information of itself, and regardless of its quality, will not lead to effective board decisions if the directors have not established appropriate goals and objectives and are unclear concerning roles and responsibilities within the boardroom.[14]
– Many boards and individual directors are inundated with information that does little to increase their understanding. A document audit could determine what is really essential in terms of documents that add value and facilitate the achievement of corporate goals and objectives.
– The energy and commitment with which specialists and experts inundate directors with papers and reports can significantly reduce their understanding.[6] A document audit could determine how information might be better formatted, presented, communicated and shared in order to improve understanding.

The relevance of knowledge

The amount of knowledge or skill required by an individual director could depend upon a number and combination of circumstances. For example, relevant considerations might include:

- the nature of the company, e.g. whether 'public' or 'private'
- the size, stage of development, vision, goals, 'next steps', etc., of the company
- the market or business context, and especially customer requirements
- the particular role (e.g. chairman, 'functional' director, etc.) of the individual director
- whether or not the membership of the board includes those with specialist knowledge, e.g. legal or financial
- the existence of particular areas of deficiency that have been identified, either in the individual director or in the board as a whole
- the individual director's existing directorial and managerial knowledge and skill base

Whatever the particular circumstances that apply, the director should (a) at least understand his or her accountabilities to stakeholders, legal duties and responsibilities, and particular boardroom role and responsibilities; and (b) possess sufficient knowledge and skill to satisfactorily discharge these responsibilities.

Another area of knowledge and skill of value to a director concerns what could be termed 'boardroom issues', i.e. various matters to do with the role, composition, structure, and functioning of the board itself; and with the appointment, remuneration, role, contribution, and conduct of the individual director.

Acquiring relevant knowledge is but one aspect of being an effective director. A competent director needs not just knowledge, but the ability to use that knowledge in the boardroom context.

Legal knowledge

The directors of a company are in a fiduciary relationship with it, and will be expected by a court to be aware of their legal duties and responsibilities. In addition to a basic understanding of legal principles and procedures, the director should be aware of areas of the law that specifically relate to (a) the duties and responsibilities of directors and boards; and (b) the work of the board. The sources of relevant law could be national or regional (e.g. the EC).

There are other specific areas of knowledge that may be of relevance to some companies but not to others. For example:

- directors of 'public' companies need to be aware of both statutory and Stock Exchange requirements.

– boards of 'owner-manager' directors can vary in structure and style from those composed of 'hired employees'.[15]

Directors of companies that operate within the global business environment may encounter a range of legal factors and considerations of which they were previously unaware while operating in a domestic context.[16]

Directors also need to be aware of the main sources of legal advice, and of their duties and responsibilities. There is little point having a legal resource which is not utilized or applied.

A board also needs to put the necessary processes and procedures in place to ensure that there is proper and professional consideration of the legal aspects of all matters concerning the company in general, and the accountabilities, responsibilities and work of the board in particular.

The chairman should ensure that all new directors fully understand what is expected of them. The company secretary should be able to advise individual directors on particular matters that concern them, update them on new legal developments, and monitor the extent to which the board is meeting its legal obligations.

Financial knowledge

There are legal duties and responsibilities of directors that relate specifically to accounts and financial information. All companies have to produce, report and file accounts that satisfy certain reporting requirements. Such accounts need to be audited, and accounting professionals are expected to conform to certain accounting standards when preparing accounts. The directors of all companies should have a sufficient understanding of accounts and accounting to discharge their reporting accountabilities and responsibilities. In particular, they should be aware of how to conduct themselves during a period when a company is experiencing financial difficulties.[17]

Directors of some companies may require special knowledge. For example, reference has already been made to the need for directors of quoted companies to understand Stock Exchange requirements. These also include financial reporting requirements.

While it is not necessary to understand all the intricacies of the process of preparing financial accounts, the director should have an awareness of the meaning and significance of financial information. This requires an understanding of financial and accounting ratios, an appreciation of the perspective of the analyst and investor, and sensitivity to financial danger signals.

A chairman should consider whether sufficient members of the board actively participate in financial discussions, or whether contribution to the review of accounting and financial information in the boardroom is limited to those members with specialist expertise.

The competent director recognizes when the use of knowledge is relevant and appropriate. On occasion it should be used to challenge and probe in order to clarify understanding. This is particularly true of the financial knowledge that is used within many boards to conceal and confuse. Consider the following representative comments from frustrated directors:

> All my business units' results show is the consequences of group overhead allocation. They do not reveal anything about our real performance.

> For too long we ran the company on accounting ratios. When choosing between return on net assets [RONA] and activities to benefit customers, RONA always won. Yet, in the long run, financial performance depends upon satisfied customers. We now put customer satisfaction 'up front'.

> We killed the product by over-pricing it to recover development costs. These were sunk costs. They were gone. They had appeared in previous year's accounts. We should have costed the products on the basis of incremental costs and revenues.

> The numbers looked fine. They all added up and met the criteria we had set. But underneath it all we did not feel a business existed. It was not real. They were just figures on a piece of paper.

> Always check the assumptions. The final numbers will depend upon certain assumptions that were made. How sound or realistic were these assumptions?

> We stopped doing it even though it contributed to the overheads. We had plenty of spare capacity and were short of orders. The opportunity cost of doing it was minimal, yet we stopped doing it because the accountants said it was making a loss.

A director needs a sense of balance when using financial information, and an awareness of its significance and implications. Professional accountants may need to be reminded that their purpose is to serve the board and not confuse it, and to assist the business and not inhibit or distort it. Some key questions that are worth reflecting upon are:

- When was the last time you encountered a board that thought it ought to spend substantially more upon accountants and auditors?
- How appropriate and fair are (a) the company's financial measures of performance and (b) the financial criteria used in decision making?
- Do the members of a board consider expenditure upon financial services to be an investment or an overhead cost?

- If an 'internal market' existed within the company, how much would other functions and business units be prepared to spend upon the 'services' they receive from the 'accounts department' or its equivalent?

6.4 Ethics and values

A director does not just deal in facts. There is often an important ethical dimension to consider in respect of many boardroom issues. Carr has raised the question of whether an executive can afford a conscience.[18] It is difficult for 'a sense of what is right' to thrive elsewhere and pervade a company, if it is absent from the boardroom. There may be a distinction between: (a) what an individual director or board might be able to get away with in terms of 'the law'; and (b) what ought to be done on moral, ethical or 'social responsibility' grounds. The BIM report *Beyond Quality*[19] suggests that values are becoming more important as a source of corporate

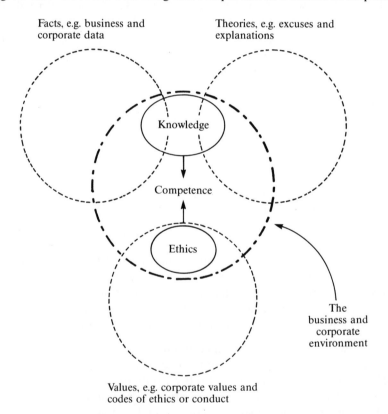

Figure 6.2 The effective director: dimensions of awareness

differentiation. As more companies operate 'total quality' programmes, reliability and efficiency may be assumed. Customers and employees may look 'beyond quality' and, where they have a choice, associate with the companies whose values they share. This suggests that an ability to understand and empathize with values may become of increasing importance in the boardroom.

A director needs to be aware of, and to relate to, facts, theories and values in (a) the external business environment and (b) the internal corporate environment. The effective director will have the competence to select and apply relevant facts, theories and values to a corporate situation and context.[20] This is shown diagrammatically in Figure 6.2.

A director sometimes needs to understand the interrelationship between (a) facts, such as business statistics, (b) theories, such as a prevailing corporate explanation of certain outcomes, and (c) values, such as the strongly held principles of certain groups. Knowledge that is largely concerned with the interrelationship of facts and theories may not be enough when values can influence perceptions of both facts and theories. The effective director needs to draw upon ethical awareness as well as relevant knowledge.

6.5 Understanding director competences

We have seen that a range of individual qualities and attributes are required by a company director. It is their combination and application in the context of board discussion and decision making that distinguishes the effective director. For example, directors need to understand how to use 'strategic processes' for such boardroom activities as formulating the vision, goals, values or objectives of a company.

A director might possess many, perhaps almost all, of the elements that could make a good director, and yet they might not come together in the boardroom. As one moves towards inserting the final pieces of the jigsaw, the picture may begin to fade. This can complicate the task of developing directors.

The director development challenge should not be underestimated. On occasion certain of the responsibilities of the board can appear deceptively simple. An example is the formulation of a vision or mission that defines a reason for the existence of a company, and inspires people to achieve. Many companies, including those with mission statements, do not have a purpose beyond the desire of the company to survive. The ability to articulate and share a distinctive and compelling vision, both inside and outside the corporation, is assuming a special significance:

– More people within corporate organizations are needing to share and

understand their company's vision, and assume personal and team responsibility for 'adding value' to customer requirements.
- Many customers, some suppliers, and business partners are also becoming effective 'participants' or 'colleagues' in the corporate enterprise. A common vision can help to hold a supply chain together.

Drafting a vision that is simple, compelling, distinctive, and acts as a guide to action is not a simple task.[21, 22] There are boards that think they have 'done it', but which have not even begun to introduce any of these desirable elements into the bland and forgettable phrases they call a vision or mission statement. In Chapter 12 we shall consider the requirements for implementing a clear and compelling vision.

The attitudes of different individuals towards directorial competence will also reflect their views concerning the function of the board. There are inherent contradictions in the assumed responsibilities of the board and the ability of many boards to deliver.[23]

Ultimately it is 'performance' that distinguishes the competent director. What constitutes 'good performance' as a director is generally relative rather than absolute, and will be largely determined by the business and boardroom context:

- In a demanding market environment, survival might represent an outcome that suggests outstanding performance on the part of the board.
- In a different market context, a rapid improvement in market share could be perceived as a sluggish response when compared with the extent of the opportunity.

The portability of directorial competences

Given the importance of relating directorial qualities to the corporate and boardroom context, it does not follow that a person who is a competent director on one board would perform equally well on another. The various elements of what makes an effective director can vary in their portability, and the extent of the variation will not be the same for all people.

Opinions differ on the question of how many directorships should be held at the same time. Some individuals can handle a larger number than others. Some boards are more demanding than others. While there are some people who 'collect' directorships, others aim for quality rather than quantity and 'manage' a smaller portfolio of appointments.

The busy executive director might be encouraged by a chairman to take on an external non-executive directorship. This could broaden and give a better sense of perspective. Another individual might prefer to discontinue a demanding full-time role with one company in favour of serving upon a number of boards as a non-executive director.

6.6 Directorial contribution to the board

Before moving from the competence of an individual director to the effectiveness of a board, let us first examine the contribution a chairman expects a director to make to the board.

The expectations that chairmen have of directors has been explored in a recent UK survey.[20] The 'top ten' expectations of the survey participants regarding contributions of members of a board are given in Figure 6.3.

The survey evidence suggests that there is little consensus concerning the contributions expected from members of boards. The responses are both consistent and inconsistent with other aspects of the same and related[6-8] surveys:

– They are consistent in some respects with the evidence we considered in Chapter 4 on the attributes that distinguish directors from managers. For example, personal qualities predominate.
– The contributions sought (Figure 6.3) are also consistent with the function of the board (see Chapter 3) in relation to strategy and direction. Over half of the respondents cited a group of qualities including 'original thinking', 'judgement', 'objectivity', 'overview', 'balance and perspective', that are related to standing back from day-to-day considerations and taking an individual view of matters under consideration in the light of the company's overall mission, strategy and objectives.

In other respects, the findings (Figure 6.3) are not consistent with either (a) other aspects of the evidence concerning the basis of the distinction between directors and managers, or (b) the evidence we shall consider in Chapter 9 on the criteria that are used to select directors. For example:

– About a third of respondents mentioned the formulation of strategy or direction as a contribution expected of members of a board. Twice as many, however, had cited the establishment of strategy, policy or objectives as a function of the board.
– Expertise or knowledge of 'their area' is the most frequently cited form of contribution. Roughly twice as many respondents cited expertise or knowledge as a contribution to the board as those who mentioned it among criteria used to select members of a board.

Certain aspects that emerged from the survey[20] of chairmen are disturbing. For example, in some interview discussions concerning the role of the board, a distinction was drawn between formulation and implementation

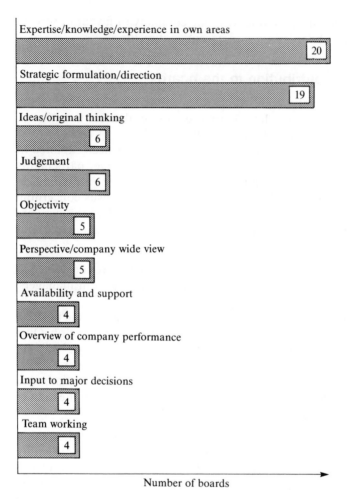

Figure 6.3 The 'top ten' expectations regarding contributions of members of a board

of strategy. It was recognized that the 'right' strategies can be inadequately implemented, but this was considered to be the province of 'management' rather than a question of 'direction'. Directors and boards need to devote more attention towards identifying obstacles and barriers to implementation, and ensuring that they are overcome.[24]

6.7 Age and directorial competence and contribution

Should one be concerned about the age of directors? The majority of directors of larger and public companies are well into late middle age.[9, 10] Some possible disadvantages of an older director are listed below. These have been adapted from a list of negative stereotypes associated with those who are older that have been identified in the BIM report *Too Old at 40?*[25].

The older director: hinders

An older director might:

– be inflexible
– resist change
– discourage the taking of risks
– act as a brake on innovation
– have outdated skills
– have more but less relevant experience
– be bored, having 'seen it all before'
– give the 'wrong signal' to younger candidates
– be resentful of younger colleagues
– favour those with similar backgrounds
– be out of touch with 'today's' customers
– stand on his or her dignity
– have strong views and prove obstructive
– have 'run out of steam'
– be looking for a 'safe haven' or 'quieter life'
– put hobbies and leisure interests ahead of the company
– be too relaxed and 'laid back'
– be reluctant to travel
– not be willing to work between meetings
– not be 'hungry any more'
– be more conscious of his or her rights
– not work well in groups and teams
– have a more cynical attitude
– be more likely to have health problems
– not wish to be stressed
– require more expensive pension arrangements
– resist director development

There are many myths and prejudices associated with 'ageism'.[25] Generalization concerning the impact of age in the boardroom should be treated with caution:

– Age does not affect all people in the same way; in fact people can 'age' in different respects at widely varying rates.

- The impact of age upon directorial attributes and qualities may be significantly different from its consequences for managerial activity.
- Within the boardroom there may be roles, such as that of non-executive director, which do not require an extensive commitment of time or of physical energy.
- Those who are aware of the negative impacts of age may be able to compensate by moving closer to their full potential.
- Certain circumstances associated with a particular age can be specifically addressed, e.g. by appropriate development activity or a particular pattern of work.

The above factors may or may not be relevant as far as any individual director is concerned. What matters is how age relates to (a) the members and activities of a particular board; and (b) those qualities that are especially relevant to the situation and circumstances of the company concerned.

In the interests of balance, it should be said that not all myths and prejudices favour the young. Some possible advantages of an older director are listed below. These have been adapted from a list of positive stereotypes associated with those who are older, and given in the BIM report *Too Old at 40?*.[25]

The older director: helps

An older director might:

- have more and relevant experience
- have a more balanced perspective
- be more tolerant
- have more patience
- be respected by others
- have more developed social skills
- understand older customers
- be a good ambassador
- calm troubled waters
- think more about the boardroom team, and less about personal issues
- take a role that a younger person might see as a 'dead end'
- be more open-minded
- be 'laid back' and more relaxed
- be relatively self-aware
- be more secure and confident
- be 'older and wiser'
- be realistic with 'feet on the ground'
- have got 'enthusiasms' out of his or her system
- distinguish between results and activity

- tell it as it is
- be free of onerous financial commitments, and hence
- be able to take risks, and be honest and objective
- not get carried away, having 'seen it all before'
- think before rushing in
- be more aware of downside risks
- not have to spend so much time 'proving things'
- be willing to share and develop others.

A continuing openness to new ideas as one gets older can be more important than age itself. According to Colin St Johnston, director of **PRO NED**, receptiveness to new ideas and challenges is especially valuable in a non-executive director: 'The willingness to learn is the key requirement . . . no-one seeks to become a non-executive director for the money.'[26]

6.8 Summary

In this chapter we have seen that the competence of directors derives from their accountabilities, their legal duties and responsibilities, and from the function of the board. The competence of directors needs to be related to the situation and context of each company. The knowledge and skill required by a company director is considered in greater detail in the author's 'companion' book on developing directors.[12]

It should not be assumed that directors are competent or that boards are effective. How directors are evaluated, and how boards conduct their business, can inhibit rather than encourage what is desirable.

6.9 Checklist

1. Has your company identified the knowledge and skills that should be possessed by the members of its board?
2. Do the knowledge and skills that have been identified match the requirements for success in the context of the business in which the company operates? Are they appropriate to the particular circumstances of the company?
3. Do the members of your company's board share an understanding of what represents a competent director?
4. Have members of the board assessed their individual competence as directors? Has a clear distinction been made between directorial and managerial competences?
5. Are the criteria used to assess director competence appropriate to the context and circumstances of the company? What is the relationship

between the competence requirements that have been identified and the vision, goals, values and objectives of the company?

6. How do the competence requirements that have been developed relate to the expectations the chairman has of members of the board?
7. Against what standards are competence and effectiveness assessed?
8. Is there a process for identifying gaps between actual and desired competence and effectiveness?
9. Which deficiencies derive from a weakness in the structure or operation of the board?
10. Does the culture of the board encourage members to assess and improve their own competence and contributions as directors?
11. Does the competence of the directors, and that of the board as a whole, extend to the translation of aspiration into achievement?
12. Has the ethical dimension been addressed?
13. Does the chairman assume responsibility for ensuring that the directors are competent?
14. What needs to be done to improve director competence?
15. Are the knowledge and skills sought in individual directors matched to the requirements of the board as a whole? How do the development needs of individual directors relate to those of the board as a whole?
16. Which deficiencies should be addressed by development activities aimed at individual directors, the board as a whole, or both at individual members of the board and the boardroom team?

Notes and references

1. McDougal, W. J., *Corporate Boards in Canada*, Research Report, University of Western Ontario, 1968.
2. Mueller, R. K., *The Incomplete Board*, Lexington, 1981.
3. Norburn, D. and Schurz, F., 'The British boardroom: time for a revolution?', in B. Taylor, *Strategic Planning, The Chief Executive and the Board*, Pergamon Press, 1988, pp. 43–51.
4. Sadler, P., 'The painful path to competence', *Director*, September 1991, 23.
5. Lorsch, J. and MacIver, E., *Pawns or Potentates: The reality of America's corporate boards*, Harvard Business School Press, 1989.
6. Coulson-Thomas, C., *Development Needs of NHS Authority and Board Members*. A report prepared by Adaptation Ltd on behalf of the NHS Training Directorate, 1992.
7. Coulson-Thomas, C., *Professional Development of and for the Board*. A questionnaire and interview survey undertaken by Adaptation Ltd of company chairmen. A summary has been published by the IOD, February 1990.
8. Coulson-Thomas, C., *The Role and Function of the Personnel Director*. An interim Adaptation Ltd survey carried out in conjunction with the Research Group of the Institute of Personnel Management, 1991.
9. Heidrick & Struggles Inc., *The Changing Board*, Heidrick & Struggles, 1987;

and Boone, L. and Johnson, J., 'Profiles of the 801 men and one woman at the top', *Business Horizons*, February 1980, 47–52.

10. Korn/Ferry, *Boards of Directors Study UK*, Korn/Ferry International, 1989 and 1992.

11. Charkham, J., *Effective Boards: The independent element and the role of the non-executive director*, Institute of Chartered Accountants in England and Wales, 1986.

12. Coulson-Thomas, C., *Developing Directors: Building an effective boardroom team*, McGraw-Hill, 1993.

13. Mumford, A., Honey, P. and Robinson, G., *Director's Development Guidebook: Making experience count*, Director Publications, 1990.

14. Aram, J. D. and Cowen, S. S., *Information Requirements of Corporate Directors: The role of the board in the process of management*. Final report to the National Association of Accountants, 1983.

15. Alkhafaji, A., 'Effective boards of direction', *Industrial Management and Data Systems*, **90** (4), 1990, 18–26.

16. Coulson-Thomas, C., *Creating the Global Company: Successful internationalization*, McGraw-Hill, 1992.

17. Institute of Directors, 'Guidelines to boardroom practice: Companies in financial difficulties', *Direct Line*, (94), January 1991.

18. Carr, A. Z., 'Can an executive afford a conscience?', *Harvard Business Review*, July–August 1970, 58–74.

19. Coulson-Thomas, C. and Brown, R., *Beyond Quality: Managing the relationship with the customer*, BIM, 1990.

20. Coulson-Thomas, C. and Wakelam, A., *The Effective Board: Current practice, myths and realities*. An IOD discussion document, 1991.

21. Campbell, A. and Yeung, S., *Do You Need a Mission Statement*, Economist Special Report No. 1208, 1990.

22. Coulson-Thomas, C. and Didacticus Video Productions Ltd, *The Change Makers, Vision & Communication*. Booklet to accompany integrated audio and video tape training programme by Sir John Harvey-Jones. Available from Video Arts, 1991.

23. Bavly, D., 'What is the board of directors good for?', in B. Taylor, *Strategic Planning, The Chief Executive and The Board*, Pergamon Press, 1988, pp. 35–41; and Coulson-Thomas, C., 'Strategic vision or strategic con?: Rhetoric or reality?', *Long Range Planning*, **25** (1), 1992, 81–9.

24. Coulson-Thomas, C., *Transforming the Company: Bridging the gap between management myth and corporate reality*, Kogan Page, 1992.

25. Coulson-Thomas, C., *Too Old at 40?*, BIM, 1989.

26. St Johnston, C., quoted in Coulson-Thomas, C., *Too Old at 40?*, BIM, 1989, p. 21.

7
The effective board

The effective board seeks answers, not yet more complex questions.
(PHILLIP JUDKINS, Director, Provincial Group plc.)

Let us now switch our attention from the competence of individual directors to the effectiveness of the board as a whole. It is the board collectively that governs a company, not individual directors.

The author has pointed out that: 'In some of the most popular management titles there is not a single reference to the board. It is as if the board does not exist.'[1] This raises some challenging questions about the effectiveness of boards:

- Is the lack of reference to boards because they 'have been overlooked, or is it because they are not discharging their responsibilities to the extent that they can be ignored?'[1]
- 'Are boards catalysts, enablers, engineers and instigators of change'; or 'are they at best bystanders, and at worst obstacles to the change process, and a burden upon the body corporate?'[1]

The 'effective' board is one that operates effectively as a team in the discharge of its collective duties, responsibilities, and accountabilities. The composition of a board, and the tone, 'atmosphere', dynamics, extent of openness, processes, etc., of the boardroom could all constitute *prima facie* evidence of board effectiveness. Whether or not a board with certain characteristics, or which operates in a certain way, actually is effective will depend upon how well it performs in relation to the company situation and business context.

A gathering of exceptional individuals will not necessarily result in an effective board. Whatever the merits and qualities of particular individuals, the value of their contributions as directors will largely depend upon how effectively the board works as a team. For reasons of interpersonal chemistry and board management, outstanding individuals sometimes find it difficult in certain boardrooms to contribute to the extent that their potential and track records on other boards might suggest.

7.1 A board or a management committee?

A legally constituted board has various accountabilities and responsibilities. It should operate as a board, and conduct its affairs as a board. Just as individuals may need to distinguish between directorial and managerial responsibilities, so a board needs to ensure that it functions as a board, rather than as a management committee composed of (a) a chief executive officer or 'boss'; and (b) executive directors, all of whom are employees of the company and 'subordinates'.

If a separate corporate management committee is thought to be necessary, the executive team could meet apart from formal meetings of the board. For example, management committee meetings could be held weekly, and a board meeting involving non-executive directors once a month.

Many 'two-tier' boards adopt a similar approach. The executive or management board could meet weekly or monthly, and then with members of the supervisory board when the latter holds its monthly or quarterly meetings. This latter situation is disturbingly common. It may appear to offer advantages such as 'unity' and 'proximity when needed', but these may be secured at the cost of other, more important, considerations such as independence and objectivity.

The composition of a board can be *prima facie* evidence of board effectiveness because of such factors as[2] (a) the presence of a strong chairman and non-executive directors on the board; or (b) a separation of the role of board chairman from that of chief executive officer. Even the most powerful of chief executives will find it prudent to seek the approval of the board on important matters. The competent chief executive, and one who is a secure personality, will want to have the advice and support of a strong board. Boards, like people, can sometimes surprise. A board may have a potential that is not being fully used. A good chairman, and on occasion adversity or a challenge, can bring out the best in a board.

Chairmen or chief executive officers who try to 'pack' boards with those whom they feel are sympathetic or 'cronies' often find that people become more robust when aware of their legal duties and responsibilities as directors. It is not unknown, particularly in the case of quoted companies, for 'strong' chairmen and chief executives to be removed by a combination of directors.[3] In a recent case involving BP, the non-executive directors are reputed to have played a significant role in the departure of the chairman.[4] The relationship between CEO and non-executive directors is significant and is 'two-way':

- The appointment, assessment and, if necessary, removal of the CEO is regarded as one of the most important boardroom contributions that the non-executive directors can make.[5]

- At the same time, the CEO may play the leading role in identifying potential non-executive directors and often controls the information the 'non-executives' receive.[6]

7.2 The conduct of board meetings

Boards vary greatly in their approach to business. Some act as a forum at which issues are raised and discussed, while others concentrate upon taking decisions.[6] Directors who feel they are shirking their responsibilities unless they are taking a snap decision should ponder the significance of the 'non-decision'.[7] It is sometimes better to reflect, or 'think again', rather than 'rush in'. Not deciding, or withholding approval, can be a potent source of directorial power.

The procedures and practices of a board should be written up, agreed by the board, and circulated to all directors. They should be reviewed periodically, and compliance should be monitored by an audit committee of the board.[8] Particular attention should be paid to ensuring that:

- all directors receive the same board papers at the same time, and sufficiently ahead of board meetings for them to be properly considered;
- the board identifies and agrees the criteria for bringing matters to their attention;
- there is an agreed procedure for handling matters that require a decision between formal meetings of the board.

Roderick M. Hills, while chairman of the US Securities and Exchange Commission, encountered boards dominated by inside directors, friends of the CEO, who were reluctant to criticize, conflicts of interest, and inadequate information: 'Information provided to boards of directors in too many cases is entirely the product of management, and no effort is made and no authority is given to outside directors to make an independent investigation.'[9]

Many boards deal with symptoms and appearance rather than reality, and are reluctant to address root causes, obstacles and barriers.[1] Discussion is based upon rumour, emotion, organizational politics, deception and departmental self-interest rather than fact and shared objectives.[1] A concern with 'numbers' should not become an obsession. A director should always probe for the significance and meaning 'behind' the figures.

Boards vary in the extent to which they are cohesive.[6] A degree of unity, a shared vision, and common goals and values may be essential if a board is to achieve fundamental change.[1] At the same time disagreement and diversity should not be driven out of the boardroom to the extent that 'groupthink' occurs.[10]

7.3 Responsibility for board effectiveness

Who should be responsible for the effectiveness of the board? In many companies, how the board operates and conducts its business is thought to be the responsibility of the chief executive officer.[11] Robert Heller has reported the view that 'the chief strategist [is] the obvious, if not the only, logical choice to take the chair'.[12]

In Chapter 3 it was suggested that in the light of a recent investigation[13]: (a) the chairman should assume responsibility for the effectiveness of the board; while (b) the CEO should assume responsibility for the effectiveness of the management team. It is a prime task of the chairman to ensure that the members of the board work together effectively as a team in discharging their accountabilities and responsibilities as a board. The chairman needs to conduct the business of the board in such a way as to achieve this. As well as drawing upon the collective strength and wisdom of the boardroom team, the chairman should also use the skills of the individual members when it is appropriate to do so in the interests of the board and its business.

Many of the contributions chairmen appear to expect of directors (see Figure 6.3), such as expertise and personal qualities, could be considered as 'input' factors. Less than one in ten respondents in one survey[13] hinted at outcomes in referring to 'problem resolution' or 'achieve objectives'. Some of the chairmen who were interviewed explained that they did not find it easy to define the 'outputs' of a board. Hence they tended to rate directors according to their personal qualities.

While chairmen stress the need to motivate and assess managers in relation to value added contribution or tangible output rather than 'input' factors such as 'appearance' or 'background', there is little evidence of a similar approach in the boardroom. We shall examine director and board performance in Chapter 11.

The learning board

Circumstances change. A board that is effective at one moment may not be effective later, and success in one particular context may not be replicated in another. A crisis situation may severely test a board, and for this reason, among others, a board needs to apply learning loops such as that in Figure 7.1,[1] which sets out the various processes that are required to ensure that corporate vision and capability remain in step with changing customer requirements. As a company evolves and passes through various stages of development, the composition of the board should be kept under review.

A board needs to be vigilant and alert. Past performance, however

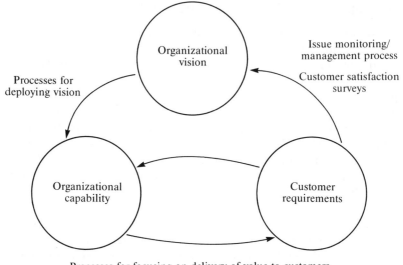

Processes for focusing on delivery of value to customers
Processes for harnessing talents of groups and teams to add value for customers
Processes for continuous learning and improvement

Figure 7.1   The learning loop

laudable, may not be a guarantee of future survival in the turbulent market-place we examined in Chapter 2. Rather than 'rest upon its laurels' or 'live in the past', the board needs to understand 'the contemporary and the emerging':

- It should focus upon the assessment of issues and trends, the evaluation of challenges and opportunities, and seek to anticipate circumstances and situations.
- It also needs to reconcile the demands and requirements of the future with the conditions and pressures of the present. While looking ahead, a board cannot afford to take 'its eye off the ball'.

Caution and prudence can lead to complacency in the boardroom. Many companies are constrained by their past, imprisoned by their own lack of imagination and fear of taking risks. Success can lead to conceit. A board may forget to continue to learn as circumstances change. In order to learn, a board, as we have already seen, needs to:

- systematically monitor relevant developments in the business and market environment;
- regularly discuss the lessons that arise from its own decisions and operations;

- periodically review and re-assess, in the light of experience, corporate vision, goals, values and objectives;
- ensure that all documents received by the board present information in a way that facilitates the building of understanding;
- make appropriate use of techniques such as benchmarking.

The active and challenging board

A board should be prepared to challenge the assumptions that form the basis of proposals from, and action by, the company's management. Standing back and working up new ideas may prove less risky than drifting by incremental decision inexorably towards the abyss. It does not really cost that much to think. As one interviewee put it: 'Whenever I'm asked to consider how valuable the time of my board members is, I remind myself of the cost to the company of getting it wrong.'

Testing new ideas and concepts need not be expensive if the overhead costs of corporate bureaucracy are kept at bay and flexibility is retained. Testing different assumptions can, at minimum, improve understanding. The key to breaking out of the 'incrementalism trap' is to ask fundamental questions in the boardroom. The following are some illustrative snippets of conversation:

> Rather than introduce a 'me-tooism' product, how could the lifestyles of customers be transformed by this technology? Rather than play the market game, could we not start a new game?

> With customer satisfaction levels of approaching 100 per cent across the industry, no wonder there is a problem of differentiation. Should we be fomenting customer dissatisfaction by sowing in the minds of customers wants they might think could only be dreams?

> Our distribution companies are reorganized almost every year; do we need them at all? If our products were sold through third parties, what price reductions could be passed on to customers?

> Each year the cost of production is cut by about 5 per cent; looking at it differently what is the minimum it could be produced for? Could we use other materials, or do the job for a quarter or a tenth of the price?

> Why do we tend to uncritically accept, and operate within, the sector classification into which the external world places us? What are we really good at, and what other needs could we satisfy?

The members of a board cannot afford to address a few issues, and then conclude that they have 'done it' for another year. Review and re-assessment needs to occur on a continuous basis. It could be perceived as a circular process along the lines of that shown diagrammatically in Figure 7.2.[14]

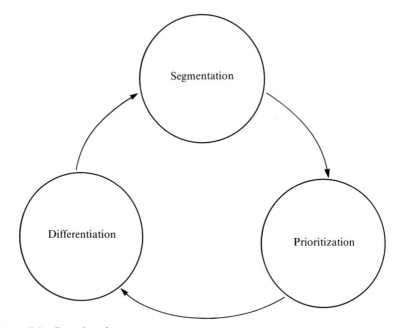

Figure 7.2 Board review process

This illustrative process addresses three key concerns of the board,[14] namely that in respect of its relationship with customers, a company should:

- differentiate itself from competitors, in order to develop a distinctive purpose and appeal;
- segment its customers into groups, in order to better understand their particular, even individual, requirements and play to its strengths;
- prioritize, so that it builds upon its unique comparative advantage, and concentrates upon those activities that provide the best opportunity for maximizing 'value added' or improvements in customer satisfaction.

A board should check that the outputs of the three stages of this iterative process are consistent with the company's vision, goals, values and objectives. Each of these should also be reviewed periodically in the light of what is learned as a result of each iteration of the process.

To identify the main sources of a company's comparative advantage a board requires a broad perspective that reaches beyond the organization and the current operators within its marketplace.[15]

The use of simplistic measures of performance in the boardroom can lead to an overemphasis of particular aspects of the directorial role. From

time to time, the criteria that are used to judge effectiveness and performance should be rematched against the requirements for competitive success
in the company's marketplace.[16]

7.4 Boards in theory and practice

Effective teamwork in the boardroom suggests an environment of openness and trust, and an atmosphere of questioning and debate. In practice,
do boards live up to the 'model' board, composed of independent and
objective directors with varied and complementary talents, and free of
vested and personal interests, who are engaged in full, free, frank and
rational debate in the pursuit of stakeholder interests? Survey evidence[13]
suggests that many chairmen do not actively seek directors who are likely
to challenge them. Many of the personal qualities that chairmen seek in
directors – such as commitment, loyalty and support – could reduce the
extent to which a chairman or chief executive officer might be challenged
by fellow directors. One might not expect chairmen to actively seek out
those who could make life more difficult; however, if commitment, loyalty
and support are obtained at the expense of independence and a willingness to challenge, the objectivity and effectiveness of a board could be
compromised.

An effective chairman would not seek an 'easy life' where this could
conflict with the full and proper consideration of boardroom business.
Non-executive directors, for example, who might ask challenging and
penetrating questions should be actively sought and not be regarded as a
threat.

7.5 The contribution of non-executive directors

Many chairmen feel constrained, when reviewing the composition of
their boards, by the qualities of the visible members of their management
team. This need not be the case. Gaps that are evident can often be filled
by the appointment of non-executive directors.

The UK Corporate Affairs Minister has expressed the view that there
is:

> a strong case in larger companies for having a body of three or four non-
> executive directors on the main board who can also sit on an audit committee,
> settle the executive directors' remuneration, and ensure that the company has
> systems to prevent fraud and to identify problems early. The Government has
> not made this a statutory requirement, because it is easy to circumvent the
> spirit of such legislation by putting on the board the chairman's or chief execu-
> tive's friends.[17]

Non-executive directors can be used to improve the effectiveness of a board in a number of ways. For example:

1. The growing private company could actively search for a non-executive director or chairman with experience of a public flotation.
2. A non-executive director appointment could bring onto the board a person, possibly an overseas national, with knowledge of particular countries or regions in order to support a planned programme of internationalization.
3. The age or experience mix of the board could be changed through non-executive director appointments in order to broaden or add diversity to the board.
4. An audit committee of non-executive directors could be appointed to liaise with the auditors and examine any deficiencies that might arise in the course of an audit.
5. The question of the remuneration of the executive directors could be handled by a remuneration committee made up of non-executive directors.

On occasion groups of non-executive directors have worked together to achieve a significant impact upon the governance of a company,[18] but the challenge of confronting an entrenched corporate leadership should not be underestimated.[19] The non-executive director may be required to display considerable moral courage and fibre in return for financial rewards that may be modest by the standards of executive colleagues.

Since 1978 the New York Stock Exchange has required all listed companies to have an audit committee composed solely of independent directors. By 1992, around two-thirds of the top 250 UK listed companies had audit committees, and the 'Cadbury Committee' recommends that all listed companies should establish an audit committee and a remuneration committee.[20]

7.6 Assessing board effectiveness

An effective board is self-critical. While the chairman should continuously monitor the effectiveness of the board, the board itself should be periodically involved in a review of its own activities, priorities and effectiveness. The board should begin with the key activities that were identified and described in Chapter 3. These are summarized in Figure 7.3.

A review of core functions could take place on an annual basis, with more extensive re-assessments every second year. An external consultant could be used as a facilitator should the board be reluctant to use a member of the management team for this purpose.

Bob Tricker has warned of the need to take account of the situation and circumstances of the particular company:

> the fact that boards and directors can be so different ... means that generalisations about how directors operate, or suggestions for change to the legal requirements on how they should operate, may well be useless, and lead to guidelines that are relevant and useful in one situation, yet irrelevant and unhelpful in another.[21]

While every board is to a degree unique, there are certain general principles that should be borne in mind when assessing the effectiveness of a board. These give rise to some relatively obvious, and grouped, questions.

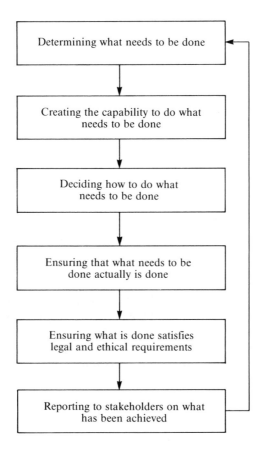

Figure 7.3   Board review process

CONSTITUTION AND COMPOSITION

1. Is the board properly and correctly constituted?
2. In terms of its composition, is the board equipped to handle the issues it is likely to face?
3. Does the membership of the board include non-executive directors, and does mutual trust and understanding exist between them and the executive directors?

CONDUCT OF BUSINESS

1. Does the board meet regularly, and conduct formal business?
2. Are the meetings of the board chaired by someone other than the chief executive officer?
3. Is the presentation of information in board papers conducive to understanding?
4. Do the processes of the board allow for the efficient conduct of business?
5. Do the processes of the board focus upon those things that are really important for customers and other stakeholders?
6. Is sufficient time devoted to the consideration of matters of importance?
7. Is the board able to handle crisis decision making?[22]

ATTITUDES AND APPROACH

1. Does the board exercise a strategic overview?
2. Are the priorities of the board appropriate to the situation and circumstances of the company?
3. Does the board confront or avoid reality?[1]
4. Is the board involving and empowering the management team?

DIRECTORIAL QUALITIES

1. How competent are the individual members of the board?
2. Do the directors understand the particular leadership requirements for successful corporate transformation?[1]
3. How perceptive, open and frank are members of the board in raising issues, and how rigorous and persistent are they in seeking to reach 'root causes'?

TEAM DYNAMICS

1. How well do the members of the board appear to work together as a team?

2. Does the board operate as a board, or as a corporate management committee?
3. Do members of the board behave as 'subordinates' of the chief executive officer?
4. Have harmony and unity been achieved at the cost of rigour, diversity and challenge?

CONTINUOUS IMPROVEMENT

1. To what extent is the full potential of the board and its members being tapped?
2. Are the expectations which the chairman has of the board, and of its members such as to encourage it to become more effective?
3. Does the board learn from its own experience, and is it prepared to challenge fundamental assumptions?
4. How self-critical is the board, and how willing is it to learn from its own evaluation of its effectiveness?

A board must recognize that relationships need to be nurtured and sustained, and that change is an ongoing process of adapting attitudes, expectations and behaviour, rather than a matter for a one-off and discrete decision.[1] The directors cannot take a quick decision and walk away.

7.7 Accountability and business development

It is important not to forget the role of the board in developing a business. This is sometimes overlooked as a result of the preoccupation with such issues as accountability and social responsibility. Peter Morgan, director-general of the IOD, has written of the draft report of the 'Cadbury Committee' on the 'financial aspects of corporate governance':

> ... the report focuses on the accountability of directors and boards almost without reference to their main function. Our definition of the objective of good corporate governance is to ensure that companies survive and thrive, and that they conduct their affairs with ethics and integrity. The Cadbury report was strong on integrity, but it did not address the challenge of surviving and thriving, nor the qualities that directors and boards of directors need to discharge all their duties.[23]

There are specific accountability questions which may need to be posed, as a result of their applicability to the situation of a particular board. For example:

– Should the role of chairman be separated from that of chief executive?

- How 'independent', e.g. composed of non-executive directors, is the audit committee, or the process that examines the nomination and remuneration of directors?
- Is the board supported by a company secretary with the 'independence' and standing to monitor the conduct of the board?

Special attention should be given to the periodic review of what might be considered a departure from usual or best practice. Care should be taken to avoid slavishly following the norm. For example, the presumption or consensus is that the roles of chairman and CEO should be separated. The *Financial Times* is of the view that 'for big companies to combine the role of chairman and chief executive in one individual is almost always a mistake'.[24]

Major organizations, such as British Gas, are separating the roles, and this can have advantages in terms of 'checks and balances', coverage, continuity, succession, and accountability to external shareholders. However, in the case of a smaller and more entrepreneurial company, requiring unity, focus and quick, authoritative decision making, a combination of roles might be more appropriate. As the business develops, circumstances and requirements could change.

7.8 Barriers to effectiveness

When assessing the effectiveness of a board it is important to examine both structure and conduct. A board with a satisfactory structure may not be efficient in its conduct of business within the framework that is provided. The following selection of quotations, from directors who have been interviewed, illustrates the variety of barriers that reduce the effectiveness of a board:

> I would like to raise it, and so would others, but we have no influence over the boardroom agenda.

> We always leave it to the end of the meeting when most people are thinking about lunch.

> We meet so infrequently that I lose touch.

> It went through. The chairman made sure it was not really discussed.

> The way it was dealt with makes me suspicious.

> The company is bound [but] the contract was not seen by the board.

> Apparently the evidence exists but we have not seen it.

> I did not like to raise it.

Some reports are so large that we cannot possibly digest them.

I hate getting things through the post the day before a meeting. Why do we always need to do it today?

Minorities are trampled upon.

We have non-executives, but they cannot always get to the meetings.

Whatever we say, what the finance director says usually goes. There is no way any of us could argue with the finance director. He blinds us with science.

The new director just arrived. I didn't know anything about it until the meeting.

He is both judge and jury. He runs the company and the board.

The chairman treats the directors like most other employees.

The two of them never seem to see eye-to-eye in the boardroom. They just don't get on. We don't know why.

I've never met the auditors.

Barriers such as those listed above should be identified and tackled. They could be symptomatic of more general underlying problems in the way the business of a board is conducted. For example, their pattern might suggest a conscious attempt to conceal material information from certain directors, or a tendency to use the board as a rubber stamp.

In the case of an effective board: (a) individual directors would feel free to raise any concerns they might have about how the board conducts its business; while (b) the chairman would periodically invite comments and feedback concerning the operation of the board. The persistence of barriers could point to inadequate chairmanship of the board, and might suggest the need to appoint a new chairman. The evaluation of the effectiveness of a board is considered in some detail in Chapter 11.

7.9 Assessing management performance

A board needs not only to review its own performance, but also that of the management team, and the extent to which the collective efforts of board and management team are leading to the achievement of corporate objectives. An effective board seeks to do this on a systematic, objective and consistent basis.

To ensure a consistent approach across a company, a board could make use of review processes supported by appropriate documentation, such as the management impact analysis shown at Figure 7.4. The management impact analysis enables the board to ensure that for each 'accountable unit' within the company:

MEASURING THE IMPACT OF MANAGEMENT ACTIVITY ON CORPORATE OBJECTIVES			
Objectives	Critical success factor	Key performance indicator	Measurement process
1			
2			
3			
4			
5			
6			
7			

Figure 7.4 Management impact analysis

- There are clear objectives that are consistent with the corporate vision, goals, values and objectives that have been established. Unit objectives should relate to activities that add value for customers or focus on opportunities to improve customer satisfaction.
- The critical success factors have been identified. These will largely determine whether or not desired outcomes are achieved. Management attention should be focused upon the 'vital few' actions and programmes that are likely to have the biggest impact upon customer value and satisfaction.

- Key performance indicators are established. These indicate the standards against which achievement will be judged. They should relate to outcomes that are desirable from the customer point of view, and may need to match or exceed competitor performance. Benchmarking could be used to set standards that are comparable with, or better than, the best.
- There is a measurement process that is both objective and fair. Third-party measures of customer satisfaction and quantitative measures should be used wherever possible. Their use ensures that management is on the basis of fact rather than opinion.

A board has to empower, support and facilitate the activities of the management team, while at the same time maintaining a degree of control to (a) ensure that business objectives are achieved, and (b) hold the network organization together. In order to communicate, motivate, enable, empower and share, the board needs to become 'involved', but not so deeply as to inhibit the objective assessment of management performance.

Close interaction with management may be necessary if mutual trust and commitment are to be achieved, and managerial attitudes and values are to be influenced. At the same time, board members must not inhibit or drive out diversity. Managers should be encouraged to question and challenge. In order to break away from an increasingly dated 'command and control' approach, directors must know when to 'let go'.[1]

The board itself should also act as a 'role model' in terms of consistency between words and deeds (Table 7.1), if its actions and communications are not to be counter-productive.[1] Gaps between rhetoric and reality can lead to a breakdown of internal trust and act as a source of division and conflict.[1]

Table 7.1   The board as a role model

The board says	*The board does*
Satisfy customers	Sets RONA targets
Build relationships	Reorganizes and disrupts relationships
Encourage teamwork	Divides and rules
Exercise restraint	Awards itself large increase in remuneration
Invest in people	Reduces training budget
Delegate and empower	Still takes the decision
Calls for long-term commitment	Over-reacts to short-term pressures

There are certain key questions that should be asked in order to determine whether or not the board systematically and consistently reviews management performance. For example:

- Does the board ensure that all people in the organization know specifically what they need to do, the standard of performance that is expected of them, and how they will be measured?
- How does the board ensure that people are equipped, empowered and motivated to act and achieve? Is the basis of their remuneration consistent with the achievement of business objectives?
- How does the board remain aware of the potential 'arenas of conflict' that can arise within the company? Does the board probe and endeavour to uncover what is hidden?
- Does the board listen to employees, especially those who are close to customers, or does it only meet the 'head office bureaucrats'? How does the board ensure that its priorities remain appropriate in relation to the changing situation and context of the company?

7.10 Board priorities

The degree to which a board is effective is evidenced by the extent to which its priorities relate to the situation and context of the company.

Too many boards deal in generalization and waffle. Many are reluctant to 'think things through' with sufficient vigour, and they are too easily satisfied. Others are more critical. According to one interviewee: 'Unless you express it in specific terms, give it to someone, tell them what performance you expect, and give them the tools to do it, nothing will happen. If it's vague, nothing will happen. Or worse, something may happen that you don't expect or want. Leaving it vague can be wasteful.'

In Chapter 2 we examined survey evidence which suggests that among companies in general:

- boards are giving considerable attention to the establishment of a clear and shared vision, and the creation of a more responsive and flexible organization
- the 'external' priority is building relationships with customers; while the 'internal' priority is harnessing the talents and potential of people.

These priorities are interrelated. For example, corporate transformation is sought in order to enable people to work better together in generating value for customers, while a clear and shared vision can provide a foundation for building and sustaining effective relationships with people, whether external customers or internal employees.[1]

A generalized priority does not indicate (a) specific outcomes that are consistent with corporate vision, goals, values and objectives, and expressed in terms of outputs that can be measured; or (b) what each person in the organization needs to do in order to contribute towards their achievement. An effective board will:

- disaggregate a 'wish list' of generalized priorities into their separate aspects or elements;
- develop and rank specific goal and outcome options;
- examine their timescales, feasibility, and resource, process and critical success requirements;
- further select and prioritize in order to develop a list of achievable actions;
- establish outcome objectives, roles and responsibilities, and standards and measures of performance; and
- ensure that output requirements, standards, measures and priorities are understood, and those concerned are equipped, empowered and motivated to achieve them.

A board has to prioritize. The list of what could be done can be endless. It may in some areas be possible to do too much. Choices have to be made and the operation of effective boards is characterized by the use of processes such as that in Figure 7.3, and the rigour and commitment with which they are used to move from the general to the specific.

A board should also be proactive. Many boards devote far too much time to achieving relatively small improvements in that which is visible, and they ignore the opportunities that may lie in that which is hidden:

- What is reported, or perceived as relevant, may amount to a small proportion of the resources that are consumed, or the time that is spent, delivering what is sought by customers.
- There may be considerable scope for cutting out waste, saving on time, etc., within areas and activities that are hidden from the board. A continuing focus upon the review and simplification of processes can enable 'larger steps to be taken'.

In the context of competitive markets and changing customer requirements, a key priority of the board should be to ensure that the company is able to learn and adapt in order to survive.[25] This requires the introduction of management and business processes for ongoing learning and adaptation. The network organization may need to establish learning partnerships and become a learning network.[1]

7.11 The changing nature of board relationships

Many boards are finding that it is becoming more difficult to exercise influence and 'make things happen'. They are having to deal with interests and groups over which they may have little control, or which may have a wider choice of alternatives than any generation in history. Boards are having to devote more effort to communicating, persuading, listening, empathizing and sharing.

We saw in Chapter 2 that, in an increasingly complex business environment, companies face a range of external demands and pressures. In less complex situations and circumstances, it might have been possible for all significant decisions to be taken by the board. More attention now needs to be devoted to:

- the 'framework' questions in terms of people, technology, organization and management, and business processes;
- sharing vision, goals, values and objectives with the management team, allocating roles and responsibilities to them, and involving and empowering them.

We saw in the last chapter that the changing focus and horizons of directors and managers can bring them into conflict. An effective board is aware of the potential 'arenas of conflict' that can arise, and seeks to avoid them by explaining, involving and sharing.[26] The maintenance of relationships based upon mutual trust and respect has now become the priority, in place of the earlier preoccupations of many boards with the preservation of status and 'distance'.

As customers become more demanding, and increasingly require tailored products and services:

- Companies are having to enter into new forms of partnership relationships with them.[14]
- It is becoming necessary for decision making to be allocated to managers throughout the organization who are empowered to act.[25]
- New account management and cross-functional management and business processes are being introduced to identify and deliver those things which add value for customers and improve customer satisfaction.
- Larger companies are finding that incremental and bureaucratic adjustment to change is no longer enough. Many are undergoing a transition to more flexible forms of organization that involve a network of relationships with customers, suppliers and business partners.[14, 25]

A board should consider whether it is devoting sufficient time to sharing, listening and the maintenance of relationships.

7.12 From company to supply chain

The limits of many organizations are no longer defined by the people that are employed or the buildings that are owned. Their boards, and the individual directors, require the capability and strategic 'overview' to cope with complex networks of interdependent relationships.

Network organizations, as we saw in Chapter 2, are emerging with electronic links forwards to customers, backwards to suppliers and sideways to business partners. As a result, directors will need to monitor a more varied set of relationships. In the case of many boards, there will also be responsibilities towards a greater number of 'external' business partners to consider. If the network organizations that are emerging are to 'hold' together, they may need to share aspirations, goals and values, as well as specific objectives. Externally, as well as internally, the board needs to create and sustain relationships that are based upon empathy and mutual and common understanding. In bureaucratic organizations periodic reorganization has often been largely a matter for the board. In emerging 'network organizations' processes for continuing learning and adaptation need to be in place. Change is ongoing, and in such circumstances the board may need to rethink its role and its responsibilities in respect of the organization.

In future, boards are likely to spend less time establishing and monitoring procedures. Instead they will devote more time to initiating and facilitating processes for ongoing adaptation and change.[13] There are important questions to address, such as:

- Does the vision and focus of the board cover the supply chain, and how is it, or should it be, extended to embrace new supply chain relationships?
- How much attention does the board give to the review and re-engineering of management and business processes; and does its perspective extend to interorganizational processes?
- Are there specific processes to ensure ongoing learning, adaptation and change?
- As the company undergoes transition to a network form of organization,[1] does the board always keep in mind, and periodically review, the purpose of the company and its vision, goals, values and objectives?

As networks and supply chains become international, and as companies 'internationalize', a board may need cultural and international awareness, and tolerance of greater diversity in order to encourage involvement and sustain necessary relationships.[27]

The stakeholders to whom a board is accountable can also be international. For example, the board may wish to 'internationalize' its shareholder base by securing a quotation on one or more foreign stock exchanges.[27] Building relationships in a global context has become a high priority with many boards.

7.13 The directorial challenge

Competent directors and an effective board welcome the opportunity to
(a) confront and understand and (b) respond and adapt to changing circumstances. Increasingly, the directorial challenge facing the board is to:

- understand the opportunities in the external business environment,
  and to derive from them a distinct purpose that matches the interests of
  stakeholders;
- express, communicate and share the essence and purpose of the company in terms of a compelling vision, and clear, demanding but achievable goals, values and objectives;
- ensure that the company has access to adequate resources of people,
  technology, organization and finance;
- establish effective management and business processes;
- ensure that the company's processes encourage, involve, facilitate and
  empower the application of its resources to the profitable achievement
  of objectives and exploitation of opportunities.

The directorial challenge is shown diagrammatically in Figure 7.5. The
chairman and board should address the question: Do individual members of the board feel a sense of 'challenge', and do they share a common
challenge? According to Richard Masterman, chairman of Key Organics
Ltd:

> the board of directors must inspire the company to create excellence through
> strategic thinking and the building of a work culture which matches the busi-
> ness strategies and can deliver them. However much the pressure, the board
> must avoid short-term orientation, shallow thinking or quick fix expectations.
> . . . People throughout the company need to know where the company is going
> and what part they are expected to play in a mission in which they can
> believe.[28]

7.14 Effectiveness and directorial remuneration

The rewards received by directors should reflect the extent to which, individually and collectively, they are effective. Without clear objectives and
agreed measures of the extent to which they have been achieved, it is not
easy to determine the basis for remunerating directors.

In the US, shareholders have become more willing to challenge the
remuneration of executive directors.[29] There is some evidence that a
greater number of companies are becoming more open, and are prepared
to disclose in annual accounts more than the legal minimum concerning
the remuneration of directors.[30] In general, there does not appear to be a

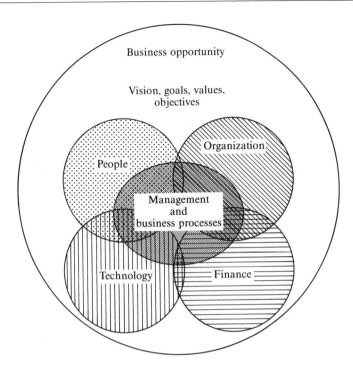

Figure 7.5   Directorial challenge

clear link between directorial remuneration and such indicators of corporate performance as return on capital employed.[31]

Those boards that have non-executive directors should involve them in the review of the remuneration of executive directors. Non-executive directors should not be paid so little that they are encouraged not to take their appointments seriously, nor so much that they become overdependent on them, and hence less inclined to be independent and critical.

7.15 Summary

In this and the previous chapter we have seen that the competence of directors and the effectiveness of boards are interrelated. They derive from the accountabilities, and the legal duties and responsibilities of directors, and from the function of the board. The competence of directors and the effectiveness of a board both need to be related to the situation and context of each company.

It should not be assumed that directors are competent or that boards are effective. How directors are evaluated, and how boards conduct their business, can inhibit rather than encourage what is desirable. In many companies more effort needs to be devoted to identifying, prioritizing and tackling barriers to director and board performance.

7.16 Checklist

1. Do the members of your company's board share an understanding of what represents an effective board?
2. Whose interests does the board of your company really serve?
3. Who really 'calls the shots' in the boardroom? How free and frank are boardroom discussions?
4. What important decisions are taken other than in the boardroom?
5. How much 'politics' is going on within the boardroom? What are the undercurrents, the 'hidden agendas', the tensions, the rivalries, the incompatibilities, the clashes of personality, etc.?
6. How many of the directors are really encouraged or prepared to speak their minds? What happens when the going gets tough?
7. Why were the last few directors appointed to the board? Are the non-executive directors really independent?
8. Against what standards is the effectiveness of the board assessed?
9. Is there a process for identifying gaps between actual and desired effectiveness?
10. Are the criteria used to assess board effectiveness appropriate to the context and circumstances of the company?
11. Does the culture of the board encourage members to assess its effectiveness?
12. Does the competence of the board as a team extend to the translation of aspiration into achievement?
13. Does the board really focus on those 'vital few' activities that add most value for customers? Are the cross-functional processes in place to allow it to do this?
14. Does the chairman assume responsibility for ensuring that the board is effective?
15. What needs to be done to improve board effectiveness?

Notes and references

1. Coulson-Thomas, C., *Transforming the Company: Bridging the gap between management myth and corporate reality*, Kogan Page, 1992.
2. ISC, *Role and Duties of Directors: A statement of best practice*, Institutional Shareholders Committee, 1991.
3. Peston, R., Betts, P. and Rudd, R., 'Bloody battle in the boardroom', *Financial*

Times, 27 September 1991; and Plender, J., 'Tougher at the top', *Financial Times*, 28 and 29 September 1991, p. 7.

4. Lorenz, C., 'Oil and troubled waters', *Financial Times*, 29 June 1992, p. 9; and Lascelles, D., 'Top-level coup in classic style', *Financial Times*, 27/28 June 1992, p. 6.

5. Weisbach, M. S., 'Outside directors and CEO turnover', *Journal of Financial Economics*, **20**, 1988, 431–60.

6. Lorsch, J. and MacIver, E., *Pawns or Potentates: The reality of America's corporate boards*, Harvard Business School Press, 1989.

7. Bachrach, P. and Baratz, M., 'Two faces of power', *American Political Science Review*, **56**, 1962, 947–52.

8. *Good Boardroom Practice: A code for directors and company secretaries*, The Institute of Chartered Secretaries and Administrators, February 1991.

9. Hills, R. M., 'Ethical perspectives on business and society', in Y. Kugel and G. W. Gruenberg, *Ethical Perspectives on Business and Society*, Lexington Books, 1977, p. 38.

10. Janis, I. L., *Victims of Groupthink*, Houghton-Mifflin, 1972.

11. Coulson-Thomas, C., *The Role and Function of the Personnel Director*. An interim Adaptation Ltd survey carried out in conjunction with the Research Group of the Institute of Personnel Management, 1991.

12. Heller, R., *The New Naked Manager*, Weidenfeld & Nicolson, 1985.

13. Coulson-Thomas, C. and Wakelam, A., *The Effective Board: Current practice, myths and realities*, an IOD discussion document, 1991.

14. Coulson-Thomas, C. and Brown, R., *Beyond Quality: Managing the relationship with the customer*, BIM, 1990.

15. Porter, M., *Competitive Strategy: Techniques for analysing industries and competitors*, The Free Press, 1980; and *Competitive Advantage*, The Free Press, 1985.

16. Pettigrew, A. M. and Whipp, R., *Managing Change for Competitive Success*, Blackwell, 1991.

17. Redwood, J., MP, *Corporate Governance*, Department of Trade and Industry Press Notice P/90/722, 7 December 1990.

18. Lorenz, C., 'Knives are out in the boardroom', *Financial Times*, 1 May 1992, p. 11.

19. Shively, J., 'Confessions of a non-executive', *Financial Times*, 15 July 1991, p.11; and Cohen, N., 'Getting directors on board', *Financial Times*, 6 April 1992, p. 12.

20. Committee on The Financial Aspects of Corporate Governance (chairman: Sir Adrian Cadbury), Draft Report issued for public comment, Committee on The Financial Aspects of Corporate Governance, 27 May 1992.

21. Tricker, R. I., *The Independent Director: A study of the non-executive director and of the audit committee*, Tolley Publishing Company, 1978, p. 35.

22. Allison, G., *Essence of Decision*, Little Brown, 1971.

23. Morgan, P., 'Cadbury presumptions on role of directors challenged by IOD', *Financial Times*, Letters to the Editor, 31 July 1992, p. 15.

24. 'The lessons of Mr Horton's exit', *Financial Times*, Editorial, 29 June 1992, p. 12.

25. Coulson-Thomas, C. and Brown, R., *The Responsive Organisation*, BIM, 1989.

26. Coulson-Thomas, C., 'Strategic vision or strategic con?: Rhetoric or reality?', *Long Range Planning*, **25** (1), 1992, 81–9.

27. Coulson-Thomas, C., *Creating the Global Company: Successful internationalization*, McGraw-Hill, 1992.

28. Masterman, R., 'Resumé of comments on creating an effective board', Institute of

Personnel Management, 1991 National Conference, October 1991, p. 1.
29. Dickson, M., 'No soft options for Oliver Twist', *Financial Times*, 9 August 1991, p.12; and 'A check on the boss's cheque', *Financial Times*, 31 March 1992.
30. Monks Partnership, *Disclosing Board Earnings in Company Annual Reports*, Monks Partnership, 1992.
31. Sullivan, T. and Bottomley, P., *Boards of Directors Study UK*, Korn/Ferry International, 1991.

8
Selection and appointment of directors

The career paths of most executives do not provide corporate experience. Regrettably long service alone is not the training which will equip an executive to direct a company. (BRIAN ROWBOTHAM, chairman, London Newspaper Group Ltd.)

How do people become directors? What criteria are used to identify suitable candidates for boardroom appointments? Are there particular requirements to satisfy, or routes to follow, that can lead automatically to a seat on the board? These are some of the questions that will be explored in this chapter.

A career as a company director should be regarded as distinct from a career as a manager. It should be perceived as a separate arena of activity, rather than as something that follows on inexorably, at an appropriate moment, from satisfactory performance in managerial roles.

8.1 A managerial career and the boardroom

In some companies there has been a tendency to appoint individuals to the board towards the end of a management career, and almost as an extension of it. A boardroom appointment might be regarded as a 'culmination' or 'pinnacle of achievement' for those who have accumulated sufficient experience, demonstrated the required qualities, or completed a process of managerial growth or development. In companies that adopt the 'extension of management career' approach, the selection process favours those candidates who have had the opportunity to obtain particular experience or demonstrate relevant qualities. Candidates with the potential to make good directors, but who have not had such experience, can be excluded from consideration.

Those who join a board typically 'turn up' at the first available opportunity and are 'thrown in at the deep end'. We shall see in the next chapter that few directors have received any specific or formal preparation for their boardroom roles. Traditionally, formal preparation *per se* has not been a criterion for a board appointment. However, the situation appears to be changing. An increasing number of large companies are now considering direction as a separate dimension. Appointments to boards are sometimes made at a younger age, when certain individuals are thought to have an aptitude for the boardroom. On joining the board, particularly in the case of a first directorial role, a person may be regarded as a novice director. An initial appointment might be seen as the first step of what may become a long boardroom career; and of what should be a lifelong boardroom learning process.

In companies that adopt the 'parallel to management development' approach, perceived potential and a willingness to learn are often important selection criteria. The selection process itself also tends to be more intuitive. Rather than mechanically 'ticking off' past job titles against a career path checklist, the focus is more likely to be upon the personal qualities of the individual and the extent to which he or she has demonstrated directorial skills, awareness or perspective.

8.2 Routes to the boardroom

There are many different routes to the boardroom, and they vary in their requirements for success. The following examples illustrate the variety of circumstances in which an individual can become a company director:

- Entrepreneurs start their own businesses, and seek incorporated status as appropriate. Such individuals in effect select themselves.
- Some individuals join the board of a family business. In such cases, being a member of the family, either by blood or through marriage, is clearly an important consideration, although not all members of the family might be thought 'suitable'.
- An employed manager might secure promotion to the boardroom. In this instance the individual is initially selected by his or her superiors within the organizational structure.
- A professional, or a specialist adviser, may be appointed to the board because of the possession of particular experience or expertise. In such a case the 'relevance' of the experience or expertise is clearly an important requirement, and the selection might be made by those who could be regarded as peers.
- An appointment of a particular person, or of a 'representative', to a board might be thought appropriate in the case of an arrangement or joint venture, or a reciprocal shareholding or technology pact. Usually

the arrangement or venture partner will be asked to nominate an appropriate individual.
- A merger or acquisition can give rise to boardroom changes. In the event of a successful 'hostile' takeover the entire board of an acquired company may be replaced.
- Certain stakeholders, such as a major provider of equity or loan finance, may press for a seat on the board. Some financial institutions maintain a panel of those from whom candidates for such directorship appointments can be chosen.
- An individual may be headhunted or 'poached' in order to fill a particular slot, or to balance or complement the attributes of the various members of an existing boardroom team.
- In order to improve the 'look' or 'status' of a board in the eyes of potential investors, or enhance its perceived objectivity, an individual of standing and independence might be sought, perhaps in the role of non-executive director.
- It might be thought that someone who would be perceived as representative of a particular constituency ought to be brought onto a board. For example, the chairman of a US multi-national might feel there ought to be a 'European', a 'college president', or a 'representative of a minority group' on the board.

In all such cases an individual may or may not have had previous board experience. With smaller companies especially, the appointment in question may represent the only board upon which the individual sits.

The route to the boardroom also varies between countries. For example, the chairman of a major French company is more likely than his or her UK equivalent to have spent a formative part of a career as a civil servant.[1] A company operating in France, Germany or Norway could be required by law to bring an employee representative into the boardroom.

Owner and family company directors

The route taken to a boardroom can have a significant impact upon directorial attitudes. Let us consider the case of the founder, owner or family company director. These present special management and directorial problems.[2]

The intensity of the commitment of an owner-director to his or her company, and of personal identification with it, can be a great strength. It can also represent a potential source of risks to both a director and a company. For example:

- Personal commitment can 'cloud' business judgement, particularly by impairing objectivity. The owner-director may be reluctant to face 'reality'. Owner-directors may 'battle on' long after the point at which a less involved director might have taken drastic remedial action.

- Owner-directors are both owners and directors, therefore, as directors they are also accountable to themselves as owners. They also have a fiduciary responsibility to the company, and should never forget that it has a separate legal personality. A number of owner-directors have made the mistake of treating company property as if it were their own.
- Because they may not have had to satisfy 'normal' selection criteria, involving objective assessment by those who are impartial, individual owner-directors may have significant and evident deficiencies. Because of the power of their positions, owner-directors may be surrounded by others who are reluctant to 'raise' or draw attention to their deficiencies.
- Any flaws in the character of a founder-director can be both exacerbated and exploited by the sycophants and adventurers the 'powerful' can attract. Directors need to be aware of the readiness of many people to crawl, bootlick, leech and exploit when it is in their interests to do so. Human nature needs to be seen as it often is, rather than as it should be.
- By employing, and selecting as advisers, those who are ignorant, naive, negligent or crooked, the owner-director may avoid the independent checks and balances found in other companies. Dubious practices may remain concealed for some time. Even when others are aware of them, they may be reluctant or afraid to act. An abuse of a position may continue until such time as it is eventually exposed, perhaps as a result of the collapse of a company.
- The directorial requirements of an expanding company can exceed the capabilities of owner-directors. When founder- and owner-directors of companies that have grown rapidly give up control of their companies, perhaps as a result of 'going public' or an arrangement with a source of finance, the process of adjustment can be painful.
- An owner-director whose own development does not match the changing situation and circumstances of a company may need to be forced off a board. On occasion 'professional' directors, brought into the boardroom by the original founders to carry a business forward, may act together to remove one or more of the original directors from the board. What is considered by the displaced director as an act of treachery, may be perceived by the instigators of such a move to be an inevitable consequence of their duty to the company and its new owners.

Competent owner-directors are aware of risks such as the selection above. They take the trouble to assemble a balanced board made up of trustworthy individuals whose qualities, skills and experience complement their own and match the situation and circumstances of the company. The question of complementing and adding to existing boardroom strengths might head the list of selection criteria that is employed. According to Dr Ingram Lenton, chairman of Compass Group plc: 'The starting point with new appointments to the board is to seek to supplement, to advantage, that body's existing qualities.'

The dangers and risks that have been identified could be shared by employee directors where independent checks and controls are weak or non-existent. In part, the 'corporate governance debate' is concerned with reducing the number of boards that fall into the hands of a narrow, self-perpetuating and self-serving clique, and go 'off the rails'.

Factors influencing routes to the board

We have already seen in Chapter 5 (Example 5.1) that there are many forms of company, e.g. public or private, and holding or subsidiary. What might be considered a feasible route to the board will vary according to the category of company being considered. For example, among companies of a similar size in the same business sector:

- in one company the board might select candidates 'internally' from the members of the management team; while
- in another company, that happens to be a subsidiary within a group, 'external' appointments might be made by the chief executive or board of the holding company.

The criteria used to select directors can vary significantly from company to company, even among companies of a similar type or category. For example, particular considerations may apply to the appointment of non-executive directors[3]:

- Company boards can vary greatly in their use of non-executive directors. Many UK boards are made up entirely of executive directors, while almost all the directors of a major US corporation might be non-executive.
- Among companies that 'use' them, non-executive directors may be appointed to fill what are perceived to be gaps in the boardroom. These will vary from board to board, depending upon the qualities and experience of the existing directors.

Many non-executive directors will be older than the executive directors and will have had broader business experience. With other sources of income, and a more varied set of perspectives, they may find it easier to remain objective than is the case with executive directors who are heavily involved in the day-to-day running of the business. The perceived attractiveness of having a non-executive director on the board could reflect the aspirations of the chairman.

The criteria used to select directors will reflect the attitudes and practice of a particular board and its chairman. The director selection criteria used by companies of a similar type, and in equivalent situations and circumstances, will also vary according to the role that is envisaged for new appointees in the boardroom, and the existing mix of skills on the board. For example, a higher priority might be placed upon the possession of professional qualifications in the case of the appointment of a financial director.

There may be the expectations of stakeholders to take into account. Certain interests in the company, for example investors, might expect a financial director to be a member of a recognized accounting body. However, from among those in possession of such qualifications, the criteria for selecting a director might put more stress upon general business awareness and the communication of financial information, and less upon technical accounting skills, than would be the case with, say, the selection of a chief accountant or treasury accountant.

A board might wish to reflect upon the routes taken by each director to the boardroom. The following are among the questions that could be asked:

- How well 'trodden', generally understood, documented, etc., was each route; and how might they have been improved?
- How has each route benefited the individual, the board and the company? What are the advantages or disadvantages, and the risks or dangers of each route?
- What factors influenced (a) the nature of the routes that were taken and (b) each individual's decision to take a particular route? What were the main 'helps' or 'hinders' that were experienced 'on the way'?
- How significant for progress along each route was (a) mentoring, 'sponsorship', favouritism or other type of 'informal' help; or (b) formal development activity?
- If they were able to start again, what route to the boardroom would each director attempt to take?

8.3 Qualities sought in directors

Before examining the criteria that are used to select directors, let us first examine the qualities that are sought, as these should influence the choice of criteria. The selection criteria used should be those that are most likely to identify the qualities that are sought.

The views of company chairmen are likely to be particularly significant when there are boardroom positions to be filled. They have been examined in a survey undertaken by Adaptation Ltd for the IOD.[4] The qualities chairmen seek in new appointees to the boards of companies are summarized in Table 8.1, which ranks the qualities in terms of 'very important' responses. The qualities sought are consistent with the basis of the distinction between direction and management (Chapter 4) and what is required of a competent director (Chapter 6).

Table 8.1 Qualities sought in new appointments to board, ranked in terms of 'very important'

Quality	%	Quality	%
Strategic awareness	48	Self-discipline	38
Objectivity	47	Team player	37
Communication skills	46	Creativity	33
Individual responsibility	45	Perspective	33
Customer focus	42	Breadth	19

Note: Some respondents considered more than one quality to be 'very important'

'Strategic awareness', 'objectivity' and 'communication skills' are ranked highest in importance, with almost half of the respondents giving them a 'very important' ranking. 'Perspective' and 'breadth' were related by interviewees to 'strategic awareness' and the ability to comprehend the company as a whole in the context of its business and market environment, and the strategic challenges and opportunities it faces. The relatively high importance attached to 'customer focus' reflects the priority given elsewhere in the same[4] and other surveys[5] to customers and customer satisfaction (see Chapter 1). A willingness to assume 'individual responsibility' needs to be accompanied by 'self-discipline' and the qualities of a 'team player', if a director is to become an effective and integrated member of a boardroom team.

Participants in the survey undertaken for the IOD[4] gave a variety of responses to an open-ended question concerning what other qualities they sought in company directors. When grouped into categories, the 'top ten' *other* qualities sought in directors of the respondents' companies are:

1. Drive, determination, enthusiasm
2. Loyalty and commitment
3. Integrity
4. Specialist knowledge
5. Broad business understanding
6. Presentation and communication skills

7. Leadership
8. Financial literacy and awareness
9. Humour
10. Intelligence/common sense.

This list of 'other qualities' sought in company directors is dominated by personal qualities and characteristics. Their relative positioning suggests that individual qualities continue to be regarded as important in respect of appointments to boards of companies.

A programme of interviews associated with the survey[4] provided an opportunity for the author to explore the rationale behind the inclusion of certain items in the priority listing of the 'other' directorial qualities sought by chairmen:

- Individual interviewees related various qualities categorized under 'drive, determination, enthusiasm' and 'loyalty and commitment' to the demanding nature of the challenges faced by many boards. A degree of sustained persistence is often required to pursue a difficult path, while certain courses of action might strain the unity of a board.
- 'Integrity' was thought to be a necessary precondition of establishing relationships of trust within the boardroom, and with 'stakeholders'. While directors may be expected to behave in an ethical manner, less than a third of large companies have been found by one survey to have a written code of ethical conduct.[6]
- Those interviewed tended to describe the 'specialist knowledge' they sought in terms of a requirement that related to a particular challenge confronting the board and the business of the company, rather than as expertise in one functional or professional field.
- 'Presentation and communication skills' and 'leadership' were related by interviewees to the need to share, to empower, and to sustain relationships based upon understanding, involvement and commitment. As a spokesperson, a director needs to think through the purposes and circumstances of communication, and the needs and interests of those with whom relationships need to be established and sustained.[7]

The development needs of a business should not be overlooked when directors are appointed. It would appear that the qualities that many chairmen seek are largely rooted in the present:

- Although 'creativity' was a 'ranked' quality, other attributes conducive to the 'prospects' of a company, such as openness or a willingness to question, often appeared as secondary considerations. This suggests that the qualities sought by some chairmen tend to relate to the present circumstances of their companies rather than to their future growth.[8]

– Even though most large companies appear to have some form of long-term plan, such control as is exercised by the board may well focus upon short-term operational performance.[9] As one interviewee put it: 'We know what we should be looking for, but at the same time we tend to focus on those shorter term indicators that people use to assess our performance.'

Many boards have not drawn up, discussed or agreed the qualities they are looking for when assessing suitable candidates for a potential boardroom appointment. If such a list exists, care needs to be taken to ensure that it matches the changing situation and context of the company.

Questions to consider include how the qualities that have been chosen relate to those sought by other boards, whether they are actually used, and whether the company has a director development capability or process for addressing specific deficiencies that emerge when potential board candidates and existing board members are matched against the agreed list of desirable qualities.[10]

8.4 Criteria used in selecting board members

Let us move on to the criteria that are used to select directors. These, as we have already noted, should reflect the directorial qualities that are sought by chairmen. The 'top ten' criteria used in selecting members of the boards covered by a 'chairman' survey undertaken by Coulson-Thomas and Wakelam[8] are presented in Figure 8.1.

Personal qualities emerge as easily the most significant criteria for selecting members of a board. Some of the criteria used do relate to the requirements of chairmen, such as 'loyalty', but, in the main, the criteria mentioned by the respondents appear to relate to the people themselves rather than their contacts, associations or networks.

Four out of ten respondents[8] mentioned age or 'track record' and experience as the criteria used in selecting board members. Those interviewed were asked to give reasons for the importance attached to 'track record' and experience, and to consider the implications of their use:

– Interviewees explained that, in the absence of any means of formally assessing boardroom qualities and competences, it was necessary for these to be demonstrated over the course of a managerial career.
– Interviewees also acknowledged that some directors might have been appointed at an earlier age had it been possible to demonstrate possession of the required qualities and competences.

The emphasis upon track record, and the practice of looking for individuals who already have boardroom experience, makes it difficult for many

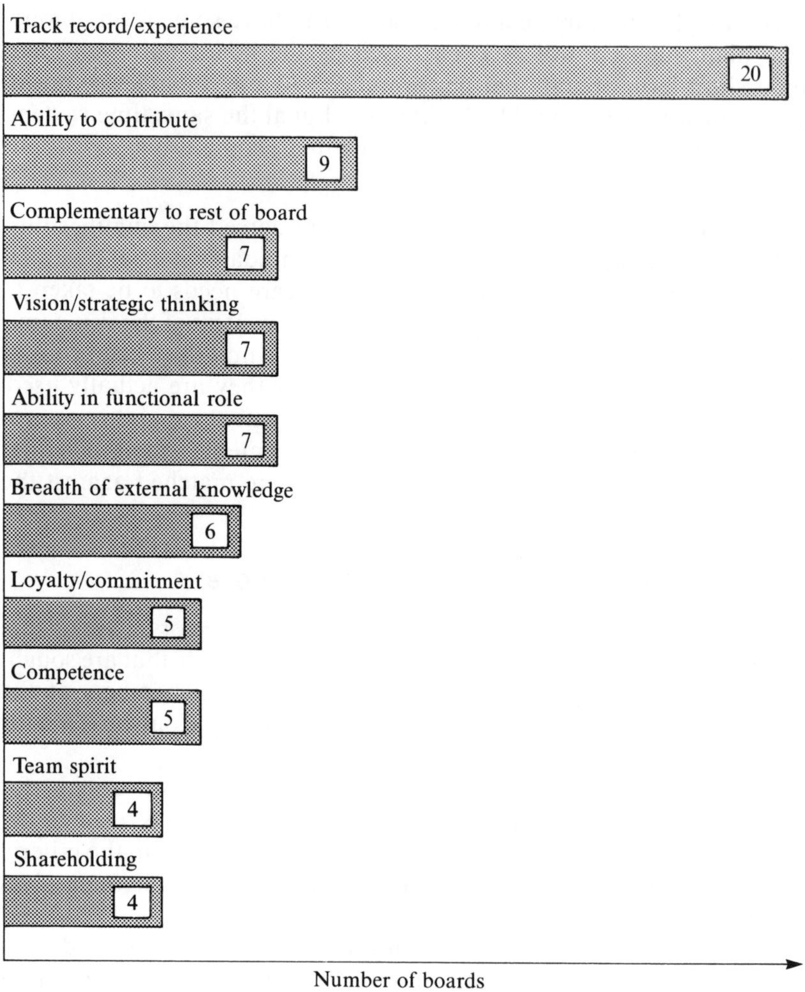

Track record/experience

| 20 |

Ability to contribute

| 9 |

Complementary to rest of board

| 7 |

Vision/strategic thinking

| 7 |

Ability in functional role

| 7 |

Breadth of external knowledge

| 6 |

Loyalty/commitment

| 5 |

Competence

| 5 |

Team spirit

| 4 |

Shareholding

| 4 |

Number of boards

Figure 8.1   The 'top ten' criteria used in selecting members of the board

women to break into the 'boardroom circuit' even though they may have relevant experience and qualities.[11]

The route taken to the boardroom can affect the age at which a person becomes a director. The youngest directors in the survey sample[8] tended to be those who had recently formed their own company. In larger companies, the younger board members tended to be those who had been brought onto the board to fill a particular functional slot.

Specialist knowledge or expertise, or ability in a functional role, was cited by only one in five of the respondents. In major companies, even when the search for a new appointee results from a feeling that a certain function ought to be represented at board level, the choice of an individual from among available candidates appears to be largely a question of personal qualities.

Not a single respondent[8] mentioned the possession of academic or professional qualifications as a criterion for selecting members of a board. The possession of a working knowledge of, or fluency in, a foreign language was also not mentioned by any of the respondents as a selection criterion.

In the survey[4] considered earlier in this chapter, 'integrity' emerged as a quality sought in directors. The ethical dimension was also mentioned in Chapter 6 as an important element of directorial competence. However, only one respondent in the 'chairman' survey[8] mentioned the requirement that a director be trustworthy, otherwise there was no mention of ethics as such.

The selection criteria in perspective

When considering personal qualities in a boardroom context it needs to be remembered that words may have a different connotation than when they are applied to the management arena. The personal qualities sought in directors are not necessarily those that are thought to be desirable in managers. For example:

– In the boardroom, drive and getting results may require moral commitment rather than the sheer physical energy that may be so important in some management roles.
– Getting results out of 'subordinates' and staff may require a different approach from that required to persuade a peer group in the boardroom.

While the boardroom deliberations of board members may be primarily concerned with strategic issues of 'what needs to be done' from a corporate perspective, executive directors around the boardroom table may play a part in the execution of policy when they are acting in an executive capacity. Such individuals may require personal qualities appropriate to both directorial and managerial roles.

The selection criteria that some companies claim to use may need to be 'taken with a pinch of salt', while general evidence should be interpreted with a degree of caution. Criteria identified in an individual survey will reflect the particular 'sample' that it covers. For example:

– in the 'chairman' survey,[8] only one in ten of the respondents mentioned

a role in the formation of a company as a criterion for board membership;
- in an earlier survey of directors,[12] over a third of the respondents were founder members of firms, and one in ten had become a director because of family links with the firm concerned.

In this case the discrepancy between the two surveys could be explained by the fact that those participating in the second survey[8] are more likely than those in the first[12] to be founder-chairmen of their companies who, in responding, were addressing the criteria to be used in making incremental appointments to a board beyond the founding group.

Wherever possible, all the surveys quoted have been cross-checked against other available evidence prior to their use in this book. Thus, for example, the views of directors (predominantly chairmen) that are cited in this chapter[4, 8] are broadly consistent with those of personnel directors in a survey undertaken by Adaptation Ltd with the Research Group of the IPM.[13]

Selection criteria and the boardroom team

Many of the selection criteria highlighted by survey respondents[8] relate to the qualities of potential directors as individuals, rather than to the qualities of the existing members of a boardroom team, and the extent to which these may need to be complemented with one or more new appointments. In the case of smaller companies there was little evidence of planning for boardroom succession:

- Few boards appeared to consider their requirements formally, or to establish selection criteria. In some cases selection consisted of responding to encounters with 'possible' directors without reference to the qualities of existing board members.
- Few boards anticipated future circumstances in which new appointments to the boardroom team might be needed. For example, many boards did not look ahead to when vacancies might arise as a result of existing directors reaching retirement age.

A newly appointed director will normally join an existing boardroom team, and will be expected to work effectively with this group of directorial colleagues. This requirement is reflected in the selection criteria that are used: 'Style appears to be important. One needs to question without ruffling feathers. Abrasiveness in the boardroom is not desired, instead qualities such as empathy and sensitivity underlie a number of the criteria.'[8]

Success in the boardroom often requires (a) the understanding and articulation of issues and moods, and (b) empathy with the attitudes and opinions of others. The arguments that are used, and any proposals that are put forward, may need to reflect the mood of a meeting, and be consistent with the way in which issues have been raised and the terminology that has been used.

Perceptive directors 'know where they stand' in respect of a particular board and its personalities. Successful directors understand the 'culture' of the boardroom and what is regarded as acceptable conduct by colleagues:

- Where there is trust, a director acting in a familiar and agreed role may be given considerable discretion. The functional director may be allowed to go a long way on his or her own initiative without having to explain the details of particular actions.
- Where trust is lacking, a director may be required to seek 'prior approval' and may be closely 'grilled' by colleagues. Close scrutiny may continue until the director concerned has earned the respect and trust of colleagues.

Commanding respect in the boardroom is an art that requires self-awareness and practice. While it can benefit from a natural talent upon which to build, and from personal qualities such as empathy and awareness, the potential of a particular individual may not be easy to detect by means of selection criteria. Some directors remain on boards for many years without securing the complete trust of all colleagues.

Not all companies use formal selection criteria when evaluating suitable candidates for a potential boardroom appointment. When selection criteria are used they may not reflect the qualities that are being sought.

Selection criteria should be reviewed periodically. How do they relate to those used by other boards? Are there omissions, gaps, inconsistencies, etc., in the selection criteria? Particular attention should be paid to the following questions:

- How significant are 'personal qualities' among the selection criteria that have been established; and how susceptible are they to relevant (e.g. focus on directorial rather than managerial qualities?), rigorous, objective, fair, etc., assessment?
- What evidence would satisfy each element of the selection criteria that have been established, and is such evidence likely to be available?
- Does the use of the selection criteria that have been established reflect the group needs of the boardroom team?
- Does the company have a director development capability or process for addressing specific deficiencies that emerge when potential board candidates and existing board members are matched against the agreed selection criteria?

The results of such questioning can be sobering. One candid chairman concluded: 'Few of us would meet rigorous selection criteria if we were subjected to them today. . . . Its all "relative", [we] aim to do the best we can. Whether that is good enough is a moot point.'

Selection criteria: the development implications

How easy is it to develop the personal qualities that might meet the criteria that are used to select directors? The conclusion of the 'chairman' survey[8] is that some personal qualities are more difficult to develop than others. For example:

> The ability to listen, think, reflect and assess are attributes which can, to some extent, be nurtured and developed. Education, training and development can have a role to play here.

> However, qualities such as loyalty, style, etc., can defy training and development, except on a very superficial level. The real foundations are normally laid many years earlier, in the family.

> Latent qualities can . . . be brought to the surface and self-awareness increased by appropriate development. In this context 'appropriate' relates to a focus upon the attitudes and qualities of particular relevance to company directors.

A competent board member should (a) have an awareness of the qualities that are generally desirable in a company director and are especially relevant to a company's situation and context, and (b) be equipped to recognize them in others. Individual and group self-awareness is particularly important in the boardroom. If deficiencies in the personal and other qualities of existing directors can be identified, it may be possible to correct or 'balance' them through the complementary qualities of new appointees to the board.

There are particular groups that may require special consideration. For example:

- Worker directors on a supervisory board may be less familiar with many aspects of corporate activity than colleagues with managerial experience. Scott Bader introduced a training programme aimed specifically at the employee director.[14]
- Women are under-represented in the boardroom.[15] According to an Institute of Directors survey, three-quarters of female company directors believe that women are discriminated against in the workplace.[16] Specific coaching and mentoring may be of value in establishing more of a 'level playing field' for male and female candidates with directorial prospects.

INITIAL AND SUBSEQUENT DEVELOPMENT REQUIREMENTS

Any directorial selection criteria that are established by a board should embrace both:

- the initial qualities needed by a new appointee to 'adjust' or 'settle in', so as to become an integrated and accepted member of a boardroom team; and
- the other qualities that the newly 'integrated and accepted' director might subsequently require in order to make a significant and distinctive contribution to the work of the board.

Before becoming a fully effective, integrated and trusted board member, a new director may require a period of 'settling in'. Some development in the form of an induction programme may be desirable at this stage. The emphasis of any such induction activity will reflect both (a) the attributes, and any previous board experience, of the individual; and (b) the nature and expectations of the boardroom team that the new director is joining.

On appointment to a board a new director will need to set about absorbing, and reflecting on, the 'background' against which its decisions are taken and its policies are made. This may require patience, a willingness to listen, think and learn, and the capacity to both understand and critically assess the points of view of others. The interest, guidance and advice of the chairman can be especially valuable at this stage.

New proposals that are brought to a board are rarely introduced into a vacuum. They, and their subsequent consideration, will reflect various shared assumptions, and a degree of common understanding in the boardroom. For example:

- The existing directors may agree and share a vision, goals, values and objectives.
- The directors may share certain perspectives and attitudes, or a sense of relevance, that may influence their perception and treatment of information. The meaning of facts is likely to derive from their interpretation in the light of an existing situation.
- The members of a board may share other common perceptions, for example, of threats and opportunities, of the capability and relevance of the company's resources and processes, or of the morale and commitment of other people.

A new director needs to understand the shared assumptions and common understanding of other board members. Empathy and awareness will need to extend beyond boardroom colleagues. In order to translate board policies into action, various groups of people likely to be affected by these policies and their implications will also need to be considered.

Having understood the various assumptions and attitudes, the shared understanding, etc., that constitutes the 'background' to board discussions and decisions, the new director is better equipped to make a distinctive contribution to the work of the board. At this point the director may need the courage and skills to question, challenge and confront the existing position and thinking of the board on certain issues.

It may not be feasible or desirable to address simultaneously the initial and the subsequent development needs of a director. Different requirements may need to be addressed in stages. An aware and competent director perceives development activities that can help to hone directorial skills as a continuing commitment.

Selection criteria: the 'route to the boardroom' implications

Many company chairmen do not find it easy to identify people with directorial qualities.[8] Is this because such people do not exist? Are the search and selection criteria that are employed too strict, or are they applied to an excessively narrow group of candidates? Are there wider pools of potential from which, possibly with suitable development, potential directors might be drawn?

One possible reason that has been suggested[8] for the perceived 'supply constraint' of potential directors could be the 'traditional' practice in many larger companies of limiting recruitment to the board to:

– those holding senior management positions within the (or a similar) corporate organization in the case of executive directors; or
– those who are already directors of significant (preferably public) companies in the case of non-executive directors.

The traditional practice, and the distinct 'directorial election' and 'management development' routes are shown diagrammatically in Figure 8.2. Those who join a board from senior positions in other companies, or who have achieved the standing to be considered a candidate for a non-executive appointment, will probably have progressed along a 'management development' route in another corporate organization.

The traditional practice (Figure 8.2) appears to be strongly in favour of those who secure senior management positions. 'Members' who are selected from this group to join a board are likely to have followed similar career paths and to have had similar management development experiences.

When directors are also drawn from similar social backgrounds, and are of the same nationality, this can lead to a board that is largely made up of those with similar attitudes and a common perspective.[17] In the case

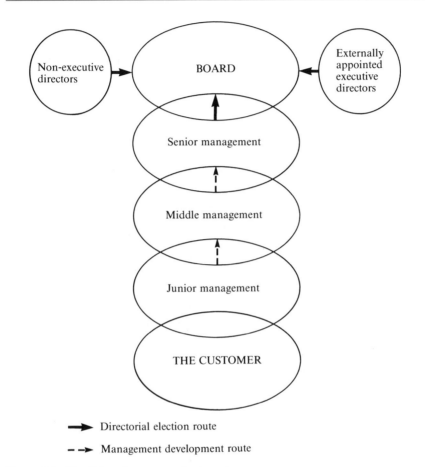

Figure 8.2 Traditional routes to the boardroom

of non-executive directors of public companies the portfolios of interlocking directorships held by some individuals has led to the suggestion
that an 'inner circle' exists of acceptable candidates who grace each other's
boards.[18] Is this always healthy or desirable? For example:

- We have seen in Chapters 3 and 7 that the presence of variety in the
  boardroom, of people with complementary skills and experiences, can
  improve the effectiveness of a board.
- We have also seen in Chapter 4 that the managerial qualities that can
  result in a senior management appointment may be quite different
  from those directorial qualities that can lead to success in the
  boardroom.

- Many senior managers in a 'head office' environment, have little direct customer contact, and are immersed in cynical bureaucratic games, office politics, and the relatively narrow concerns of a particular functional department.
- In Chapters 4 and 6 we saw that it is possible to identify the personal qualities and skills that are desirable in a director. Why should these personal qualities not be found in other groups, i.e. beyond the ranks of senior management?
- In later chapters we shall consider how directors should be developed, both as individuals and as a boardroom team. There may be many people outside a cadre of senior managers who are closer to customers and who would respond well to such development.[19]

A recent survey by PRO NED has revealed little satisfaction with the criteria and process used to select non-executive directors, and there is a feeling that many non-executive directors are not making an effective contribution to the board.[20]

The 'Cadbury Committee' has recommended that non-executive directors should be independent, be entitled to seek professional and independent advice, be nominated by the board as a whole, be selected by an agreed and formal process and be appointed for specified terms.[21] The Committee is of the opinion that: 'Companies have to be able to bring about changes in the composition of their boards to maintain their vitality. Non-executive directors tend to lose something of an independent edge over time. Furthermore, the make-up of a board needs to change in line with new challenges.'[21]

Widening the directorial recruitment and development arena

A more open approach to director recruitment that has been suggested[8] recognizes that some individuals with 'director' qualities might well be found within the ranks of middle, junior or supervisory management (Figure 8.3). The people below senior management level should not be 'written off' in the search for directorial talent. In the network organization, they share vision and values, and are motivated and empowered to add value for *their* customers.[19] As selected interviewees put it:

These people are honest. They tell you what they think. They don't rely upon position. They know who they are.

Some even believe in the mission. They believe not because they think it will help their careers, but because they meet the customers. They don't really need to be told. They know.

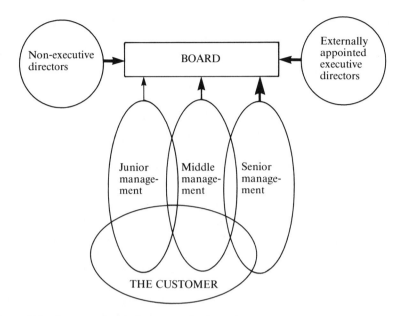

Figure 8.3 Suggested recruitment to the board

> The atmosphere of the boardroom can be unreal. Every day the troops face what we only sometimes glimpse through the fog of management reports.

We saw in Chapter 4 that the focus and horizons of managers are changing. As a result of quality and other programmes more (and more junior) managers are thinking 'longer term', and focusing on external customer requirements. They are acquiring general facilitating competences, and becoming involved in company-wide task forces and projects. More of them may have an opportunity to acquire a sense of the 'company as a whole'.

A key policy decision concerning the development of directorial competences relates to the number of people who should be exposed to various training and development activities. There might be an advantage in having a pool of people with directorial qualities outside the boardroom.

In deciding how many people may and ought to benefit from some conscious and formal development of their directorial potential, the following should be borne in mind:

– In the case of those who are founder-directors of their companies it would appear that not all of those participating in the surveys cited in this book[4, 8] had been 'drawn from' the ranks of senior management. Successful directors of significant companies were interviewed who

thought they might never have become directors had they remained as employees of someone else's business.
- In the area of local government, and the field of public appointments, competent committee chairmen, and effective members of national and regional committees and boards, have been drawn from many groups outside the ranks of senior management, including those who in their regular employment work in various blue-collar occupations.
- In the arena of national politics many Cabinet Ministers have hailed from relatively modest occupational backgrounds. While such examples might appear to some as 'exceptions', many boardrooms would benefit from an input of exceptional directorial talent.

Widening the pool from which non-executive directors are drawn would allow more boards to set up audit, nomination, remuneration and other subcommittees of the board. Almost nine out of ten larger US companies, and over nine out of ten UK listed companies already have remuneration committees, and the appointment of additional non-executive directors could allow their use to spread to smaller companies.[22]

A board should aim to identify and tap as wide a pool of potential directorial talent as possible, in order to produce a flow of people who are eligible to be considered for a boardroom appointment. How balanced is the board? Do the selection criteria that have been established favour certain groups within the company rather than others? How many people are aware of them? What groups that might contain individuals with directorial qualities would appear to be excluded?

The age implications of the criteria used in selecting board members

We have seen that the approach of many companies to director selection tends to put senior executives at a significant advantage. Are there particular groups that appear to be excluded or favoured when directors are appointed?

Those who are older can benefit from the approach of many companies to director selection. A half of all managers appear to be over 40 years of age, and directors tend to be older than managers.[23] We have already encountered some reasons why this might be the case in larger and relatively bureaucratic companies:

- It can take many years for an individual to progress through the ranks of management to reach the senior levels from which new appointees to the board are drawn (Figure 8.2).
- The importance that many chairmen attach to 'experience' and 'track record' as selection criteria (Figure 8.1) also favours older candidates.

We saw in Chapter 6 that age could be a positive or negative factor, according to the individual, the circumstances of the particular company, and the profiles of other members of the boardroom team.

8.5 Building a balanced boardroom team

Lists of 'helps and hinders' similar to those on pages 129–131, and applicable to a particular board, could be drawn up in respect of members of groups that appear to be 'under-represented' on the board. Such an analysis could be used to assess women or foreign candidates for a boardroom appointment, or those from a 'minority group'. Drawing up such a list can ensure that:

- there is a fuller and more rounded consideration of the various qualities and attributes of each candidate; 'positives' sometimes emerge that might not otherwise have been identified;
- 'hinders' are not only identified, but categorized, understood and addressed, where it is applicable by appropriate development activity; such a response might open up a new route to the boardroom.

From time to time, a review should be undertaken of the major characteristics of the existing members of the board, and how balanced and 'representative' they are. Questions to consider include:

- What other characteristics, qualities, experiences, etc., would improve the balance of the board, and should these be actively sought?
- For those likely to have the required characteristics, what 'helps' or 'hinders' would encourage or inhibit their identification by, application to, selection by, or appointment to the board?
- Do the qualities that are sought in directors, or the selection criteria that are used, discriminate against those with certain characteristics?

A chairman might wish to consider whether particular prejudices, myths and stereotypes colour the perceptions of members of the board concerning the directorial qualities and characteristics that are sought. In some cases it may be possible to encourage or build certain of the desired characteristics, or overcome the 'hinders' by appropriate development activity.[10]

The re-assessment of directorial qualities

A discussion of 'selection', and the consideration of 'hinders', raises the question of whether there should be 're-selection' and the periodic review of the existing members of a board and the criteria for board membership. The continuing service of a 'self-perpetuating board oligarchy' or a 'group of cronies of the chairman' can keep 'new blood' out of the boardroom. For companies that operate in dynamic and competitive markets, this is a situation to avoid.

When re-assessing directorial qualities, it needs to be borne in mind that all members of a particular board may hold director's service contracts. Directors tend to be adept at looking after their own interests, and the termination of their service contracts can be an expensive business. The term of a director's appointment establishes a point at which it will be necessary to consider whether or not the person concerned should remain a member of the board. For board membership to continue an appropriate resolution will need to be put to the shareholders. The continuation of an appointment should not be seen as a formality:

- A re-appointment review provides an opportunity for both parties, the individual director and the chairman, to give their views and discuss deficiencies and development requirements.
- The term of an appointment, within the context of the 'constitution' of a company, should not be so long that individuals might 'outlive' their usefulness as the business situation and composition of a board changes.
- However, a term of appointment needs to be long enough to encourage independence and objectivity, and allow a proper assessment to be made of a director's contribution, given the strategic nature of directorial responsibilities.

In the sections of Chapter 11 concerning 'personal effectiveness in the boardroom', it will be seen that there appears to be some inconsistency between the qualities thought desirable in directors, the contributions chairmen seek in directors, and the criteria they use in assessing these contributions:

- The ability to adopt the perspective of the company as a whole, and personal qualities, rather than specialist expertise, are held to be of decisive importance in selecting new board members.
- However, in practice the most commonly cited criterion for assessing the effectiveness of individual directors is 'performance within their departments'.

The adequacy of the selection process

Over time, the process used to select directors can have a very significant impact upon the effectiveness of a board and the competence of its members. There are various criteria that can be used to assess the adequacy of the process for selecting and appointing new members to the board:

- Does the process begin with a comprehensive review of the existing composition of the board, and of the qualities of its members?
- Do the specifications which are drawn up reflect the nature of the identified requirements?
- Is the selection process in accordance with such requirements as applicable company law, the company's own 'constitution', any agreed board procedures, and the participation of shareholders?
- Has the selection and appointment process, and have the participants in the process, been duly authorized?
- How broad and exhaustive has the selection process actually been on those occasions on which it has been used?
- How adequate were the selection criteria that were established, and how systematically were they used?
- How many members of the board, if not all, were involved in the process prior to a final decision to appoint a new director?
- Where applicable, were the non-executive directors involved?
- Do the conditions of the appointments that have been made, in respect of term, remuneration, responsibilities, etc., match the initial requirements and the qualities of the successful candidates?
- Have all those who were candidates, whether successful or unsuccessful, been treated fairly and honourably?

When assessing the adequacy of the selection process of a particular company much will depend upon:

- the nature of the board – for example, whether of a holding company or a subsidiary company; and
- the positions that need (or have needed) to be filled – for example, whether of a 'functional' director, a non-executive director, a chairman or a chief executive.

8.6 Effective director selection

An experienced director or manager is likely to be aware of the 'dos' and 'don'ts' that need to be considered when using such selection techniques as interviews or formal testing. Are there special considerations that apply when selecting directors?

There are particular factors that need to be taken into account when directors are to be appointed. These derive from the nature of the directorial role. The selection of directors can be especially problematic. For example:

- An effective board operates as a team, and the contributions of individual directors may not be easily distinguishable from those of their colleagues.
- Each board is composed of a particular combination of personalities. The individual who relates to one group may not be 'at home' with another.
- Skills applicable to the situation and circumstances of one company may not easily translate to the needs and priorities of another enterprise.
- A variety of factors can determine corporate performance independently of the calibre of a board.
- A number of the personal qualities that are sought in directors are difficult to assess outside the boardroom.
- Some selectors are reluctant to address the moral dimension, and find ethical qualities difficult to determine.
- Traditional qualifications, and various tests of competence, are generally not considered relevant to the directorial dimension.[8, 12]

Effective directorial selection will generally require a series of direct personal contacts with those individuals concerned. These may extend over a period of time, and may involve both formal and informal contacts. The selection process is likely to be 'two-way'. A competent director, aware of directorial accountabilities, and the legal duties and responsibilities involved, is likely to require a considerable amount of background information, and may seek certain assurances before agreeing to a board appointment. The selection process used will also reflect:

- the nature of the company concerned, and of the particular boardroom role to be filled; and
- the route to the boardroom that is likely to be applicable, e.g. 'internal' promotion or 'external' introduction.

The use of a 'traditional' selection technique such as the formal group interview might be limited to particular roles on the boards of a certain type of company. For example, there may be a number of possible candidates for the position of financial director of a European subsidiary of a multi-national company.

The directorial interview

When interviewing a potential director it is important to maintain a focus upon directorial qualities and avoid being sidetracked by managerial considerations. For that reason, use should be made of the 'output' rather than the 'input' focused questions given below.

'INPUT' FOCUSED QUESTIONS

1. What is your specialist expertise?
2. What qualifications do you have?
3. What boards have you served on?
4. What types of boards were they?
5. What was your directorial or managerial job title?
6. Who did you report to?
7. What was your salary and benefits package?
8. How did the move, or your service on the board, benefit you?
9. Why do you want to join this board?
10. What are the attractions of this particular boardroom role?
11. What would you hope to gain from the other directors?
12. For how long were you a director?
13. What would you most like to be?
14. What golf clubs or 'networks' do you belong to?

'OUTPUT' FOCUSED QUESTIONS

1. What are your key competences?
2. What in your view distinguishes a director from a manager?
3. Which of your qualities and attributes are especially relevant to this board?
4. What did you learn from your directorial, or managerial, experience?
5. What did you achieve on your last board, or in your previous job?
6. What did you bring to the directorial team or situation?
7. Who did you work with?
8. What value did you create for the company?
9. What is the greatest benefit the board and the company obtained from you?
10. How did customers and stakeholders benefit?
11. What can you contribute to this board and company?
12. How might you complement the other members of the boardroom team?
13. What qualities and experiences did you acquire?
14. What were your major accomplishments during this period?
15. What challenges did you successfully overcome?
16. What would you most like to do or contribute?
17. What board, or other, project groups or task forces do you belong to?

Using an interview checklist

The 'input' and 'output' focused questions presented above are adapted from those suggested in the BIM report *Too Old at 40?*[23] Such questions can be used to assess the extent to which a person might contribute to a board, meet particular experience or skill requirements, and strengthen an existing boardroom team.

An interview checklist, along the lines of that in the appendix to this chapter, could be used (a) to ensure the consistent treatment of all the candidates to be considered; and (b) to enable the members of an interview panel to better compare the comments they have recorded. (The director assessment form presented in the appendix to this chapter is an example of one that has been used, and is given for the purposes of illustration. It does not represent a model that all companies should necessarily use.)

The use of an interview checklist can ensure that essential directorial requirements are not overlooked. Candidates who do not appear to meet an acceptable level of directorial awareness and competence should never be appointed to a board to 'make up the number'.

In the case of certain directorial roles – for example, a non-executive director or a director 'without-portfolio' – there may be neither a particular 'vacancy' to be filled, nor an expectation that an appointment has to be made. In such circumstances, there may be no need to 'make do' with someone who will not contribute very significantly to the work of the board. The 'marginal' person can sometimes adversely affect the atmosphere, dynamics and quality of a board.

8.7 Selection and availability of candidates

Overall, the selection criteria that have been identified in this chapter are not thought by chairmen to be easy to satisfy. A number of interviewees during the course of the 'chairman' survey[8] indicated that it was not easy to identify suitable candidates for boardroom appointments. Those with the required qualities were seen as 'few and far between', and already likely to be in demand.

It should not be thought that all those with the personal qualities that are required will be beating a path to the door of the boardroom. Some evidence emerged in interviews[8] of highly qualified and sought-after individuals preferring to avoid or limit non-executive board appointments in favour of working upon ad hoc projects for negotiated fees.[8]

Potential board members appear to be increasingly aware of their potential liabilities. In the case of smaller companies the cost of directors' fees is also a constraint upon the appointment of additional board members.

A company may need to take steps to increase the availability of candidates. Involving a wider community of people in a range of director development activities could be one means of doing this. Other initiatives could include a 'younger director talent programme' of putting senior managers with directorial qualities onto subsidiary company boards. A consortium of non-competing companies could open up subsidiary board opportunities to suitably qualified members of each other's executive teams. This might create a cadre of younger directors, and widen the pool from which non-executive directors could be drawn.

From time to time, a board should examine the process that is used to select new board members, and how it might be improved. The review could address whether the questions used in interviews are 'input' or 'output' focused; how they relate to directorial criteria; and whether they are posed in such a way as not to discriminate between candidates. The selection process should encourage rather than discourage the availability of candidates.

8.8 Becoming a company director

So far we have considered the appointment of company directors from the perspective of the company and the board. Let us now briefly consider the perspective of a person seeking a directorial appointment. What advice should one give to someone who is seeking to become a 'director person'? The key points that emerged from interviews with company chairmen are presented in Example 8.1.

Keep listening and learning
Cultivate an overview perspective
Develop people and communication skills
Be aware and sensitive to others
Relate to feelings and values
Safeguard your health
Don't become a 'clone' or avoid reality
Maintain a sense of balance and proportion
Avoid the introversion of 'specialism'
Differentiate your qualities and contribution
Develop your own positions on issues
Be your 'own person'
Be true to yourself and your strengths

Example 8.1   Becoming a 'director person'

Personal qualities, or the 'calibre of the person', feature prominently in this example, while 'trappings' such as qualifications do not, as these might be held by people of widely differing directorial potential. Experience *per se* may or may not be relevant:

- People do not always learn from the experience they may have had.
- Directorial qualities are largely personal qualities, and fundamental changes of attitude and perspective occur more readily in some than in others.

Acting upon a list such as that in Example 8.1 will not guarantee a seat on a board. Much will depend upon retirements, vacancies and perceived needs. In many companies whether or not a particular person becomes a director appears to be largely a matter of individual choice on the part of the chairman or chief executive.[24]

Directorial qualities need to be developed and demonstrated, but demonstration is not always easy outside the boardroom context:

- A candidate's particular qualities and potential to contribute need to be apparent if others are to relate his or her attributes to a boardroom requirement. If the substance or mettle of someone is not clear, how will others know whether or not the candidate might complement the qualities of the existing team of directors?
- A board is composed of people with personalities, who exchange ideas, discuss and debate. Many boardrooms can be an unpleasant environment for those who deal in generalizations, obfuscate and avoid commitment.

Awareness, empathy and sensitivity are important directorial qualities. They are also viewed with suspicion in some management cultures. The 'hardness' that has enabled the 'tough' manager to climb above others may need to be complemented by a 'human side' if the threshold of the boardroom is to be crossed. According to Sir John Harvey-Jones: 'It does not always follow that the best executive manager will become the best director, and, indeed, I have sometimes wondered whether we should stream and select directors quite differently to the way we stream and select chief executives.'[25]

Career planning and the boardroom

How should a career be managed in order to secure a directorship? This is not an easy question to answer because, as we have seen, there are many different routes to the boardroom. Each route will make its own particular demands upon those intent upon travelling along it.

Success, when it comes, is likely to result from a matching of the qualities of the individual with the special requirements that relate to a particular boardroom opportunity that arises at one moment in time. Opportunities are easier to bring about in respect of some routes than others. For example:

– A person can become an 'owner-director' by being proactive and establishing and launching a business into the marketplace at an appropriate moment.
– Another person may occupy a succession of senior management roles within the bureaucracy of a large company without ever encountering the 'right opportunity' to become a director.

Let us examine the case of the executive with directorial ambitions in the larger company. The lessons that emerge from this and the earlier chapters of this book for career planning are set out in Example 8.2. An individual with directorial aspirations needs to understand that:

– managers and directors can require distinct sets of qualities; managerial moves and experience *per se* will not necessarily lead to the development of directorial qualities;
– career options should be assessed in terms of their potential for the development of directorial qualities; activities that enable a person to acquire a strategic perspective, or an understanding of the company as a whole, are especially valuable;
– in many companies, in the absence of any formal director development

---

Think through the director/manager distinction
Acquire a strategic overview and perspective
Never forget the customer
Obtain multi-function experience
Participate in multi-functional/multi-location teams
Seek cross-functional and inter-organizational process experience
Join international task forces and teams
Develop an international perspective
Understand the business environment
Avoid introversion – build a 'directors' network'
Match career moves to directorial skills
Maintain visibility
Demonstrate contribution to key business objectives

Example 8.2 Lessons for aspiring directors

programme, the individual may need to assume responsibility for his or her own directorial development;

– self-awareness and honesty are very important, and personal qualities should be seen as they are, rather than as they should be, if disappointment is to be avoided.

We have seen that it can help a person's chances to be regarded as a distinctive individual. However, the drive to 'differentiate' should not be taken too far, as this may result in suggestions that a person is an 'awkward customer' or is 'likely to rock the boat'. While many boardrooms would benefit from being 'stirred up', chairmen appear to have a strong preference for the 'safe pair of hands':

– Loyalty, particularly to the chairman and chief executive officer, 'team spirit' and generally 'fitting in' appear to be valued more highly by many chairmen than originality and creativity.[8]
– Creativity *per se* does not rank highly as a boardroom quality, and those who go out of their way to appear bright and full of ideas can reduce rather than enhance their chances of a boardroom appointment.[8, 11]

Becoming a director is about the capability (a) to 'add value' and contribute in a particular boardroom context and (b) to complement and enrich the qualities and experience of the other members of a boardroom team. It concerns accountability and legal duties and responsibilities. It should not be about the pursuit of standing and status, or satisfying an ego or individual sensitivities. A person should become a director primarily in order to 'put in' rather than to 'take out'.

8.9 Summary

In this chapter we have examined routes to the boardroom, the qualities that are sought in directors, the criteria that are used to select them, and issues relating to each of these areas. The qualities that are sought in a new director will depend upon the situation and context of a company, and the qualities of the existing boardroom team. The selection criteria and process that are used should be appropriate to the qualities that are being sought.

In many companies, the routes to the boardroom could be more open, and there could be a wider search for directorial talent. The adequacy of the selection process should be re-assessed periodically. We have also examined the implications of our findings for those with directorial ambitions.

8.10 Checklist

1. How should a directorial career relate to a managerial career?
2. In the case of your company, what route did each director take to the boardroom?
3. In each case, how much was either judgement or 'planning', or simply luck and chance 'accidents'?
4. What criteria are used to select new members of the board of your company?
5. Who is responsible for establishing them, and are they kept up to date?
6. Do the criteria and the selection process used adequately reflect the needs of the company and the board?
7. Are the criteria and selection process understood by existing and potential members of the board?
8. Are the criteria and selection process made explicit and communicated to members of the management team in such a form as to represent a useful guide to aspiring directors?
9. Does the training, career development and succession planning undertaken by your company take account of the criteria used to select new members of the board?
10. To what extent could the selection process and organized development activity be used to widen the pool of people from whom directors might be drawn?
11. Are the routes to the boardroom in your company transparent and open, or concealed and blocked?
12. In the context of the particular situation and circumstances of the company, what ought to be the 'normal' route (or routes) to the boardroom?
13. What changes in the 'normal' route should be made to accommodate the needs of particular boardroom roles (e.g. chairman, non-executive director, particular functional director, etc.)?
14. What route to the boardroom (or a boardroom) would you recommend your son or daughter (or a representative young manager) to take?
15. How often does the board review (a) its existing membership, and (b) the criteria for board membership?
16. What happens, or should happen, when directors 'come up for re-appointment'?

Notes and references

1. Pitt, W., 'How many routes to the top?', *Director*, June 1991, 45–50.
2. Rock, S., *Family Firms*, Director Books, 1991.
3. Lindon-Travers, K., *Non-executive Directors: A guide to their role, responsibilities and appointment*, Director Books, 1990.
4. Coulson-Thomas, C., *Professional Development of and for the Board*. A question- naire and interview survey undertaken by Adaptation Ltd of company chairmen. A summary has been published by the IOD, February 1990.
5. Coulson-Thomas, C. and Brown, R., *Beyond Quality: Managing the relationship with the customer*, BIM, 1990.
6. Webley, S., *Business Ethics and Company Codes*, Institute of Business Ethics, 1992.
7. Bartram, P. and Coulson-Thomas, C., *The Complete Spokesperson*, Kogan Page, 1991.
8. Coulson-Thomas, C. and Wakelam, A., *The Effective Board: Current practice, myths and realities*. An IOD discussion document, 1991.
9. Horovitz, J. H., 'Strategic control: A new task for top management', *Interna- tional Studies of Management and Organisation*, III (4), 1979, 96–112.
10. Coulson-Thomas, C., *Developing Directors: Building an effective boardroom team*, McGraw-Hill, 1993.
11. Howe, E. and McRae, S., *Women on the Board*, Policy Studies Institute, 1991.
12. Wakelam, A., *The Training & Development of Company Directors*. A report on a questionnaire survey undertaken by the Centre for Management Studies, Uni- versity of Exeter for the Training Agency, December 1989.
13. Coulson-Thomas, C., *The Role and Function of the Personnel Director*. An interim Adaptation Ltd survey carried out in conjunction with the Research Group of the Institute of Personnel Management, 1991.
14. 'Worker director training at Scott Bader', *Industrial Relations Review and Report*, No. 478, 21 December 1990, pp. 11–14.
15. Holton, V. and Rabbetts, J., *Powder in the Boardroom*. Report of a Survey of women on the boards of top UK companies, Ashridge Research Group, Ashridge Management College, 1989.
16. Institute of Directors, *Women's Participation in the Workforce*, Director Pub- lications, 1992.
17. Coulson-Thomas, C., *Creating the Global Company: Successful internationalization*, McGraw-Hill, 1992.
18. Kay, H., 'Inner City circle holds the key to top boardrooms', *The Sunday Times*, Business section, 14 June 1992, p. 3:8.
19. Coulson-Thomas, C., *Transforming the Company: Bridging the gap between management myth and corporate reality*, Kogan Page, 1992.
20. PRO NED, *Research into the Role of the Non-executive Director*, PRO NED, July 1992.
21. Committee on The Financial Aspects of Corporate Governance (chairman: Sir Adrian Cadbury), Draft Report issued for public comment, Committee on The Financial Aspects of Corporate Governance, 27 May 1992, pp. 13–14.
22. Korn/Ferry, *Boards of Directors Study*, US (1989) and UK (1992), Korn/Ferry International, 1989 and 1992.
23. Coulson-Thomas, C., *Too Old at 40?*, BIM, 1989.
24. Coulson-Thomas, C., 'What the personnel director can bring to the

boardroom table', *Personnel Management*, October 1991, 36–9.
25. Harvey-Jones, Sir J., *Making it Happen: Reflections on leadership*, Fontana/Collins, 1989, p. 186.

Appendix

DIRECTOR ASSESSMENT FORM

Candidate's name: ....

Board (e.g. group, subsidiary, etc.): ....

Directorial role: ....

(a) Directorial skills/experience (e.g. strategic awareness, etc.)
....
....
....

(b) Personal qualities (e.g. able to work with other board members, etc.)
....
....
....

(c) Level of commitment to corporate vision, goals, values, and objectives
....
....
....

(d) Understanding of corporate processes (i.e. comfortable with process)
....
....
....

(e) Role model assessment
....
....
....

Any other comments
....
....

Does the candidate understand the accountabilities, and the legal duties and responsibilities of a company director?
....
....

Overall, is the candidate a fit and proper person to be a director?
....

Interviewer's signature: ....
Date: ....

[Note: This form, which has actually been used, is given for the purposes of illustration. It does not represent a model that all companies should use.]

9
Developing directors

Directors lead busy lives. Too often, they address every development need except their own. Directorial competence cannot be assumed. (RICHARD FIELD, chairman, J. & J. Dyson plc.)

Having considered the role of the director, and directorial qualities and requirements, we turn in this chapter to the preparation of directors for their directorial accountabilities and responsibilities, and their boardroom roles. How should directors be prepared? Can they be prepared? Before examining these questions, we shall first consider how directors have been prepared, and in many cases still are prepared.

Current practice, and 'traditional' development preferences have influenced the quality of existing directors, and they have implications for the emergence of future generations of directors. Neither the influences, nor the implications should give rise to complacency.

It is very difficult to generalize about how directors and boards should be developed. Boards and companies both vary enormously in their nature, situation and context, and development requirements need to reflect the composition and circumstances of each individual board. The subject of developing directors is considered in greater detail in a 'companion' book by the author.[1]

9.1 Preparation for the board

There would appear to be a significant role for relevant and tailored director development in (a) improving the effectiveness of many boards, (b) enhancing the competence of their members and (c) raising the quality of new entrants to the boardroom. Consider the following characteristic comments:

> I did not receive any form of preparation. Until I got onto the board I did not know what was required.

> Luck played its part in my case. I must have been seen as just a bit better than

the alternatives available at that moment. I did not satisfy any absolute criteria as these did not exist.

My preparation was totally inadequate. I was thrown in at the deep end, and had to pick it up as I went along.

I would not have known what to do to prepare myself. No one said anything to me at this stage.

I would like to have done more, but I had no idea what was expected of me. I'm still not sure what I could have done.

Looking back on it, my appointment must have been a gamble. Once on the board, everyone gives you the benefit of the doubt.

Directorial qualities are largely personal qualities. How could I have prepared?

Understanding the very limited extent of past preparation for the boardroom does not lead one to assume, or expect, directors to be competent or boards to be effective. The existence of competent directors and effective boards is a tribute to much persistence, determination and needless uncertainty and anguish.

Preparation for excellence in the boardroom should be ongoing. According to John Harper of the Institute of Directors: 'Becoming a director is not the end of a career path or an end to a process of learning and improvement. Rather it is an area of activity in which people can progress from novicehood to excellence, just as they can in management, and other professional activities.'[2]

The extent of the development challenge

What sort of preparation have directors received for their boardroom roles? Some clues are provided by: (a) surveys undertaken by Adaptation Ltd for the IOD[3] and in conjunction with the Research Group of the IPM[4]; and (b) surveys undertaken by the author and Alan Wakelam.[5, 6]

In an 'open-ended' section of the questionnaire used in the IOD survey[3] participants were asked a series of questions about their preparation for the boardroom. Their responses suggest:

– Formal preparation for the boardroom is almost non-existent. Over nine out of ten respondents either had not received any preparation for the board, or had been prepared by such informal means as 'experience'.
– The training received by those with directorial potential rarely embraces the specific requirements of the company director. For the majority, any 'formal training' that was received appears to be mainly

concerned with 'management' rather than 'direction' skills and competences.

The general thrust of these findings is corroborated by the initial results of the IPM survey.[4] For example:

– All but one of those referring to some form of preparation prior to a directorial appointment cited either 'experience', or one or more management or professional courses, rather than an activity specifically concerned with company direction.
– Not one of the respondents had attended a course or formal programme designed explicitly to prepare them for the role of company director.

A board should consider whether its members have been properly prepared for their directorial roles. Questions to address include:

– Did the formal and/or informal preparation (if any) that was received address: (a) the needs of members as individual directors; or (b) their requirements in relation to the board as a team?
– Was the formal and/or informal preparation (if any) that was received in any way concerned with 'making it happen'?[7]

The directors should reflect upon how their preparation could have been improved, and assess what needs and deficiencies might be tackled by formal and informal development activity.

ACCUMULATING EVIDENCE OF THE NEED FOR ACTION

There has been a steady accumulation of evidence concerning the need to focus attention, commitment and action upon the development of competent directors and more effective boards. The findings of the IOD and IPM surveys are further supported by the surveys undertaken by Coulson-Thomas and Wakelam.[5, 6] For example:

– Among chairmen, there is little satisfaction with the performance of their board. Three out of four respondents believe the effectiveness of their board could be improved.[5]
– Nine out of ten respondents did not receive any preparation for their role as a company director before their appointment.[6] (This is a similar proportion to that in the IOD survey.[3])
– The lack of formal preparation prior to board appointments does not appear to be made good during the post-appointment period. Over two-thirds of respondents did not receive any formal help after their appointment.[6]

The results of these surveys[3–6] are not encouraging. However, it should be said that at the time many of the survey participants were coming up to their directorial appointments, the range of available and formal director development programmes was relatively limited. As a result of their inadequate preparation, many directors are not able to cope with fundamental change.[7] There is some evidence that many boards adapt to discontinuous or 'frame-breaking' change by bringing on board new members rather than by developing the existing directors or expecting them to cope.[8]

More recently, there has been a marked expansion in the number of activities aimed specifically at existing and potential directors, including the courses of the IOD itself. Does this mean that a significant increase in formal 'director development' is likely to occur? The answer to this question will depend upon obstacles to director development, and experiences with, and attitudes towards, informal preparation.

OBSTACLES TO DIRECTOR DEVELOPMENT

There are many practical obstacles to director development, and these need to be acknowledged and addressed. Understanding the barriers and the 'hinders' is best done at the outset, if a practical programme is to emerge.

The preparation of individuals for the boardroom is an activity that is not free of controversy. Director development is not always assumed to be a 'good thing'. Activities, such as 'top team development', that neither reflect the distinction between direction and management nor focus upon the distinct requirements of the directors of a particular board, might do more harm than good. Much will depend upon who is being developed, by whom, and for what.

Many directors are very reluctant to acknowledge or address their development needs. A position on a board can be a source of great personal satisfaction, the culmination of a lifetime of endeavour, an acknowledgement that one has 'arrived'. Therefore, addressing the development needs of directors and boards requires sensitivity and tact.

Given the obstacles to director development, the support of the chairman and the chief executive is clearly desirable, but it should not be assumed. Many chairmen are cautious, and have a sceptical approach towards director development. They appear to adopt the view that directors are 'born not made'.[1]

Informal preparation

In the perceived absence of organized and formal alternatives, preparation for the boardroom has been largely informal:

- The preparation of the participants in the IOD survey[3] has been overwhelmingly informal. Only a small minority have taken advantage of the special courses and workshops for directors which are provided by the IOD.
- The preparation of three-quarters of the participants in the IPM survey[4] has been informal, consisting of observation, discussion with colleagues, background reading, and asking relevant questions.

Individual directors with a desire to better equip themselves for their boardroom roles have had to 'take the initiative'. Even in the case of formal courses, the initiative for action is coming from individual directors, rather than as the result of a formal corporate or board programme. The participation of two-thirds of the delegates at IOD courses has been 'a result of the individual's own interest'.[6]

There is much that an individual director can do to learn actively from work experience,[9] and we shall examine a number of the opportunities later in this chapter. Given the lack of formal corporate or board programmes, to whom do directors turn for informal help? Other directors (including non-executive directors) and chairmen are those to whom individuals turn most frequently in respect of their preparation for the board and specific boardroom roles.[3]

WHY INFORMAL APPROACHES PREVAIL

There are many reasons for the persistence of informal approaches. Some of these could also be said to represent problems for director development in general. For example:

- There is an inadequate understanding of both the role and function of the board (see Chapter 3), and the distinction between direction and management (see Chapter 4).
- The requirements for competent directorship and effective boards (see Chapters 6 and 7) are often not 'thought through'.
- There is uncertainty concerning how best to develop many of the directorial qualities that are sought, and satisfy directorial selection criteria (see Chapters 6 and 8).
- There does not appear to have been a generally accepted, understood and practised route to the boardroom.[3]

Some directors pursue an informal approach to their self-development because of the perceived disadvantages of formal development, while others are positively attracted by the advantages of learning from experience.

THE LIMITATIONS OF FORMAL DEVELOPMENT

Formal development is thought to have some drawbacks. For example:

- The diversity of 'recorded' views on how individuals should be prepared for the board reflects the varied nature of the experience of survey respondents and the differing nature of the boards and companies they serve.[3] Those that do recognize the need for director development may come from diverse backgrounds and may have differing reasons for seeking help.[10]
- We saw in Chapter 5 that there are many forms of board, in terms of type, composition and operation. Standard approaches, courses and training packages designed for managers are unlikely to meet the needs of a particular board and its individual directors.
- The strategy and structure of a company is likely to evolve as its operations become more extensive and complex.[11] The development needs of a particular board may change significantly over a period of time.
- Many formal programmes lack credibility, or are not sufficiently tailored to the special needs of directors. We saw in Chapter 4 that directors differ from managers in their development requirements. For example, they need to understand their particular accountabilities and duties, the awareness and perspective of the director, and the peculiar pressures and dynamics of the boardroom.
- Compared with an extensive provision of management programmes, there remains a shortage of people and institutions equipped to offer courses, and provide other activities, that are specifically aimed at directorial requirements. The use of 'retreaded' training originally designed for managers may encourage those who receive it to blur the distinction between 'director' and 'manager'.
- Some areas of director skill needs that can be addressed by formal programmes, such as financial understanding and knowledge of legal duties and responsibilities, do not rank highly among the personal development priorities of individual directors.[4]

The sceptics remain to be convinced that the services they have encountered would significantly change directorial attitudes, awareness and perspective.[1] As one chairman put it:

> I would like to be persuaded that something existed along the lines of management development which I could buy. But, heaven knows, changing managerial attitudes and behaviour is bad enough. How much more difficult it is in the boardroom, especially when those supplying services do not even attempt to understand the attitudes and personalities involved. The options that are safe tend to be bland and cosmetic.

There are approaches, tools and techniques that have been used success-fully within a relatively small number of 'benchmark' companies to con-front the problems faced by many boards.[7] However, such formal 'solutions' tend to remain hidden within these organizations. Those equipped to use them are generally in great 'internal' demand. Hence many workable approaches, tools and techniques are not 'publicly' available for 'external' use.

THE BENEFITS OF INFORMAL PREPARATION

There is also a positive demand for informal development as a result of what are thought to be its advantages. For example:

- Informal contact with fellow directors is perceived to have considerable value.[5] Directors learn from each other, and, as we shall see later in this chapter, discussion with colleagues is the most common means of remaining 'up to date'.
- The value of informal evening discussions and the opportunity to meet other directors appears to be an important consideration in the deci-sion of directors to participate in formal development activities.[6]
- In the case of many issues on the boardroom agenda, generalized and abstract debates are of little value. It may also not be possible for an expert, such as a 'teacher' on a formal programme, to produce a 'right' answer. In these circumstances, each board should determine its own positions and solutions in the light of the particular situation of the individual company.

Networking with other directors can both broaden an individual and help to put an issue into context. The problems faced by a board may not be unique, but shared by other companies. Many directors value the opportunity to develop a more rounded perspective on a certain issue as a result of discussion with other directors facing similar challenges.

The role of formal professional development

There would appear to be a very significant potential role for formal pro-fessional development. In the case of the participants in the IOD survey,[3] who are broadly representative of the total population of directors:

- there is little satisfaction with the current situation, and it is clear from their responses that 'experience' on its own, gaining it as one goes along, is not thought to be a sufficient preparation for the boardroom.
- the need for 'director development' is acknowledged; three-quarters of

respondents believe that there are particular boardroom roles for which specific preparation is required.

However, a recognized requirement may not be a priority action. Less than a quarter of the respondents[3] thought 'preparation for appointment to the board' was 'very important', while a fifth thought it either 'not very important' or 'unimportant'. There is some evidence that those who participate in appropriate director development find that their 'appetite is whetted'. For example, in a survey undertaken by Alan Wakelam,[6] over two-thirds of those obtaining the IOD's Diploma in Company Direction expressed an interest in undertaking further formal development.

9.2 From development need to development action

Let us examine the question of turning a latent requirement for director development into a reality. The 'chairman' survey[5] suggests that the acknowledgement of development need is rarely matched by an understanding of how it might be met:

– When prompted, directors who were interviewed readily acknowledged that 'both their individual performance and that of their boards could be improved by relevant training'. However, in the absence of such prompting, there appeared to be little awareness of how to remedy deficiencies in direction as opposed to management skills.
– Among those who acknowledged the existence of a development problem there was little evidence of an active search for solutions. Boardroom skills and competences do not appear to be a priority. Awareness of the need for action is more widespread than the motivation to act.
– Opportunities to spend time with 'role model' business leaders are few in number. At a superficial level they can appear a disparate group, and it may be necessary to associate with, or observe, them for a period of time in order to discern the combination of actions that distinguish them from less successful directors.[12]

In view of the demanding nature of the business environment, and the onerous duties and responsibilities that have been placed upon directors, it is important that they are competent, well chosen and properly prepared for the boardroom. In changing circumstances they also need to keep up to date, and may benefit from taking time out to broaden their thinking and regain a balanced perspective.

In general, while recognizing the long-term importance of creating and maintaining an effective board, many directors do not find it easy to identify the practical steps they might take that would lead to a measurable improvement in board performance. Taking necessary action to identify possible 'next steps' does not appear to rank high on the agendas of many boards.

A board should assess whether director development needs are explicit and acknowledged, or latent and hidden. Barriers to action, and 'helps' and 'hinders', should be identified, specific objectives set, and roles and responsibilities allocated in order to move from aspiration to achievement.

Implementation requirements

One area in which action is needed in many boardrooms concerns the drive towards corporate transformation, which we examined in Chapter 2. Very few directors appear to have been equipped with the skills and qualities to 'make it happen'.[7] Determining a strategy may require one set of skills, and implementing it another. Adrian Davies points out: 'The board must not [only] establish and sell a challenging strategy, but also deploy its resources and skill over the time needed to achieve that strategy.'[13]

In some cases there is only a vague acknowledgement that more effort on the part of the board is needed. The following are the views expressed by some interviewees.

> Once strategy is determined that tends to be it. We then hope for the best, monitor, and report what happens.

> For the board the agreed strategy is the output, not an implemented strategy. We do our best, and circumstances decide the outcome.

> We point the ship in the right direction and hope that management will take up the challenge. That's leadership. Becoming involved, that gets into management.

> Some of these things have to be aspirations, . . . a wish list. Of course we talk about implementation, and we try to implement. . . . If we are honest we must accept there are things we cannot do.

The determination of vision, goals, values and strategy, however excellent these might be, should only be regarded as a beginning. All that can be gained from an excellent strategy that is not implemented is selfish intellectual satisfaction for the participating directors. The company will not have benefited. Stakeholders may have been 'taxed' in order that the directors might feel important.

A board should recognize its responsibilities in relation to bringing about fundamental change. Objectives may be stretching, but they should be capable of achievement. The board should do whatever is necessary and practical by way of sharing, empowering, enabling, motivating, monitoring, facilitating, supporting, etc., to ensure that objectives are accomplished.[7]

The effective board ensures that: (a) vision, goals, values and strategy are shared; and (b) the resources, processes, motivation, etc., are put in place to enable them to be achieved. In particular, it needs to ensure that the necessary processes are in place to identify and deliver the value sought by customers.[7]

9.3 Keeping directorial skills and awareness up to date

Once appointed, how do directors ensure that their qualities and skills remain relevant to the situations and contexts of their boards? In a 1989 survey,[6] directors were asked how they remain up to date with changes in the business environment and developments relating to their directorial roles. The most common means of staying up to date was discussion with colleagues, which was cited by eight out of ten respondents.

This finding is consistent with the results of the 1991 IPM survey,[4] in which 'discussion with colleagues' is ranked as the most valuable source of information:

- Two-thirds of the respondents consider 'discussion with colleagues' to be 'very valuable', while all but two respondents consider it to be either 'very valuable' or 'valuable'.
- A half of the participants who are board directors seek the advice of boardroom colleagues, while the other half turn to 'network' colleagues such as specialist or professional advisers, peer colleagues in other companies, or the IOD.

A general picture emerges of directors who: (a) are in receipt of a flow of 'external', or non-company, information resulting from decisions taken over many years to subscribe or 'plug in' to certain sources; and (b) 'keep their eyes open' with varying degrees of commitment for items that might be relevant to their directorial roles.

The role of the chairman

The approach adopted by many directors appears to be passive rather than active:

- They have not prepared adequately for the boardroom, or significantly changed their priority sources of updating information since becoming directors.
- They have not thought through the updating information they should receive in their directorial roles, or taken active steps to obtain it.

The chairman should ensure that:

- all new directors are properly prepared for the boardroom; at least they need to be made aware of their accountabilities, duties and responsibilities;
- the directorial skills of all directors remain current and relevant to changes in the situation and circumstances of the company; the board and its individual members should 'grow the business' and 'grow with the business'.

All members of the board should demonstrate a positive commitment to remaining up to date. There is no substitute for thought, and a challenging attitude, on the part of directors themselves.

Directors operate in a rapidly changing business environment. Their updating information should reflect prevailing circumstances and requirements. Some of those who appear to rely heavily upon the printed word and management courses may be drawing upon past experience that might not be relevant to their particular situation or current roles as directors.

As and when significant requirements for new forms of specialist skills arise, the board can make use of external consultants to supplement its own understanding.[14] Those seeking advice on director development can turn to the Centre for Director Development of the IOD. The IOD is a professional association that was set up specifically to promote professionalism in direction. It offers an extensive range of courses, workshops and updates for directors. Individual directors can undertake a programme of course modules leading to the IOD's Diploma in Company Direction.

The board as a learning environment

In the area of directorial knowledge and skills, the board should assume responsibility for its own development. Within the boardroom, the chairman has a special responsibility for ensuring that the directors are competent and the board operates effectively.[5, 15] Competence and effectiveness will reflect directorial accountabilities and responsibilities, and the particular challenges and opportunities faced by the board.

There is a strong preference for the integration of working and learning.[16] This is when effective learning occurs. The boardroom itself represents the primary learning environment for most directors:

- The boardroom is 'where it happens'. A chairman should ensure that the culture and dynamics of the board are conducive to learning.
- The context of the boardroom, the nature of the individual company and the nature of the business and market environment can be major

influences upon director development needs. Within the boardroom the director is aware of these factors.
- Each board is made up of a combination of people to suit the situation and circumstances of the company. The subtleties and distinct culture of a particular boardroom may take some time to absorb. This process of absorption best occurs in the boardroom.
- A director is appointed to sit upon a specific board. The point was made in Chapter 6 that the competence of an individual director needs to be assessed in relation to a particular board. A director who makes a significant contribution to the work of one board may struggle to add value to another.
- A director is a member of a team. The qualities that individual directors need to develop and display are often those that relate to, and complement, the qualities of colleagues. It may not be easy to determine or assess them in the absence of other directors.
- The process of learning to be a better director should continue throughout a directorial career. The changing nature of the development requirement will reflect the evolving directorial challenge that faces a board. Detaching learning from the boardroom may give it the appearance of being a periodic, rather than a continuous, requirement.

Before embarking on a director development programme, it is advisable to assess and discuss relevant directorial views, attitudes and prejudices. How receptive is the board to the concept of director development? What are the main concerns and reservations, and how might these be tackled? Who are likely to be the champions of director development? It may be necessary to identify particular directors who are cautious or sceptical, as they might have a significant influence upon the extent of director commitment to, and involvement in, development activities. Concerns and reservations should be brought into the open in order to increase the extent of self-awareness in the boardroom.

9.4 Meeting the requirements of new directors

Having 'taken the temperature', or assessed a board's attitude towards director development, where should one begin? A good place to start, if the occasion presents itself, is with the appointment of new directors to the board. The preparation of new directors for the boardroom may not be perceived by the existing directors to be as 'threatening' as directly confronting their deficiencies. New directors, even experienced directors, will need to be inducted into the practices and ethos of a particular board. The individual who is not sensitive to those things that distinguish one board from others may be less successful as a director than colleagues who are more aware.

A successful induction will not happen overnight. For example:

- It may take time to appreciate how the board relates to, and communicates with, the various stakeholders in a company. In many companies the communication of financial results is an activity that takes place once a year, while others 'go public' with half-year or quarterly results.
- The mix of business that is conducted will in all probability vary from meeting to meeting. Any meeting might spring surprises when certain issues are encountered for the first time by a recent appointee.
- It may be thought desirable for a new director to visit a number of business units or overseas operations. Arranging such a programme can take time.

Some directors may only feel at home when they have sat through an annual cycle of board meetings. During this period they should be encouraged to ask questions, and supplementary briefings may need to be arranged.

The chairman will be expected to give a lead in inducting the newly appointed director into the ways of the board, and in particular, how it conducts its business. Particular attention should be paid to informal contacts between meetings, practice regarding the presentation of information, and how issues find their way onto the boardroom agenda.

Existing directors may take many practices of the board for granted. The alert chairman might want to learn from the initial reactions of someone who is an experienced director, but new to a particular board.

The induction programme

Most new directors will be joining an existing team. Some chairmen make it a practice to 'profile' each of the existing members of the board. A thumbnail sketch might include past experience and the rationale for an appointment to the board.

Newly appointed directors ought to be made aware of the criteria that were used to select them. They should also understand how their particular qualities and attributes complement those of other members of the boardroom team. The director who understands the strengths of each boardroom colleague may find it easier to become a team player.

What else should be included in a formal induction programme? New directors should be made aware of:

- their legal duties and responsibilities as directors
- relationships with the various stakeholders in the business

- relevant policy guidelines or corporate codes covering such matters as disclosure of interests, price-sensitive information, corporate hospitality, how to handle offers of gifts, etc.
- past, recent and any likely future developments relating to the board
- what is generally expected of them in the boardroom
- any particular contribution they might be expected to make
- the roles and responsibilities of other members of the board
- how their performance as directors will be judged
- how they should relate formally and informally to each other, the chief executive and the chairman
- how they are to be briefed and supported in their role as directors
- to whom they should turn – for example, to the company secretary or the chairman – when they require information, counselling, or there are issues they would like to raise
- the vision, goals, values and objectives of the company.

It is particularly important that the role of the director is understood. According to David O'Brien, chief executive of the National and Provincial Building Society: 'It is difficult to build competencies for a role which is not understood. The director role is different from that of a manager, and if its particular competency requirements were understood people would be able to choose whether or not to occupy director roles.'[17]

When discussing roles and responsibilities, particular attention should be paid to the roles of chairman and chief executive.[15, 18] Wherever possible, legal, procedural and accountability requirements and expectations should be put in writing. A briefing from the company secretary on the more technical aspects of board procedures, and legal duties and responsibilities, is also advisable. The chairman should check not only that these documents have been received and briefings have been held, but also that they have been understood.

The chairman should also make sure that new directors have an adequate understanding of corporate finance and financial accounts to enable them to discharge their financial and reporting responsibilities. While specialists may be responsible for preparing the various financial statements and reports that are made available to directors, the director should be able to understand and interpret them, and ask pertinent questions.

Directors who are new to a company – for example, a non-executive director – may require a more extensive briefing on plans, policies, products, services, processes, values and culture of the company. More familiar faces may also need to be briefed. In the case of those who have been employed as managers, it should not be assumed that past events and current circumstances are understood from a directorial perspective.

Some introduction to the background and history of a company can be of value in understanding current attitudes and practices. A director might have a particular interest in boardroom 'personalities' of the past. Company expectations, attitudes and confidence can be significantly 'conditioned' by corporate history and the collective experience of both directors and employees.

The existing boardroom team

The introduction of a boardroom induction programme will not of itself create an effective board:

- Boards vary in the time it takes for their membership to 'turn over'. In the case of some boards it would be many years before a majority, let alone all, of the directors had the benefit of a formal induction programme. In the meantime, certain directors might continue to serve on the board with deficiencies that could be addressed by appropriate development activity.
- Individual directors, whatever their merits, and even those who have had the benefit of an excellent induction programme, still need to be integrated into a boardroom team. Excellence in the boardroom is the product of relationships, the chemistry of interaction, the dynamics of the group or team.

A company should periodically review its director induction programme. Questions to consider include:

- Are all 'new' directors properly prepared for their directorial accountabilities, legal duties and responsibilities, and boardroom roles and responsibilities?
- Does the induction of new directors include their integration into the boardroom team? Is the impact of 'new' directors upon the existing members of the board assessed?
- Are 'new' directors encouraged to ask questions, and do they have access to all the information they need? How easy is it for a 'new' director to be accepted as an integrated and trusted member of the boardroom team?
- How might the induction programme affect the attitudes, conduct or commitment of a 'new' director? Does the induction process allow the other directors to learn from the initial impressions of a 'new' director?

Special development needs

The use of an overall development needs 'map' should not be allowed to obscure the fact that individual directors may require highly tailored programmes. A strong view has emerged in interviews with chairmen[5] that there are particular boardroom roles for which specific preparation is required. For example:

- It is felt that the role of chairman deserves 'special treatment'. In particular, the chairman needs to be made aware of his or her special responsibility in relation to developing an effective board.
- Non-executive directors are thought to require special preparation for their role. On many boards, the non-executive directors have responsibilities that are not shared by other directors – for example, relating to the fixing of the remuneration of executive directors.
- Many owner-directors regard themselves as a distinct group with special needs. The future of their companies can be closely tied to their own ambitions, expectations, and lifestyle preferences.

Meeting the needs of the business

What about the 'needs of the business'? Have these been addressed? Before implementing a director development programme, a useful last check is to consider:

- Are the knowledge and skill needs being addressed appropriate to the nature, situation and circumstances of the company? A distinction should be made between skills that are nice to have and those that are essential in relation to key objectives. Priority should be given to the latter.
- In particular, are the business and market environments in which the company operates understood? Changes in the business environment can have a profound impact upon a company,[19] and we saw in Chapter 2 that a board needs to monitor and respond to significant developments in the external environment.
- Do the knowledge and skills that will result match the development needs and future 'ambitions' of the company? If the board does not have the potential to 'grow' with the capability of the company, it could itself become a constraint.
- Has sufficient attention been given to facilitating and transformation skills? The board needs to be able to 'implement' or 'make it happen'.[7]

As a result of enthusiasm to tackle the needs of directors and boards, and a focus upon their requirements, it is sometimes possible to overlook the situation of the company. Excellence in the boardroom is not sought for its own sake, but in order to better serve the company and satisfy its stakeholders.

Once identified and mapped, director development needs have to be matched to appropriate activities.[1] Using the overall picture that emerges, some further categorization is usually necessary. For example:

- A view might need to be taken as to whether a particular requirement would best be met by formal or informal activity.
- There may be some requirements that are best met by means of development programmes for individual directors, while in other cases an exercise involving the board as a whole might be more appropriate.

9.5 Future directors

The existing board members and those who have been considered for an appointment to the board are not the only people for whom director development may be relevant. The development of future directors should also be addressed. How many of the existing directors will still be in the boardroom in five years time?

It appears that many companies do not find it easy to identify potential directors.[5] Succession appears to be a significant problem for many boards, and particularly for their chairmen.[3] Some assessment of direction competences and qualities in a 'wider population' might assist the selection of candidates for boardroom appointments. Could management development activity help in the identification and preparation of directorial talent? While recognizing that directors do have distinct requirements (Chapter 4), certain development activities can sometimes be aimed at members of the board and at those identified as potential future members of the board. Examples might be:

- activities to share a vision, goals, values or objectives in order to secure a common board and senior management commitment.
- 'awareness-creating' activities to 'internationalize' attitudes and perspective, or increase understanding of the business environment.[20]

It might be possible for some management development activity to anticipate the requirements of directors, and those of their management colleagues who need to share their perspective. We have seen that directors need to understand the business environment. Such an understanding has also become a priority management requirement[21] that needs to be addressed by corporate development activity.

In many companies, development activities have concentrated on immediate requirements, and only senior managers have been exposed to

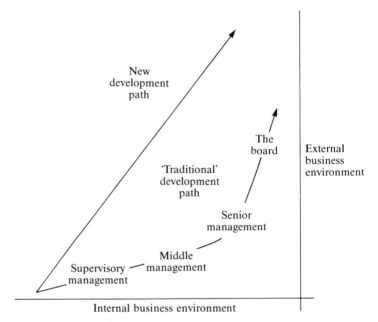

Figure 9.1   Corporate development activity: the internal/external balance

issues concerning the business environment.[5] The focus of supervisory, junior and middle management was thought to be largely 'internal'. However, as we saw in Chapter 4, with the spread of 'quality', and an emphasis upon building relationships with customers, many more managers now need to develop external awareness.

To equip people to understand and satisfy the needs of both internal and external customers, a new development path[5] may be needed – one that pays equal attention to internal and external requirements (Figure 9.1). Director development in such circumstances can be incremental rather than remedial, building upon earlier foundations rather than introducing a dimension that has hitherto not been addressed.

9.6 The changing route to the boardroom

In Chapter 8 we saw that in many companies the 'traditional' route to the boardroom has been via a steady climb through the ranks of corporate bureaucracy. However, as we saw in Chapter 2, in order to respond to a myriad of developments in the business environment, many corporate organizations are undergoing transition to flatter and more flexible forms.[21, 22] This has implications for director development.

In the case of the emerging 'network organization',[23] the route to the boardroom is likely to consist of a movement around the network in order to gain some understanding of its various processes and components (Figure 9.2) rather than a series of steps up, or movement between, functional ladders within a corporate head office.[5]

Within the context of the network organization a different sense of development priorities can emerge. For example:

- If the network is not to fragment, there needs to be a sharing of core vision, goals, values and objectives.[7] More people are likely to be exposed to these earlier in their careers.
- Greater emphasis needs to be placed upon empathy, awareness, tolerance, etc., in order to build and sustain relationships. Director development

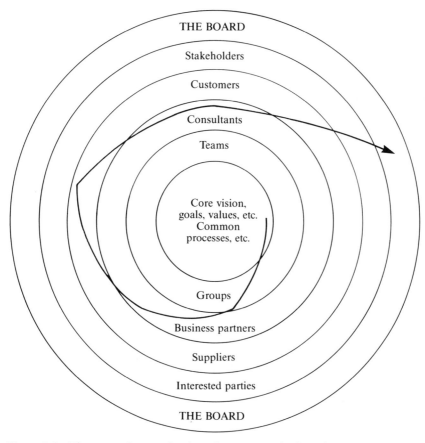

Figure 9.2   The network organization: the route to the boardroom

can focus upon incremental requirements, such as refining such qualities in terms of relationships with particular stakeholders.
- As people move around the network, they may need access to common tools and processes in order to work effectively with all the varied groups they might meet, and to ensure that network activity is focused on those things that generate value for customers.[7]

As executive directors are appointed from those who have moved around the network organization, the development needs of non-executive directors who are 'brought in' from beyond the network should not be overlooked. A survey of non-executive directors has shown that while 'companies rightly want non-executive directors to participate actively in board decision-making, . . . many of them have not been picked or trained to provide the added value of independence. Some have not even been told what is expected of them.'[24]

9.7 Learning methods and preferences

Many directors believe that the best way to learn is by direct face-to-face contact; and that they can often learn more from each other than from the traditional 'teacher' or 'trainer'.[5, 25] They have specific concerns[5]:

- Some directors feel that many of the issues and matters that concern them cannot be 'packaged' in such a way as to be delivered by the printed word, or some other means of audio or visual communication.
- There is also a concern that, given the source and 'management nature' of much distance learning, the material that is made available in this form might not be tailored to the specific needs of directors.

At the same time, they often expect more from a facilitator than an 'understanding of process'. Their preference tends to be for a development adviser; someone who

- is mindful of such matters as the learning process, participation, group dynamics, etc., but at the same time
- understands the distinction between direction and management, has a directorial perspective, and is aware of boardroom issues.

Many consultants and business school authorities, as one interviewee put it, 'learn from their clients rather than vice versa'. Boardroom matters can be relatively sensitive. An international consultancy firm may have the capability to 're-package' and popularize a useful tool or approach that a board has quietly used to secure competitive advantage. A much slower and less harmful 'leakage' of corporate 'know-how' could result from the use of an individual facilitator.

The prime consideration when selecting a source of director development services should be the personal qualities and experience of the person who will actually be working with the boardroom team.

While many directors of major corporations express a preference for 'company specific' programmes, their equivalents in small and medium-sized companies (SME) sometimes take a different view. Participants in an Adaptation Ltd survey for the IOD[3] preferred, by a ratio of two to one, an open course over a course for directors that was tailored to the needs of their own company.

Those interviewed from smaller companies feel that open courses can allow them to compare how issues of concern to them are tackled by other boards. As one owner-director stated: 'I would like to know how the challenges we face are tackled by other boards. I don't want a theoretical answer. I want to know what boards are actually doing about them.'

Encouraging informal learning

We saw earlier in this chapter that many directors express a preference for informal over formal learning. Informal learning can be more effective when it is conscious and actively encouraged.[9] Too often it is accidental and is not acknowledged.

Many directors lack confidence in their ability to learn. Their insecurity may have originated in some unfortunate past experience with formal learning. Active learning from experience can be both relevant and rewarding. It could be encouraged in a number of ways. For example:

- A chairman or a chief executive officer could consciously become a role model by actively learning from experiences, and sharing what has been learned with other directors. Learning should become a way of life.
- The habit of reviewing each day or week what has been learned can make directors aware of insights that can be derived from events and situations that might otherwise be forgotten.
- Directors, and the board itself, could review all significant decisions and discussions in order to assess what has been learned. Such a review could be undertaken in the boardroom prior to moving on to the next agenda item.
- An openness to new ideas and a willingness to learn can be harnessed by means of 'benchmarking' or organized learning from others with similar problems in non-competing companies. All employees could be encouraged to adopt such an approach.
- A review or learning element could be built into certain or all key board

and management processes. At an appropriate stage in each process the question could be inserted: What have we learned?
– Directors could be encouraged to seek new challenges that might force them to re-assess and question. The 'learning trigger' could be a public appointment, or an invitation to join the board of another company as a non-executive director.

The opportunities for informal learning are many and varied. They are not confined to the boardroom, the company, or to the 'working day'. Some of these opportunities are presented in Example 9.1.

The relevance of a 'learning opportunity' can vary from person to person, and according to the 'directorial quality' in question. For example, travel could result in general 'international awareness', but a professional activity might result in a better understanding of a functional aspect of internationalization.[20]

Board and management meetings
Living through major corporate developments
Visits to corporate locations
Travel and external visits
Corporate and social events
Contacts with customers, suppliers and business partners
Professional activities
Recreational activities
The family and friends

Example 9.1 Opportunities for informal learning

Just thinking about opportunities to learn may make some directors aware of the fact that they may have been learning effectively, although unconsciously, by intuition over many years. This can encourage them to become more proactive and disciplined in their approach to informal learning.

A standard approach to informal learning should not be forced upon a board. We do not all learn in the same way.[26] Each director should be encouraged to understand his or her own learning potential and preferences and to adopt a personal approach to informal learning that builds upon natural strengths. Members of a board should identify those opportunities for informal learning that offer the most potential in relation to their current boardroom role and particular responsibilities. They should be encouraged to learn actively from each other, subordinates and customers.

Key questions to consider are whether the board is committed to learning and regularly reviews what it has learned. Is the board itself a learning 'role model'?

A director who ceases to challenge, probe, question and learn can become a liability in the boardroom. The chairman should assess whether each director actively participates in learning activities. Do the directors 'network' and sound out the views and opinions of others prior to, or between, board meetings? Do the directors listen to the views of others during board discussions?

The board itself has a responsibility for the creation of a learning organization.[7, 27] Do the culture and values of the company encourage active learning? Is learning built into key board and management processes? Are there techniques such as 'benchmarking' that could be used to encourage learning throughout the organization?

It should not be assumed that larger and more complex organizations will necessarily provide richer learning opportunities at board level. Sir John Harvey-Jones, a former chairman of ICI, has recounted that, in his experience,

> ... it is surprising how little guidance is available to people who become directors ... you try getting advice, guidance, a course, or a specialist book on the skills of being a good director of a company, and you will find almost nothing except a great deal of mystique. ... Not only is there little external guidance about the changes required of you, but all too often no one inside the company guides you either.[28]

Chief executive learning

Chief executive officers can find it particularly difficult to create informal learning opportunities within their own companies. The following points put by CEOs illustrate the 'problem':

> All I did was ask for an opinion on another company. The next day the building was full of rumours that we were planning to take it over.

> A simple informal discussion led to suggestions that I was flying a kite or 'trying to tell them something'. I just wanted their views.

> He thought I was going behind his back and challenging him. I had no idea the directors were so sensitive until I started wandering about and talking with managers.

At the same time, gathering a wider range of views may yield benefits. The last chief executive quoted went on to say:

> The sensitivity in this case was not without reason. I discovered another option

existed which had not been put to the board. . . . There were inputs we had not tapped. I learned . . . we needed to do more to involve these people.

Sensitive issues are not easy to discuss with colleagues. Chief executives may need to develop their own networks of contacts with people outside their own organizations. For them a 'sounding board', or access to a confidant, can be particularly beneficial. Participating in courses with other chief executives could help establish a network of contacts.

Director networks

Other directors can also benefit from networking. Directors are often reluctant, for a variety of reasons, to discuss certain issues with management colleagues. Contact with fellow directors on external courses can allow discussion of such sensitive matters. Exchanging ideas with other directors from non-competing companies can also allow ideas and points of view to be floated, and arguments tested, ahead of exposing them to one's own board.

Those who are self-aware can arrange to 'network' with individuals that have complementary skills. It helps if those to whom directors turn for insight and perspective are themselves still learning and active in commercial affairs. The former colleague with whom one felt comfortable may soon have views that are out of date when freed from executive responsibilities. Playing a round of golf with 'cronies' may be relaxing, but of little 'networking' value.

To some extent one can judge directors by the company they keep. Some have a penchant for associating with those who have already retired. Others are seeking opportunities to gain fresh insights into new worlds of experience. The latter may be more desirable in a turbulent business environment. The sort of people who might be included in a director's network are illustrated in Figure 9.3.

Many executive directors have access to various sources of professional advice on matters relating to their management responsibilities. Fewer directors acknowledge the need for a 'direction' as opposed to a 'management' input which needs to be accessible on a continuing basis. To involve and contact advisers and other directors effectively, one needs some form of 'directors' network'.

THE 'INTERNAL' NETWORK

The members of a board could form a 'network' themselves to create opportunities for interaction outside the formal structure of meetings in

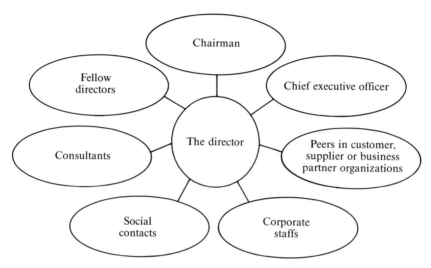

Figure 9.3   The director's network

the boardroom. This can help to break down departmentalism and build a board team.

A directors' network today could take a number of forms. Computer, video and telephone conferencing can allow members of the board 'team' to discuss an issue as a group, although a directors' network will need to be secure given the confidential nature of certain items that may need to be discussed. For the larger company with an international board, advantages include an obvious saving in time and money. Communication with an individual director can be by a variety of means, including telephone, fax and E-mail.

Many organizations are taking advantage of developments in telecommunications to facilitate a transition to more flexible forms of working involving networks of people drawn from different functions and locations who work together on defined tasks.[17, 20] There is less evidence, however, of this same technology being used to change the way boards operate. 'IT and the boardroom' seems largely a question of presenting information for consideration at traditional meetings, rather than using audio or visual conferencing to allow the board to operate in new ways.

There is much to be gained from the non-executive director who remains 'detached'. Being drawn in too closely to a mass of operating issues can blur a critical perspective. A balance may have to be achieved between the need for involvement and contact to build understanding and remain in touch, and the requirement for independence and objectivity.

A sometimes sensitive issue in the case of boards with both executive and non-executive members is how much information to provide to non-executive directors. The principle of supplying or giving access to whatever is necessary to allow individuals to discharge their responsibilities as directors is easier to state than to apply. The robust non-executive director demands access to whatever information is available to the executive directors.

Board meetings need to take place sufficiently often to enable business to be transacted smoothly. For example, the timing of meetings should relate to the need for decisions concerning the annual report and accounts and the annual general meeting. At other times in the year, the cycle of meetings will depend upon matters to be discussed.

Additional board meetings can always be called in 'crisis' situations, such as the occasion of a possible takeover. Some flexibility might be built into the timing of meetings by supplementing them with document circulation via a directors' network.

9.8 Summary

We have seen in this chapter that there is little evidence of systematic and thorough preparation for the role of company director. If it occurs at all, preparation appears to be 'informal' and unstructured in the sense that individuals 'pick things up' and learn from each other in the course of their various activities. There are many obstacles to director development, including the scepticism and caution of directors themselves.

Many of the director development services that are available do not meet the needs of individual directors or the requirements of particular boards. However, informal learning, and learning in the context of the boardroom, can be particularly effective.

The drive for director development is not strong, and many directors and boards are uncertain how to proceed. In order to move ahead they may need a better understanding of 'where they are'.

A director development programme should reflect the needs and preferences of individual directors, the 'routes' to the boardroom, and the requirements of both the board as a whole and of 'the business'. Whether development activity should be formal, informal, individual, or undertaken by the board as a team, will depend upon the nature of the knowledge or skill deficiency. However, the potential of informal learning, and the value of directors' networks, should not be overlooked.

9.9 Checklist

1. How are the directors of your company prepared for membership of the board?
2. Is this preparation adequate, or how might it be improved?
3. How committed are the individuals concerned to formal and informal preparation for the role of company director?
4. Is director development really a priority of the board?
5. What are the likely implementation barriers that lie between development need and development action?
6. By what means do the members of the board of your company remain current and up-to-date?
7. To whom does your company turn for professional advice concerning preparation for the board?
8. Does any training that is provided reflect the distinction between direction and management, the particular requirements of the board, and the individual needs of its members?
9. If you could 'start again', what formal and/or informal preparation (if any) would you undertake?
10. Does your company take account of the learning preferences, potential and requirements of each individual director when setting development objectives?
11. Do these relate to and reflect the needs of the board as a whole?
12. Do the chairman and the chief executive act as role models in respect of their commitment to ongoing learning and development?
13. Does the board of your company actively take steps to learn from its own experience and activities?
14. Have the main barriers to formal and informal learning been identified, and how might they be overcome?
15. Does the board of your company review its own performance and establish development objectives for itself and its individual members?
16. How does your company ensure that training and development at board level take account of the directorial as opposed to managerial needs of those concerned?

Notes and references

1. Coulson-Thomas, C., *Developing Directors: Building an effective boardroom team*, McGraw-Hill, 1993.
2. Harper, J., *Developing Competent Directors*. Paper presented at Institute of Personnel Management Annual Conference, Harrogate, 1991.
3. Coulson-Thomas, C., *Professional Development of and for the Board*. A questionnaire and interview survey undertaken by Adaptation Ltd of company chairmen. A summary has been published by the IOD, February 1990.

4. Coulson-Thomas, C., *The Role and Function of the Personnel Director*. An interim Adaptation Ltd survey carried out in conjunction with the Research Group of the Institute of Personnel Management, 1991.
5. Coulson-Thomas, C. and Wakelam, A., *The Effective Board: Current practice, myths and realities*. An IOD discussion document, 1991.
6. Wakelam, A., *The Training & Development of Company Directors*. A report on a questionnaire survey undertaken by the Centre for Management Studies, University of Exeter for the Training Agency, December 1989.
7. Coulson-Thomas, C., *Transforming the Company: Bridging the gap between management myth and corporate reality*, Kogan Page, 1992.
8. Tushman, M., Newman, W. and Nadler, D., 'Executive leadership and organisational evolution, managing incremental and discontinuous change', in R. Kilmann and T. J. Covey (eds), *Corporate Transformation*, Jossey-Bass, 1988, pp. 102–30.
9. Mumford, A., Robinson, G. and Stradling, D., *Developing Directors, The Learning Process*, Manpower Services Commission, 1987; and Mumford, A., Honey, P. and Robinson, G., *Director's Development Guidebook: Making experience count*, Director Publications, 1990.
10. Batchelor, C., 'The boardroom beckons', *Financial Times*, 3 March 1992; and *Boardroom Agenda*, (2), May 1992, 16 and 17.
11. Chandler, A., *Strategy and Structure: Chapters in the history of American industrial enterprise*, MIT Press, 1962.
12. Bennis, W. and Nanus, B., *Leaders*, Harper & Row, 1985.
13. Davies, A., *Strategic Leadership*, Woodhead-Faulkner, 1991.
14. Beer, M. and Walton, E., 'Developing the competitive organization, interventions and strategies', *American Psychologist*, **45** (2), February 1990, 154–61.
15. Cadbury, Sir A., *Company Chairman*, Director Books, 1990.
16. Coulson-Thomas, C., *Human Resource Development for International Operation*. A survey sponsored by Surrey European Management School, Adaptation Ltd, 1990.
17. O'Brien, D., *Quality of Management or Management of Quality*. Presentation to IRR Conference on Total Quality Management in Financial Services, 15 October 1991.
18. Copeman, G., *The Managing Director*, 2nd edn, Business Books, 1982.
19. Lawrence, P. R. and Lorsch, J. W., *Organisation and Environment*, Irwin, 1967.
20. Coulson-Thomas, C., *Creating the Global Company: Successful internationalization*, McGraw-Hill, 1992.
21. Coulson-Thomas, C. and Coe, T., *The Flat Organisation: Philosophy and practice*, BIM, 1991.
22. Burns, T. and Stalker, G. M., *The Management of Innovation*, Tavistock, 1961; and Lawrence, P. R. and Dyer, D., *Renewing American Industry*, The Free Press, 1983.
23. Coulson-Thomas, C. and Brown, R., *The Responsive Organisation*, BIM, 1989; and *Beyond Quality: Managing the relationship with the customer*, BIM, 1990.
24. Redwood, J., MP, *Corporate Governance*, DTI Press Notice P/91/172, 27 March 1991, speaking at launch of a survey report, *Non-Executives in the Boardroom*, PA Consulting Group and Sundridge Park Management Centre, 1991.
25. Coulson-Thomas, C., *Development Needs of NHS Authority and Board Members*. A report prepared by Adaptation Ltd on behalf of the NHS Training Directorate, 1992.

26. Coulson-Thomas, C., 'Building Europe's learning foundations, the European learning network', *IT in Europe Journal*, February 1990, 14–19; and 'Breaking through the information barrier: Management development and IT', *International Journal of Computer Applications in Technology*, **3** (4), 1990, 269–71.
27. Garratt, R., *Creating a Learning Organisation: A guide to leadership, learning and development*, Director Books, 1990.
28. Harvey-Jones, Sir J., in *Making it Happen: Reflections on leadership*, Fontana Paperbacks, March 1989, pp. 185 and 186.

10
Building the boardroom team

The directors determine whether or not a company survives and thrives. The extent to which the board liberates or constrains the energies and talents of the people of a company is determined by the competence of the directors, and how effectively they work together as a team. (PETER MORGAN, director general, Institute of Directors.)

Of course boards should operate as a team but not to the degree that team building suppresses the opportunity to challenge and say the unthinkable. (DAVID THOMPSON, chairman, Rank Xerox (UK) Ltd.)

Developing individual directors is only one means of creating excellence in the boardroom. In this chapter we turn our attention to the development of the board as a team, and, in particular, to activities that are undertaken by the directors as a group.

10.1 Barriers to board performance

We have seen in earlier chapters of this book that there are many types of board. Each will consist of a particular combination of people, and may face specific demands and pressures from stakeholders, while the situation and circumstances of the company may be distinct from those faced by any other board.

There are also many barriers to board effectiveness. Some of these barriers, in the area of director contribution alone, are listed in Example 10.1. For those concerned with director development, there is an almost endless number of combinations of personalities and problems to address. Hence, it is important that development activities meet the needs of each board and its members.

No influence on agenda
Infrequent meetings
Discussion discouraged by 'strong' chairman
Use of board as a rubber stamp
Little opportunity to question or record minority views
Inadequate information
Little time to read board papers
Poor attendance or little continuity in attendance
Powerful external constraints, e.g. holding company board or major shareholder
Little or no say in new appointments to the board
Powerful or manipulative chief executive
Office of chairman and chief executive combined
Lack of non-executive director involvement
Incompatible interests or accountabilities
Lack of common vision, goals and values
Conflicts of personalities
Limited contact with staff or auditors
Inadequate access to specialist advice
Lack of processes and tools
Short-term focus
Lack of mutual trust and understanding between executive and non-executive directors

Example 10.1 Barriers to director contribution

Given the lack of preparation for the boardroom (Chapter 9), the effectiveness of a board should not be assumed. According to one interviewee: 'Good people sitting around the boardroom table are just that. They won't necessarily form an effective team unless appropriate steps are taken.' One study has suggested that 50 per cent of chairmen and chief executives are dissatisfied with the performance of their 'top teams'.[1] If the performance of a board is to be improved, it may need 'to be seen as it is'.

More effort needs to be devoted to understanding how boards actually operate in practice as opposed to how it is assumed they operate or should operate. We have seen already that myths abound, and that these may hold the key to what needs to be done to enhance board effectiveness. For example:

– Directors focus upon the 'external' business environment rather than the 'internal' requirements of a company (Chapter 4). Is there an 'arena of conflict' arising out of the conflicting focus and horizons of directors and managers?

– 'Direction' and 'leadership' are synonymous; or board membership is largely a matter of outstanding professionalism (Chapters 4 and 8). It is vital that the distinction between direction and management in the context of the contemporary company is understood.

– All boards are of a similar size and composition (Chapter 5). Is the size and composition of the board appropriate to the nature, situation and circumstances of the company?

Although not all myths are shared by all directors, some may be present to some degree in most boardrooms.[2] A high degree of rationalization often occurs, and some boards become more concerned with the observance of ritual than with the confrontation of reality.[3]

10.2 Improving board performance

We saw in Chapter 8 that when directors are selected little importance appears to be attached to technical or specialist skills. Knowledge *per se* was regarded as much less important than attitude and perspective. Similarly, improving board performance is generally a matter of changing attitudes, awareness, approaches, perspective and behaviour within the context of a group. There are many activities that can be undertaken to improve the effectiveness of the board as a team. These include:

1. Involvement in establishing the basic boardroom agenda. This tends to be set by the CEO in consultation with the company secretary and is submitted to the chairman for approval, but all directors could be invited to review the core agenda and suggest items for inclusion.
2. Effective chairmanship of board meetings. A good chairman should ensure that all directors are given an opportunity to make relevant contributions.
3. 'Grasping nettles' in terms of being more open about, and tackling, the factors that inhibit board performance. Some of the 'inhibitors' may be hidden. These should be flushed out, and personal concerns shared with the group.
4. Changing the membership of the board, or altering the frequency of meetings. If effectiveness is really to improve, there may have to be some inconvenience and casualties.
5. Directors could be broadened and the barriers of specialism broken down by giving them a cross-functional process or some business unit

responsibilities, initially in addition to, and eventually in place of, departmental or functional roles. Each director could in effect become a general manager of a portfolio of distinct businesses.

6. It is particularly important that a balance is maintained between the various roles of the board and the qualities of its individual members.[4] As the roles change and new ones emerge, the membership of the board may need to be reviewed.

7. Changing the conduct of business during the course of board meetings, or the information supplied to directors ahead of board meetings. Information *per se* may not lead to better understanding. Many directors receive too much and poorly presented information.

8. 'Motivated teamwork training' through which members of the board learn more about each other as a result of being engaged in some other activity such as agreeing a vision or strategy, or acquiring communication skills.

9. Encouraging directors to join development groups or 'networks' with other directors from the boards of non-competing companies that have certain development needs in common. Benchmarking could be brought into the boardroom.

10. Locating board meetings where there are opportunities to broaden perspectives – for example, in a prime overseas market. An international company could rotate meetings between Europe, the US and Japan.

11. The use of periodic and residential strategy reviews, or roles and responsibilities exercises. There are many approaches and tools that have been specifically designed to support boardroom activities.

12. Self-assessment. Annual reviews could be undertaken of board accountabilities, performance and effectiveness, linked with agreed individual and group activities to remedy deficiencies.

13. External assessment. The independent assessment of board effectiveness can ensure that a comprehensive review is undertaken. A 'peer review' could be undertaken by the chairman of, or a team from, the board of a non-competing company.

14. The use of business games or outward bound activities to pose a challenge to the board as a team. Enthusiasts of such approaches at management level should think through their applicability to certain boards.

15. The employment of specialist facilitators to work with the board in examining and meeting its development needs. The extent to which sensitive matters can be addressed will depend upon the degree of trust that is established.

16. The boardroom itself can become a forum for learning, and the

'action learning' approach can be adopted in the boardroom.[5] Some aspects of informal learning were considered in Chapter 9.

Many of the options that are available are not mutually exclusive. They can be used in various combinations to meet the circumstances of an individual board. It may be important to have a balanced overview of development requirements if the key deficiencies are to be given priority consideration.

As with corporate transformation, undertaking individual initiatives may not of itself lead to significant improvements in performance until certain major barriers or inhibitors are addressed.[3] Progress may only be made when all the pieces are in place. For this to occur, the full and sustained commitment of the board may be needed.

The board should examine the main barriers, obstacles or inhibitors of improved board performance, and prioritize them according to the nature of the board, and the situation and circumstances of the company. It should then consider which deficiencies should be addressed by individual development activity, and which by activities involving the board as a team.

10.3 Unity and the unitary board

In the case of the unitary board, particular attention may need to be paid to the relationships between executive and non-executive directors, and to ensuring that each understands the other's roles.[6, 7] An executive director who has just joined a board may have extensive knowledge of one or more functions within the company, while lacking board experience. In comparison, the non-executive direction may have extensive boardroom experience, while lacking knowledge of the particular company and its capabilities and activities (Figure 10.1).

In many companies and public sector bodies there is an urgent need to reduce a degree of mutual suspicion between executive and non-executive board members. Their respective roles and responsibilities may need to be clarified. Non-executive directors should not become so involved in the detail of operational matters that they lose their sense of independence, detachment and objectivity.

Peter Morgan of the IOD has warned that a strengthening of the independent role of the non-executive director in the interests of 'good corporate governance' should not be allowed to result in two distinct groups within the boardroom – 'the doers and the checkers'.[8] Such an outcome could undermine the principle of a unitary board.

EXPERIENCE OF COMPANY

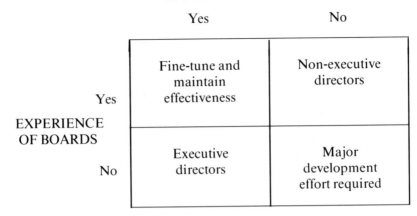

Figure 10.1 The 'executive' and 'non-executive' dimensions

10.4 The role of the chairman

Reference has already been made in earlier chapters to the special role of the chairman in improving board effectiveness. The chairman, particularly when the role of chairman is separated from that of chief executive officer, is in a privileged position to assess and reflect upon (a) the composition and operation of the board and (b) the contributions and interactions of its individual members.

A number of experienced chairmen who were interviewed acknowledged that they have put too little emphasis upon this aspect of their role. Consider the following selection of comments:

> What would I do differently if I could start all over again? . . . I would have been tougher on the board. In some cases I should have said 'goodbye' much earlier.

> I used to be so obsessed with getting through the business. Much was of a routine nature in any case. If I had put more effort into getting the board to operate right, that would have been a legacy, something I would have left behind.

> For the Managing Director the board was just another meeting. They were his people and he was driving for results. If I didn't think about the board, no-one else would have done. They all had other priorities.

> What intrigues me is that we never did customer satisfaction surveys or the like. We did not know what customers wanted, let alone what activities were relevant. We really had no way of knowing whether what we did added value or not.

> Looking back we took so much for granted. It was our board. There was so much that we could have done, but we didn't. We operated as the board always had done.

A common theme of these comments is the recognition that more could have been done. Activities to ensure the effective performance of the board need to be integrated into the ongoing work of the board. Directors need to understand that one of the most significant contributions they can make to a company is to ensure that they work together effectively as a team.

The effectiveness of a board should be reviewed at least once a year. It should not be taken for granted, even when a board has been through a development process to improve its effectiveness. Circumstances change:

- Externally, new challenges and opportunities may arise in the business environment that subject the board to pressures that are different from those that have been experienced before.
- The world of the boardroom is a dynamic one. Internally, a board may 'drift back to old ways', divisions may arise over particular issues, or a chairman may lose his or her 'touch'.
- The composition of the board may change as a result of retirement or illness. New directors may have been appointed to the board who have not been through the team-building experiences of colleagues.

The chairman should consider how open the board is at identifying its deficiencies. What are the sources or 'root causes' of the problems? Are there particular myths, shared by certain members of the board, that need to be confronted? How committed is the board to appropriate action? To what extent do the chairman and the chief executive officer act as role models? A secure chairman (and a confident chief executive) will invite comment and feedback upon his or her own performance.

10.5 Teamwork in the boardroom

So where should we begin? An obvious consideration is how the directors, however competent they may be as individuals, work together as a team. Do they share a vision, goals, values and objectives? Do they recognize, respect and complement each other's qualities and contributions?

In a survey of 218 directors, over three-quarters of whom were chairmen or chairmen and chief executive officers of their companies, 'teamwork' emerged as the number one boardroom issue.[9] Those interviewed during the course of the survey tended to portray their boards as a 'collection of individuals' rather than a team. Individual director development may need to be complemented by some form of team-building activity if executive members of the board are not to focus excessively upon their own viewpoints and departmental concerns.[10]

For those who favour the integration of working and learning, the board itself can constitute an action learning set.[5, 11]

Many boards comprise individuals with strong ambitions and 'hidden agendas'. Boardroom colleagues may be perceived as rivals, obstacles to future career moves. There may be those who harbour resentments, or who are aggrieved 'from the past'. There are chairmen who encourage rivalry, and who seek to 'divide and rule' or play strong personalities off against each other. These realities of boardroom life and politics need to be understood.

Opportunities for teamwork

Opportunities for the directors to work together as a team arise naturally from the responsibilities of the board. Many of the board's most vital tasks are best done by the board operating as a team. Examples include:

- stakeholder or accountability reviews
- preparation for the annual general meeting
- sharing responsibilities for presentations at an internal 'year start meeting'
- issue monitoring and management discussions
- determination of a corporate vision or core purpose
- agreement of the main threats and opportunities in the business environment
- assessment of corporate strengths and weaknesses
- determination of what is distinctive or different about the company
- review of accountabilities, roles and responsibilities
- agreement of a corporate mission, goals, values and objectives
- formulation of indicators of mission achievement or success criteria
- identification of 'helps and hinders' and likely barriers to implementation
- prioritization of key or 'vital few' actions
- identification and review of management and business processes, especially those that cross departmental or functional boundaries
- establishment of the board's own information, process and support requirements
- review of the board's effectiveness, and the extent to which it 'adds value'.

An examination of these selected opportunities for teamwork (a) reveals the extent to which the performance and contribution of a board can be compromised by a failure of the directors to work effectively as a group, and (b) illustrates the dangers of directors focusing excessively upon their departmental responsibilities at the expense of group tasks.

The consequences of some group reviews in the boardroom may be far-reaching for both the company as a whole and for individual departments. It is essential that sufficient time and commitment is devoted to them.

Group tasks

In many companies there may be little need to contrive discussion sessions at the level of the board. Certain necessary tasks of the board can themselves represent useful development opportunities that may extend across a number of meetings. For example, a sequence of sessions could be organized for the board to initiate or review the following:

THE DETERMINATION OF VISION AND MISSION

This provides an opportunity for the board to pose and discuss some fundamental questions concerning the purpose of the company.[12] For example:

- What is special or distinctive about the company?
- Why should it continue to exist, and what would the world lose if it ceased to exist?
- Who is the customer, and why should any customer be interested in the company?
- What value does, or could, the company add for customers?
- Why should anyone want to work with, or for, the company?

THE ESTABLISHMENT OF GOALS AND OBJECTIVES

This creates opportunities for the board to consider:

- the extent to which goals and objectives relate to a vision or mission;
- how they relate to the interests and perceptions of stakeholders in the company;
- whether, and how, they are to be measured;
- the achievement of a balance between motivation and the desire to stretch, and realistic attainment;
- the extent to which multiple goals, if set, are consistent;
- the match of simplicity and relevance when establishing quantitative objectives.

FORMULATING A STRATEGY FOR THE ACHIEVEMENT OF BUSINESS GOALS AND OBJECTIVES

This requires:

- an understanding of what represents value to customers;
- an awareness of actual and potential competition;
- prioritization, segmentation and focus;
- the identification of opportunities for sustained competitive advantage and differentiation;
- commitment to quality, and the building of closer relationships with customers.

ESTABLISHING A FORM OF ORGANIZATION, AND ALLOCATING ROLES AND RESPONSIBILITIES

This involves:

- determining and negotiating who is responsible to whom for what;
- identifying gaps and overlaps in roles and responsibilities;
- considering whether certain directors should assume responsibility for particular cross-functional processes.

DETERMINING THE CORE VALUES AND BUSINESS PHILOSOPHY OF THE COMPANY

This involves:

- agreeing, communicating and sharing values;
- establishing the corporate culture, and commitment to customers and employees;
- articulating a philosophy of management that embraces the values of the company;
- relating the role of the individual to that of the team;
- ensuring that members of the board, and the board itself, act as role models in terms of morality and conduct.

ESTABLISHING FACILITATING PROCESSES AND SUPPORTING TECHNOLOGY

Areas to consider include:

- a process for handling the business of the board;
- management processes, with supporting subprocesses and technology;
- business processes, with supporting subprocesses and technology;
- an audit of the creation, flow and use of documents throughout the organization;

– ensuring that the key processes are in place that add value for customers, and that all processes are documented and their purposes are understood.

AREAS OF RESPONSIBILITY

Many management processes that 'begin and end' in the boardroom may involve the active participation of managers in various parts of the corporate organization. From time to time it may be necessary to clarify where the responsibilities of the board end, and where those of managers begin. The board should consider whether it is an assembly of individuals or a team. How secure or insecure are members of the board? How loyal or disloyal are the members of the board towards each other? Do those who attend board meetings respect confidentiality, or does the board 'leak like a sieve'?

10.6 Analysing director and board requirements

The analysis of director and board requirements could be undertaken by means of a process along the lines of the people strategy process (see Figure 2.3) which we examined in Chapter 2. Such a process is illustrated in Figure 10.2. This should not necessarily be viewed as a 'model', although variations of it have been used by certain boards.

The director and board requirements process of Figure 10.2 could be undertaken in stages, or during the course of a board 'away day'. Progression to the next step in the process should only occur when there is agreement and shared understanding at each of the preceding stages:

1. Firstly, the purpose of the company and its board needs to be determined. The process begins with the agreement of vision, goals, values and objectives in the context of a shared understanding of the nature of the business and market environment. The 'visioning' part of the process should not be rushed. It should be possible to measure the extent to which objectives are achieved.
2. A roles and responsibilities exercise should be undertaken to determine what needs to be done and by whom. Outputs should be defined in customer and stakeholder terms.
3. Having established and agreed what needs to be done, skill and process requirements need next to be determined. These should be such as to harness the potential of individual directors and enhance the capability of the board as a team.
4. At this stage in the review process skill and process deficiencies may

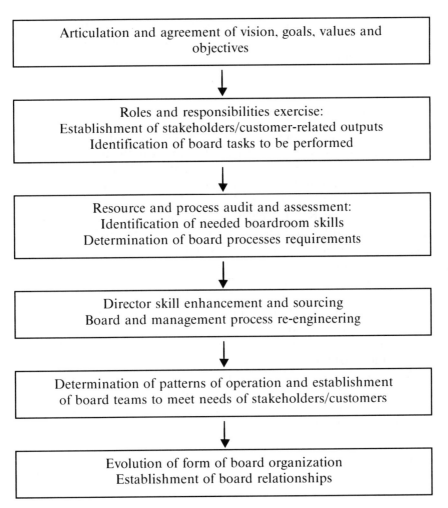

Figure 10.2   Director and board requirements analysis

emerge. Both will need to be addressed. A board will not be effective, in spite of the evident qualities of its individual members, if the processes are not in place that allow it to ensure that the company's resources and capability are focused upon the requirements of customers and stakeholders. Additional skills may need to be brought into the boardroom, and certain key processes may need to be re-engineered.

5. A pattern of board operation, organization and relationships with stakeholders will emerge from the analysis.

6. Many boards are overly constrained by a traditional form of operation

and organization. These should not represent a starting point or straitjacket, but should be seen as a consequence of what needs to be done to achieve corporate goals, values and objectives and turn the vision of the company into a reality.

Teamwork in the boardroom

We have seen that teamwork should not be assumed. Given both the importance of, and opportunities for, teamwork in the boardroom, what is being done to ensure that directors work effectively as a team? The 'top ten' ways of ensuring teamwork in the boardroom for participants in a survey of board chairmen[13] are shown in Figure 10.3.

Teamwork appears to be achieved by 'process' rather than by 'structure'. Effective teamwork is regarded as an issue independent of board structure. Getting the structure 'right' can be helpful, but may not of itself lead to effective teamwork in the boardroom.

In general, it is thought that the members of a board should share understanding and agree significant developments, and that such agreement should follow full and frank discussion. One in five respondents stress the need for good communications. Follow-up interviews suggest that in many companies there is limited cross-functional communication inside and outside the boardroom.

A degree of trust and a willingness to be open in dealing with others facilitates teamwork in the boardroom. An atmosphere of openness and trust in the boardroom does not 'just happen'. It may result from a process of building upon helpful trends, and a willingness to deal with particular barriers:

- Working together over a period of time can build collective empathy and shared experience and understanding. Adversity can help to 'bind' a board.
- Values that are 'lived' as well as articulated tend to be reinforced. A board can get into a 'virtuous circle' or an 'ascending spiral' in terms of the more positive attitudes of its members.
- On the other hand, the 'chairman' survey[13] suggests that those who do not 'fit in' are unwelcome in the boardroom. Certain directors may be less willing than others to make the required commitment to working as a team. A bad apple may need to be removed from the barrel.

Formal training is not ranked highly as a means of ensuring effective teamwork in the boardroom. One chairman who was interviewed explained:

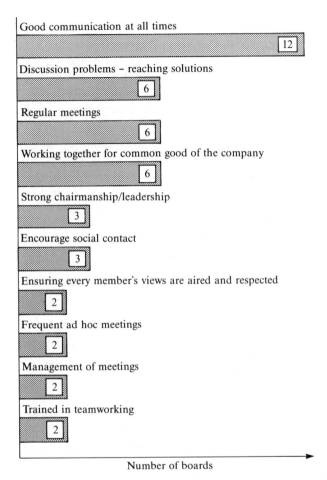

Figure 10.3   The 'top ten' ways of ensuring teamwork in the boardroom

Training tends to be associated with skills, when teamwork in the boardroom is all about attitudes, expectations, climate, trust, empathy ... all things that are difficult to 'teach'. The board needs to confront and challenge its own attitudes. The onus is upon the chairman to ensure that the directors feel they are part of a team.

Team development activities designed for managers may not be applicable in the boardroom. Teamworking in a situation of collective responsibility in the boardroom requires skills that are different from those required when working in a management group on an assigned task, either as a subordinate or a project leader.

The role of the chairman and balancing interests

Those interviewed in the course of the 'chairman' survey[13] considered the chairman to be the most appropriate person to monitor and evaluate how effectively the board works together as a team. This view has been expressed earlier in this chapter, as well as earlier in the book.

The IOD has been a consistent advocate of the importance of the chairman:

> In practice, a board of directors will only function effectively if it is given a sense of purpose and direction by its chairman. . . . The way that a chairman leads and manages the board, organises its work and sets its priorities will be a major factor in the board's relative success. . . . The choice, development and counselling of the other members of the board is one of the chairman's tasks. How the board comes together as a team will depend very largely on his skill and leadership.[14]

Chairmanship is an art, and a question of balance[15]:

- The management of boardroom business and discussion has to steer a course between: (a) the need for a collective view to emerge, and (b) ensuring that all members, should they desire it, have an opportunity to put a particular point of view.
- Closing a debate when all are not convinced, in order to 'progress the business', may be shortsighted if subsequent implementation is delayed as a result of a lack of motivation or commitment.

Chairmen tend to allow a reasonable time for debate, but often draw the line at allowing all those who would like to contribute to do so. In the 'chairman' survey,[13] almost 80 per cent of respondents referred to the need for a collective view ('working together', 'removing non-team players', 'avoiding unnecessary friction' and 'pre-empting adversary issues') against 20 per cent who identified the need for each board member's views to be 'aired and respected'.

If an effective boardroom team is to be created, the chairman will need the support of other directors. John Adair has suggested a 50/50 principle, with 50 per cent of the success in creating a successful team being due to the leader and the other 50 per cent resulting from the efforts and contribution of the team itself.[16]

Membership of a board *per se* can create the potential for conflict between individual and group interests:

- The remuneration and promotion prospects of many directors depend upon their departmental performance, even though it may be possible to pursue departmental initiatives and objectives at the expense of the company as a whole.

– A new 'fresh blood' director may have been brought onto the board to 'stir things up', and with a brief from the chairman to 'challenge' and encourage debate. Pursued to extreme, such an approach may shatter a 'positive' consensus that has taken some time to achieve.

A board needs to work together effectively as a team to achieve common objectives rather than the aims of its individual members. At the same time, the risk of complacency or the danger of a comfortable group of people who are unwilling to challenge each other should be avoided.[6, 13]

A director is unlikely to get his or her preferences accepted at every board meeting. The subsequent attitude and response of those who disagree with a decision of the board will reflect the nature of the matter in question, how the decision was arrived at, and the weight attached to the judgement and experience of those who put contrary views. Following 'full and frank' discussion there needs to be some respect for a collective decision.

How best to improve teamwork in a particular boardroom will depend upon such factors as the nature, size and composition of the board. Many boards are composed of a relatively small number of people. Four out of ten of the boards covered by the 'chairman' survey[13] had five or fewer members. A team-building programme might involve relatively few people who meet infrequently, particularly in the case of non-executive directors.

A larger number of directors may not of itself make it more difficult for the board to operate effectively as a team. Only one respondent to the 'chairman' survey[13] referred to the size of a board ('keeping the team small') as a factor contributing to effective teamwork in the boardroom.

Communication skills

A board and its members may need to sustain relationships with a number of stakeholders, and arbitrate between their competing interests:

> the modern company is not a machine to be run or driven by its board but rather it is a complex organism, a network of interests co-operating in some areas and conflicting in others. One of the jobs of the board is to arbitrate between the various interests in the company, the publics with whom [it] is or ought to be communicating, and to allocate scarce values and resources. In essence this is a political activity. Its critical component is communication.[17]

A lack of communication skills has been identified as the main barrier to both internal and external communication.[18] Interpersonal skills and communication within a group can be an important determinant of team effectiveness. The communication skills that need to be addressed are those concerning attitudes, approach, perspective and behaviour.[18] These are often most apparent and best dealt with in a team context.

The BIM report *The Responsive Organisation*[19] suggests that more 'work will be undertaken in teams with clear accountabilities and a focus upon delivering what constitutes value in the eyes of the customer', and that 'teamwork and communication skills will be highly prized'. The report, based upon a survey of 100 organizations employing some three million people, makes the point that 'effective team working cannot be assumed. It needs to be consciously developed. The board itself should review how effectively it is working as a team.'

Against this background, chairmen are seeking improved communication and team-working skills within the boardroom.[9] Executive directors with specific responsibilities for finance, marketing and personnel need to be able to communicate and build relationships with investors, customers and the people of the network organization, respectively.[17]

As more boards (a) define corporate objective and priority tasks in the form of measurable outputs and (b) undertake role and responsibility exercises to allocate tasks to particular directors, greater numbers of executive directors are likely to require project management skills. The 'vital few' actions to achieve corporate objectives need to happen, and when inputs are required from a number of divisions or business units, individual directors may be made accountable for the 'delivery' of certain project teams.

According to a survey undertaken by Adaptation Ltd for the Association of Project Managers (APM),[20] communication skills are one of the 'top two' competences in project management when these are ranked in order of 'very important' replies. The other key competence, 'understanding the anatomy of a project', or seeing the project as a whole, is one the 'good' director should have. When APM respondents were asked to specify the 'qualities' they considered were most desirable in project managers, communications skills emerged as top of the list in terms of 'very important' replies.

COMMUNICATIONS STRATEGY

The board as a whole needs an overview understanding of the communication process and how it relates to other elements that need to be in place if a company is to operate effectively and renew itself.[3] Examples of matters with which the board is concerned that impact upon the communication process are shown in Figure 10.4.

Too often boards authorize or initiate communications activity without first thinking through why they are communicating, and what is being communicated to whom.[21] Communications activity consumes resources, and the time of board members can be particularly valuable. A board

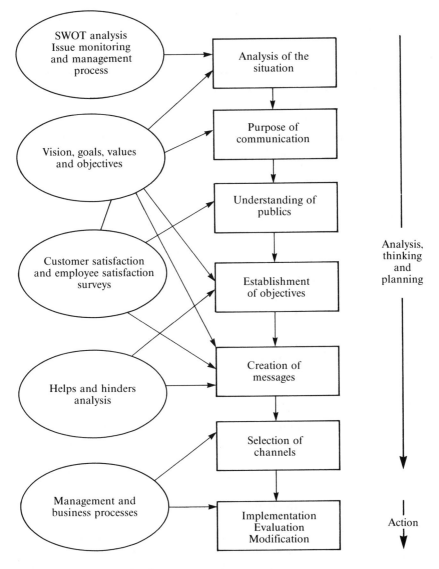

Figure 10.4 Communication process

should always consider a number of factors before 'rushing into action', for example:

– What is the nature of the situation? Why does the communication need to occur? What is the problem? (Has the root cause been identified?)
– Have appropriate objectives been set? What are we trying to achieve? (Does what is sought relate to corporate goals, values and objectives?)
– Who are the audiences or 'publics' to be addressed? To whom do we need to communicate? (Have these been defined, subdivided, prioritized, etc., with sufficient vigour?)
– Do the messages relate to the objectives that have been set, and the interests of the audience? Are the messages clear, concise, appropriate to the audience, etc.?
– What are the most effective channels for putting the message to the priority audiences? Are we going direct to the people we really want to reach? (Is enough priority being given to the key channels?)
– Have we formulated a practical and focused programme of communication activities? Are we doing too much, being too general, etc.?
– What is the objective assessment of the results? What has really been achieved (i.e. in terms of initial objectives)?
– Has the company, or those concerned, learned from experience? How should the programme (e.g. message, channels, etc.) be modified in order to better achieve the company's communication objectives?

Motivated teamwork training

In many companies traditional 'effective teamwork' development activity does not extend to the boardroom and senior management team. Where it does, its relevance and purpose may not be perceived unless 'team skills' are related to a particular issue.[10] In other companies little effort is made to assess the effectiveness of team-building exercises, even when they occur at senior management levels.

Bringing a work group together to discuss a problem area can be very conducive to team building.[22] Some directors who are reluctant to undertake specific teamwork training may be receptive to other activities that focus upon deficiencies they are more willing to recognize, while incidentally developing a group awareness. As an example, consider the role of the board in agreeing, communicating and sharing a compelling vision and mission:

– As responsibilities are delegated, and more work is done by multifunctional and multi-location teams, it is important that all the members of an organization share a distinctive vision and mission. The common

vision can be the cement that holds the network organization together (Figure 2.2).
- According to the BIM survey-based report *Beyond Quality*,[23] the mission or purpose of an organization can also be a key source of differentiation. Members of the board may need to devote considerable effort to articulating or propounding a distinct vision or mission.
- If a vision is to be shared it must be communicated. Many directors are having to assume the role of external spokesperson. The media is devoting more coverage to business issues, and as a consequence larger numbers of directors are being interviewed. They need to be equipped to operate in what, for many, may be an unfamiliar arena.

10.7 Vision and mission

A priority for the board as a team (see Chapter 3) should be the determination of a 'purpose' for the company, and the articulation and communication of a distinctive vision. We saw in Chapter 6 that a recent Adaptation Ltd survey *Communicating for Change*[18] suggests that a 'clear vision and mission' is the first requirement for management of change.

The importance of vision and mission has also been emphasized by other surveys. For example, a BIM survey-based report[24] has found that in the creation of a new philosophy for managing the flat organization 'every respondent assessing it believes clear vision and mission to be important'. About three-quarters of them consider it 'very important'.

According to Peter Drucker: 'Only a clear definition of the mission and purpose of the organisation makes possible clear and realistic business objectives.'[25]

A vision should be a shared view of an attractive and achievable future:

- The vision should inform stakeholders and other interested parties of where the company would like to be.
- It should be distinctive and sufficiently compelling to attract the interest of customers and of those whose active cooperation will be needed to bring it about.

Customers, employees, suppliers and business partners all have a greater choice of whom to form relationships with than any generation in history. Even those on the other side of the world are accessible within seconds by telephone, fax and electronic mail. For people to work together they need to feel that they have a certain empathy and that they believe in common aims.

The vision is neither a mission nor an objective. For example:

- A vision tends to be broader than a mission statement, which can be relatively precise. There is a danger that a mission statement can become over-detailed and bland. It may close off options that the right vision could open up.
- A vision cannot always be measured like an objective. Its purpose may be to influence thoughts, feelings and values, and it may be qualitative rather than quantitative. A vision is not a dead document. It lives and grows. It spreads.
- The vision is not a detailed plan, but it should act as a guide to action. It should enable someone, as one chief executive officer put it, to 'jump out of bed in the morning and know what to do'.

Establishing a clear and compelling vision

Few boards approach the task of establishing a clear and compelling vision with a clean slate. Most companies already have an image in the marketplace – an existing 'corporate personality' that may be firmly entrenched in the minds of those with whom the company deals.

Many companies formulate and communicate a vision or mission without first understanding where they are in terms of their existing image, or thinking through the image they would like to create. It may not be possible to bridge too big a gap between a current and desired image. The experience of one chief executive officer illustrates the dilemma:

> We have tried and tried, and we have spent millions, but we cannot shift the image. We have the capability to deliver, but everyone out there sees us as something else. They have been dealing with us for years. They have made up their minds. They have labelled us, and we can't persuade them we are something else.

Some boards find it is helpful to think in terms of 'corporate personality', perhaps using a checklist along the lines of Figure 10.5 to assess a current personality and profile the personality the company would like to have. The subject of 'corporate personality' is one that can encourage a lively debate in the boardroom.

Figure 10.5 is one of a number of checklists in *The Complete Spokesperson*[26] which might prove helpful to a board undertaking the task of formulating and implementing a communications strategy. A key concern of the board must be: To what extent does the personality of the company reflect corporate vision, goals, values and objectives?

A useful board technique is to list separately all the factors that are likely to help or hinder the achievement of a particular goal, objective or task. This enables barriers to be identified and permits an overview of what is likely to be involved in implementation. Activities can then be

Determining the elements of corporate personality

Under each of the following headings describe in a few words or phrases the distinctive image that your company wants to portray. If you feel a particular heading is not important to your corporate personality, leave it blank.

VISION: ....

....

MISSION: ....

....

VALUES: ....

....

HISTORY: ....

....

CULTURE: ....

....

NATIONALITY: ....

....

LOCATION: ....

....

OWNERSHIP: ....

....

STRUCTURE: ....

....

PEOPLE: ....

....

MARKETS: ....

....

PRODUCTS AND SERVICES: ....

....

TECHNOLOGY: ....

....

COMPETITION: ....

....

STRENGTHS AND WEAKNESSES: ....

....

Figure 10.5   The elements of corporate personality

identified that build upon helpful factors and alleviate those that are unhelpful.

For example, a board could relate its corporate personality (Figure 10.5) to the development of the business by considering how it might help or hinder the achievement of each of its key business objectives. The value of helps and hinders analysis is that it can enable a board to identify the full range of actions that may need to be initiated. Very often, boards only identify some of the relevant factors, and although these may be addressed, those that are overlooked may prevent the occurrence of desired outcomes.[3]

Communicating the vision

An effective 'vision' message is interesting, relevant to those receiving it, believable in relation to existing perceptions, authoritative, credible and distinctive. The vision should not represent an unrealistic leap forward from current capability and perceptions.

A message should carry conviction and be backed by commitment, unity, determination and purpose. No amount of expenditure or copywriting can compensate for a lack of intrinsic interest, reality, honesty, empathy and integrity. A contrived or manufactured message will be perceived as 'words on paper' and will not convince.[3]

An ideal message is short, simple, accurate and jargon free.[26, 27] Pitching a message at the right level means 'relating to' and 'sharing with' rather than 'talking down to' an audience. Wherever possible, a message should be tailored to the needs and interests of those receiving it. In the case of a vision, there needs to be a degree of consistency across the groups receiving the message.

The most exciting vision in the world will not motivate anyone if it is not communicated and shared. The authority of the vision will derive from its agreement or endorsement by the board. Hence, the responsibility for initiating the communication of the vision lies with the board. The following questions are typical of those that should be considered by the board:

1. Is the vision just 'words on paper', or 'floating about', or does it relate to actual or potential requirements in the marketplace?
2. Does it differentiate the company from other organizations? (Is it distinctive and memorable, or bland and instantly forgettable?)
3. Does the vision represent a realistic step forward from an existing image or 'corporate personality'? Does it stretch people?
4. Will the vision message encourage a response and lead to action?

(What would, could or should anyone do differently having been exposed to the message?)

5. Is the vision likely to live and spread by word of mouth? (Is it in a form that can be easily communicated? Will people want to communicate it?)

6. Will its communication aid understanding, and help to build relationships with those with whom it is shared?

The author's 'companion' book on developing directors[10] considers how a workshop could be used to (a) formulate a distinct vision and mission and (b) assess and test how each might best be communicated and shared.

We have seen that directors have a strong preference for learning from each other.[9] Board workshops can encourage greater openness and mutual trust. Getting the board to work together on a particular task outside the normal boardroom environment, and perhaps assisted by an experienced facilitator, can yield a number of incidental development benefits.[10] The experience of participants confirms that motivated learning – that which has a particular focus and is perceived as both relevant and practical – is the most effective.

10.8 Summary

In this chapter we have examined both barriers to, and ways of improving, board performance. The chairman has a key role in balancing interests and encouraging open communication within the boardroom team. Teamwork in the boardroom is a critical determinant of board effectiveness. We have also considered the importance of articulating and communicating a clear vision. Board workshops and exercises for 'visioning' and other purposes can be particularly effective at team building. There are many opportunities to create learning situations in the boardroom.

10.9 Checklist

1. To what extent are the interests and priorities of the board synonymous with those of the company?

2. Who is responsible for developing the board as a team?

3. How effectively do the members of your board work together as a team?

4. What activities of the board could give rise to teamwork or group discussion opportunities?

5. Is there an atmosphere of openness and trust in the boardroom?

6. Does any teamwork training that is undertaken by the board of your company take account of their distinct needs and shared responsibilities as directors?
7. Does the board operate as a board, or as a 'management committee'?
8. Do members of the board learn from the work of the board?
9. Has the board articulated and communicated a distinct and compelling vision?
10. Is the vision a 'so what' statement, or does it make people sit up, interest them, and motivate them to act?
11. Whose vision is it? Why should anyone care about it?
12. Do directors and managers all share the same corporate vision, goals, values and objectives?
13. Is there a conflict of interest or perspective between board and management? Does the board really understand the concerns of management? Does the board listen?
14. What should be done to achieve a better relationship between the board and management?

Notes and references

1. Kakabadse, A., *The Wealth Creators*, Kogan Page, 1991.
2. Coulson-Thomas, C., 'Competent directors: boardroom myths and realities', *Journal of General Management*, **17** (1), Autumn 1991, 1–26.
3. Coulson-Thomas, C., *Transforming the Company: Bridging the gap between management myth and corporate reality*, Kogan Page, 1992.
4. Sadler, P., 'On shaping the balance of power', *Director*, March 1992, 25.
5. Revans, R. W., *Action Learning*, Blond & Briggs, 1979.
6. Demb, A. and Neubauer, F-F., *The Corporate Board: Confronting the paradoxes*, Oxford University Press, 1992.
7. Coulson-Thomas, C., *Development Needs of NHS Authority and Board Members*. A report prepared by Adaptation Ltd on behalf of the NHS Training Directorate, 1992.
8. Morgan, P., 'Cadbury presumptions on the role of directors challenged by IOD', Letter to the Editor, *Financial Times*, 31 July 1992, p. 15.
9. Coulson-Thomas, C., *Professional Development of and for the Board*. An Adaptation Ltd survey for the Institute of Directors, IOD, February 1990.
10. Coulson-Thomas, C., *Developing Directors: Building an effective boardroom team*, McGraw-Hill, 1993.
11. Mumford, A., Honey, P. and Robinson, G., *Director's Development Guidebook: Making experience count*, Director Books, 1990.
12. Van Sinderen, A. W., 'The board looks at itself', *Directors & Boards*, Winter 1985, 20–3.
13. Coulson-Thomas, C. and Wakelam, A., *The Effective Board: Current practice, myths and realities*. An IOD discussion document, 1991.
14. 'Could you be a chairman?', Chairmanship, *Boardroom Agenda*, (3), August 1992, 18 and 19.

15. Cadbury, Sir A., *Company Chairman*, Director Books, 1990.
16. Adair, J., *Effective Teambuilding*, Gower, 1986.
17. Coulson-Thomas, C., *Public Relations is Your Business: A guide for every manager*, Business Books, 1981, p. 59.
18. Coulson-Thomas, C. and Coulson-Thomas, S., *Communicating for Change*. An Adaptation Ltd survey for Granada Business Services, 1991.
19. Coulson-Thomas, C. and Brown, R., *The Responsive Organisation: People management, the challenge of the 1990s*, BIM, 1989.
20. Coulson-Thomas, C., *The Role and Status of Project Management*. A survey undertaken by Adaptation Ltd for the APM, 1990; and, 'Project management: a necessary skill?', *Industrial Management & Data Systems*, (6), 1990, 17–21.
21. Coulson-Thomas, C., *Public Relations: A practical guide*, Macdonald & Evans, 1979.
22. Dyer, W. G., *Teambuilding: Alternatives and issues*, Addison-Wesley, 1977.
23. Coulson-Thomas, C. and Brown, R., *Beyond Quality: Managing the relationship with the customer*, BIM, 1990.
24. Coulson-Thomas, C. and Coe, T., *The Flat Organisation: Philosophy and practice*, BIM, 1991.
25. Drucker, P., *Management: Tasks, Responsibilities, Practices*, Heinemann, 1974.
26. Bartram, P. and Coulson-Thomas, C., *The Complete Spokesperson*, workshop and workbook, Policy Publications, 1990; and Kogan Page, 1991. Details of *The Complete Spokesperson* workshop and workbook can be obtained from Policy Publications Ltd, 29 Tivoli Road, Brighton, East Sussex, BN1 5BG (tel.: 0273 565505, Fax: 0273 550072).
27. Coulson-Thomas, C. and Didacticus Video Productions Ltd, *The Change Makers, Vision & Communication*. Booklet to accompany integrated audio and video tape training programme by Sir John Harvey-Jones. Available from Video Arts, 1991.

11
Evaluating performance

We should expect from directors . . . an approach to dealing with people inside and outside the business as if they were your best customers. This means understanding people's needs and wants and fulfilling them wherever possible. Where this is not possible explaining why and managing expectations. (ROGER GRAHAM, chairman, The BIS Group plc.)

A board of directors has many accountabilities and responsibilities. What constitutes effective performance can depend upon one's perspective and sense of priorities. Thus the owners, customers, employees, business partners, and the directors themselves, may all form very different judgements of the performance of a particular board.

Directors are likely to have a strong interest in their own personal performance. The chairman of a board should be concerned both with the individual performance of each member of the board, and with the collective performance of the board as a whole.

We saw in Chapter 1 that there has been much criticism of the performance of boards. What value does the board add? The question has been asked: 'Do directors earn their keep?'[1]

11.1 Comparing like with like

There are an enormous number of companies. Over a million of them are registered at the UK's Companies House alone.[2] In recent years, over 100 000 new companies have been incorporated per annum, and there have been a similar number of net removals from the register.[2]

A company might have been formed for any one of a number of purposes. We have seen that there are many different types of company, and those companies that are similar in some respects may face very dissimilar market environments. The degree of challenge faced by different boards varies enormously. Boards do not all begin at the same starting block.

How the performance of the board of an individual company is measured must reflect the nature of the company and its situation and circumstances.

Customer loyalty, the existence of barriers to entry, the extent and quality of competition, the level of margins, and the availability of skills can all vary significantly between business sectors.

A view may then need to be taken concerning whether to measure performance by (a) objective or external data, such as an industry league table, or (b) in terms of the board's own aspirations as expressed in the vision, goals, values and objectives it establishes for the company. In practice, a combination of both approaches may be adopted according to the perspective from which performance is to be assessed.

Among formal surveys and studies of board performance, various approaches have been adopted. For example:

- A link has been sought between director compensation and corporate performance.[1]
- The impact of different types of board and, particularly, the relative power of the CEO on board effectiveness and corporate performance has been examined.[3]
- The role of the board in respect of a particular corporate activity, such as the determination of corporate strategy, has been examined.[4]
- The responses of boards to certain challenges have been examined.[5]
- The impact of board structure and style has been investigated.[6]
- The extent to which a desired outcome such as organizational change is achieved has been assessed.[7]

Given the wide variation in the nature and composition of boards, and in the situation and circumstances of individual companies, generalization on the basis of formal studies is problematic. Hugh Parker has found it impossible to 'define precisely a set of criteria for board performance that can be strictly applied to all boards'.[8]

Directors should be wary of applying standard models and approaches without thinking through their applicability. Each board needs to agree a means of monitoring and evaluating its own contribution. The process used by one board is shown diagrammatically in Figure 11.1. This is not intended as a suggested model, but illustrates one of many approaches that could be adopted.

11.2 Agreeing the basis of measurement

What can be learned from the efforts of practising directors to evaluate board effectiveness? To evaluate performance in the boardroom, and of the board, it is necessary to agree certain 'ground rules'. For example:

1. The main functions of the board for the purposes of assessment need

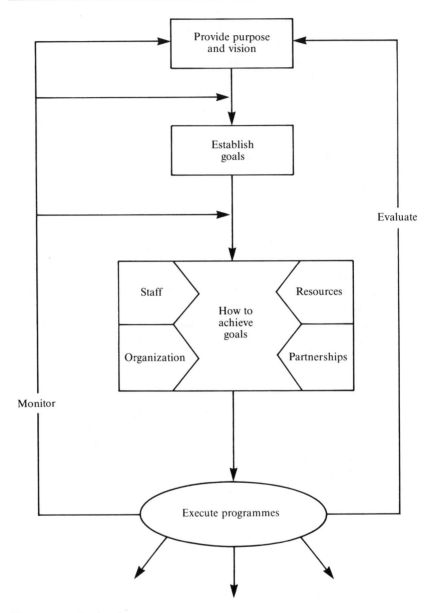

Figure 11.1 Evaluation process

to be agreed. How these are defined, and the relevance of vision and values to the corporate context, could itself be an indicator of board effectiveness. One board may set itself a demanding brief that is not easy to fulfil, while another has little difficulty satisfying the requirements of a relatively simple view of the role of the board.

2. In respect of each agreed function, clear objectives need to be set. These could be accepted as a basis for performance measurement, or questioned in terms of how they relate to the interests of customers and other stakeholders, or the extent of marketplace potential.

3. The priority of objectives, or how the interests of one group of stakeholders are traded off against another, can be particularly significant. The behaviour and focus of a board that puts customer satisfaction as the first priority may be very different from that of another which is 'going all out' to maximize short-term improvements in return on net assets. The two boards may come up with very different answers to such questions as: What are the key cross-functional management and business processes?

4. Criteria need to be established for distinguishing between effective and inadequate performance. Some boards are more easily satisfied than others. One board may be content with achieving an industry average performance, while another seeks to equal or exceed 'benchmark' performance in all respects.

Actual performance needs next to be assessed against the criteria that have been agreed. Quantitative performance targets are often easier to measure than those that are qualitative. An increasing number of 'benchmark' companies are adopting relatively objective measures of performance such as independently measured 'customer satisfaction'.

'Internal' measures of business performance include such calculations as return on capital or net assets, whether or not adjusted for the risks involved, liquidity and other ratios, and net income or profit growth. 'External' measures include market share data, credit ratings, corporate and brand image, and various indices of satisfaction, motivation, loyalty and participation.

What constitutes adequate performance will vary according to circumstances. The 'ground rules' adopted should reflect the nature of the company and the context. For example, the criteria for judging the adequacy of financial reporting could be significantly different between (a) communication with the 'external' investors in a major 'plc' and (b) the owner-directors of a smaller and private company.

11.3 Performance in relation to the function of the board

In Section 3.1 in Chapter 3 we considered a number of aspects of the role of the board. These could be used to develop a series of directorial responsibilities against which the performance of the board could be assessed on a scale of one to ten. A list of board responsibilities to be assessed could be selected from the following :

- Determining a purpose for the company, a reason for its continued existence.
- Articulating, communicating and sharing a compelling and distinctive vision.
- Establishing, reviewing, communicating and sharing goals, values and objectives derived from the vision.
- Understanding the aspirations, drives, preocupations, needs, interests and requirements of the company's stakeholders.
- Ensuring that the vision, any associated mission, and the goals, values and objectives of the company are consistent with the aspirations, drives, preoccupations, needs, interests and requirements of its various stakeholders.
- Formulating, reviewing and communicating strategies for the achievement of the defined goals, values and objectives.
- Allocating roles and responsibilities within the boardroom team for the achievement of the defined goals, values and objectives.
- Establishing quantifiable targets against which corporate progress towards the achievement of the defined goals, values and objectives can be measured.
- Ensuring that the company has adequate finance, people, organization, supporting technology and management and business processes to implement the agreed strategies and subsequent plans.
- In particular, appointing a management team and establishing the values, principles of conduct and policies that define the framework within which management operates.
- Delegating responsibilities, as appropriate to the management team, and ensuring that these, together with the operating framework and environment of the company, are understood by management.
- Negotiating quantifiable targets against which management contributions towards the achievement of the defined goals, values and objectives can be measured.
- Ensuring that members of the management team are involved, empowered and equipped to do what is expected of them.
- Examining proposals, and approving and reviewing various proposals and plans, submitted by the management team.

- Monitoring performance against agreed 'output' targets, taking corrective action where appropriate.
- Establishing and sustaining cooperative, collaborative and supply chain relationships with business partners and other organizations that share or can contribute to the achievement of the company's goals, values and objectives.
- Establishing and sustaining relationships with the stakeholders in the company.
- Reporting performance to the stakeholders in the company, and particularly its owners.
- Maintaining a balance between the various stakeholders in the company, including a duty of care to the company itself.
- Maintaining a balance between short-, medium- and long-term pressures and requirements.
- Ensuring that the business of the company is conducted in an ethical and responsible way.
- Ensuring that all the activities of the company observe the laws of those countries within which it operates, and are compatible wherever possible with local customs.
- In particular, ensuring the observance of those laws which particularly relate to companies and the duties and responsibilities of company directors.
- Sustaining the vision, and maintaining the capacity to care and cope in the face of adversity, uncertainty and surprise.

Working through such a list serves to remind members of the board of their various responsibilities as directors, and of the function and purpose of the board.

11.4 Aspiring to boardroom excellence

Some boards may wish to do more than discharge their core responsibilities, demanding and onerous though they are. At this stage the reader may wish to form an overview of the effectiveness of the board of his or her company. To do this, a checklist could be compiled by reviewing the earlier chapters of this book and considering which of the questions that arise are particularly applicable to the situation and circumstances of the specific board. Such a checklist, representing the author's selection, is presented as an appendix on page 292. Of course, other matters could be of greater significance to a particular company, depending upon its context and business development needs. Further approaches to assessment are considered in the author's 'companion' book on developing directors.[9]

Particular attention should be paid to the performance of the board in relation to business development, corporate renewal and corporate transformation.[10] The excellent board may be distinguished by attitude, behaviour, will, vision and commitment rather than by structure and credentials.

Structure and conduct

The formal structure of a board can itself be a source of concern, independently of how a board performs.[11] There are many forms of board structure which could be adopted, and how boards operate in practice may be at variance with the formal position. Thus, in the UK, the

> traditional *de jure* model has a unitary board running the legal entity, the company, by dealing with various interests on behalf of and in the interest of shareholders. In practice, as reflected in the *de facto* model, the shareholders tend to be just another interest with which the board deals, albeit a rather special one and one that is reported to by independent auditors.[12]

There are other models that could be adopted. For example:

> The two-tier model, regarding the employees as constituting, like the shareholders, a special group, establishes a supervisory board upon which there are both shareholder and employee representatives and which then appoints an executive board which runs the company.[12]

> The representational model, while returning to the unitary board, is based upon the view that rather than limit boardroom representation to one or two special interests, a much wider range of interests such as creditors and customers should be represented.[12]

> A number of models aim to place some intermediary organization between shareholders and the board. Perhaps shareholders, especially significant institutional shareholders, could be represented upon a separate nominating committee whose job it is to select candidates for non-executive positions.[12]

Experience with two-tier boards 'has been misunderstood in that the second tier existed prior to worker directors. The two-tier system was introduced to separate the advisory role from the executive function'.[12] The author has expressed the view that: 'The single board is as capable as the upper tier in reconciling competing political interests with the added advantage of being closer to the implications of policy decisions.'[12]

What matters is conduct and performance in the demanding and international market environment we examined in Chapter 2. The challenge of corporate renewal and transformation, governing the emerging network organization, and coping with an increasingly complex regulatory environment is resulting in similar attitudes and responses irrespective of board structure. Demb and Neubauer have also been struck by the similarities of approach across different board types.[13]

The author has cautioned that while structure needs to be appropriate to the situation and context:

> Too great a concern with structure is a reflection of mechanical thinking, which leads to the search for an ideal structure. Viewing the company [and board] as an evolving organism leads to the conclusion that no one form of structure is likely to be the best for all companies. . . . While communication and structure interrelate, structure should be the servant of communication and not *vice versa*.[12]

A board structured according to the best principles of corporate governance could preside over a declining company, meticulous in its stewardship and reporting of accumulating losses to shareholders. People often do grow old gracefully and die with dignity, but the demise of a company can be a messy business, characterized by the sudden shock of redundancy, the losses of investors and creditors, allegations of incompetence, and suspicions or investigations of fraudulent trading.

Directorial and board effectiveness

Competent directors may serve upon a board that is not effective. It will also be necessary to distinguish between:

- The performance of individual directors and that of the board as a whole. Individual and group deficiencies, although interdependent, are likely to have distinct consequences and to require different treatment. The board itself is a mechanism for complementing and building upon individual strengths within the team, and ameliorating individual weaknesses.
- The activities and dynamics of the board, 'as a board', and its impact upon the business. The assessment of a board in terms of the quality of its processes and debates, the efficient conduct of its business, and the relevance and clarity of its strategy and objectives, is sometimes difficult to reconcile with such 'outcomes' as 'bottom line results' or whether desired changes occur. Boards that are effective at strategy formulation are not always able to 'implement'.[14]

Performance evaluation requires judgement, and a conscious perspective. Consider the following 'looking back' comments of interviewees:

> At the end of the day what we did was a failure. We topped the league tables for a period, but look at the situation now.

Do we apply hindsight and judge on the basis of what we know now, or do we judge on the basis of what we then knew? I suspect almost any good board given the same information and the view of the time would have come to very much the same conclusions.

Success has brought its own problems. Lose the momentum and you go to sleep and are 'taken out'. People are waiting out there for us to loosen our grip on the marketplace. We hit all the standards, and we are now having to set our own objectives which is tougher.

There are no absolutes. The perfect board does not exist. We just need to be that bit smarter and sharper than the competition.

All the resources and talent in the world would not have helped. We were not focused on the customer. Never ask me how good we are, ask the customer.

At the time I prided myself on the long hours I worked. That commitment was rewarded in terms of promotions, and this encouraged me to work harder. I scheduled earlier meetings, later meetings, and went on extra trips. All this activity gave me too little time for reflection. When I most needed it, I didn't give myself time to think.

There were so many things that we did right. There was so much activity going on that was 'good stuff'. What we missed at the time were the one or two obstacles that prevented us from breaking through.

So much of what went on was 'gloss'. So much that was fun, or made us feel important, was actually quite irrelevant. Yet so much of what has happened subsequently is the product of a few key decisions of the board that did not seem significant at the time.

I can see now what we should have done, but I'm more detached. It was all there bar 'a couple of clubs'. Then I was so involved, and working so hard. It requires real self-discipline to ease off, stand back and retain an overview perspective.

Vital clues can be obtained as to the effectiveness of a board, and the attitudes, perspectives and priorities of its members, from an examination of the boardroom agenda, and the focus and preoccupation of boardroom discussion (see Table 11.1).

A common characteristic of those interviewed in the course of the various surveys of directors and boards cited in this book is a degree of humility, associated with a wish that more had been achieved. Many directors appear to have their own private aspirations for the companies on whose boards they sit. These are sometimes relatively demanding. The potential, or what could be, is frequently understood and it is often alluring.

Table 11.1 The boardroom agenda: positive and negative symptoms

Positive symptoms	Negative symptoms
Break-out/transformation	Spiral of descent to marginal commodity supplier status
Long-term focus	Short-term orientation
Re-deploy to activities that add value for customers	Headcount reduction
Concern with customer satisfaction	Concern with financial numbers
Investment approach to quality, training and IT	Preoccupation with costs of training, IT, etc.
Build added value opportunities	Lower price/price competitively
Securing commitment	Wordsmithing
Speed up service to customers to increase customer satisfaction and generate value	'Screw customers' to increase margins and generate cash
Emphasis on building relationships	Bargaining and negotiation orientation
Empowering and sharing culture	Control culture
Focus on fact, reality and intention	Expressions of opinion, surmise and hope
Fair and honest reporting to stakeholders	Concealment or misrepresentation of actual situation
Holistic approach	'Line by line' approach

Focusing upon essentials and the longer term

The sense of disappointment, rather than satisfaction, that many directors express when looking back often results from the time it generally takes, and the difficulties that are encountered, in attempting to turn vision into reality.[10] As one chairman put it: 'the board is generally a better vehicle for determining what needs to be done, than ensuring what needs to be done *is* done. We all seem to suffer a blockage. Why, when we all know what we want, is it so difficult?'

Many executive directors also appear to 'pay a heavy price', in terms of lack of perspective and awareness, for the time they commit to their 'managerial' tasks as opposed to their 'directorial' role. The 'managerial' day of the senior director can consist of a stream of meetings and interruptions, with only a few minutes available for each encounter or task.[15] Within such a hectic schedule there is rarely time to think.

Directors who, while 'in harness', consciously strove to remain detached, and who endeavoured to assess and question, are often those with fewer 'looking back' regrets. As one former chief executive officer put it: 'I may have got some things wrong, but at least I thought about what I did. I know that at the time I did my best. I actually did the job I was paid to do rather than be distracted by everything but my core duties as a director.'

A great many boards do not focus on the 'vital few' tasks that need to be done to achieve corporate objectives. Often, whatever the efforts devoted to such varied activities as quality and other training, or investments in information technology, desired outcomes or success is elusive because a crucial piece of the jigsaw puzzle is missing.[10] Boards wonder why they are not achieving a measurable return from 'investments' in training of information technology, while failing to identify the key obstacles to progress.

To ensure that the board concentrates upon essentials, basic questions along the lines of the following could be asked:

- Does the board understand what constitutes value to customers? (Has it ever 'asked customers', or sought to learn from them, by means of a customer satisfaction or requirements survey?)
- Has the board identified the key cross-functional management and business processes that generate the value that is sought by customers? (Does the board, or should it, employ equivalents of the various proven techniques that benchmark companies are using to identify and re-engineer business processes to achieve massive improvements in customer requirements, such as response time?)
- Have the barriers and obstacles that are standing in the way of the effective use of these processes been identified? (Are actions in place to deal with them?)
- Is information technology, training, etc., being applied (a) to the key processes that turn customer requirements into customer satisfaction and (b), in particular, to tackling the barriers to their effective use? (If not, why should the board assume that expenditure in these areas will lead to a 'return', or that business objectives will be achieved?)

11.5 Evaluation of personal effectiveness in the boardroom

How do chairmen measure the contributions of their directors? This question has been considered in a survey of chairmen undertaken by Coulson-Thomas and Wakelam.[16] The 'top ten' methods of assessing the effectiveness of individual members of a board are given in Figure 11.2. The terminology employed in this illustration is somewhat vague and imprecise, but it is the terminology that was used by the participants in the survey. The evaluation of the effectiveness of individual members of boards is overwhelmingly informal and intermittent:

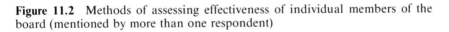

By performance within their departments

11

By performance at board meetings

6

Annual appraisal

6

Observation/judgement

5

By results

5

Contribution

2

Promote and suggest useful ideas

2

Number of boards

Figure 11.2   Methods of assessing effectiveness of individual members of the board (mentioned by more than one respondent)

- Over three out of ten respondents actually used the word 'informal', while most of the approaches of the remaining two out of three responses (including some of those described as 'formal') could be categorized as informal.
- Only one in eight participants claim that their boards operate any form of periodic and formal appraisal. Any formal assessment that does occur tends to be on an annual basis.
- Only about a fifth of respondents evaluate effectiveness in terms of the demonstration of personal qualities and competences. Personal qualities that are important in securing access to a board do not appear to be as relevant to continuing membership.
- One in ten respondents cited 'results' as a measure of the personal effectiveness of individual directors. The 'results' that those interviewed had in mind were 'the company results'. These would appear to be more of an indication of the performance of the board as a whole.
- When assessing directors, many chairmen appear to draw upon the

views of 'others', such as staff or customers. 'Impression' may be as important as 'reality' for many board members. One in three participants assess the impact of directors upon 'others', or seek the views of 'others'.

We saw in Chapter 3 that monitoring management performance is regarded by directors as an important function of the board. More participants in the 'chairman' survey[16] cited 'monitoring top executive performance' as a board function, than formally assess the contribution of individual directors to the performance of the board:

- It would appear that many boards either consider managerial performance to be a factor that is largely independent of the board, or confuse the respective roles and responsibilities of directors and managers. The board establishes the strategy and sets objectives, their achievement being regarded as the responsibility of managers.
- Many boards do not appear to accept that while there are distinct directorial responsibilities, directors share some responsibility for ensuring that strategy is translated into action. The board needs to ensure that managers are involved, empowered and equipped to make their contributions to the achievement of corporate objectives.

One approach to involving directors in the evaluation of their own directorial competences is (a) to draw up a matrix of directorial knowledge and skills and (b) to ask members of the board to undertake a self-assessment of their own competence against the standards established in the matrix. An example of such an approach is given in the author's 'companion' book on developing directors.[9]

A number of matrices of directorial skill requirements are in existence, and more authoritative definitions of directorial competence are under preparation. These need to be treated with some caution, as what constitutes a competent director can depend in large part upon the nature, situation and circumstances of a company.

The implications of how directors are assessed

By measuring the effectiveness of executive directors in terms of their performance within their departments, chairmen are employing managerial rather than directorial criteria. This can, and does, have many undesirable consequences. For example:

- Many directors are not encouraged to behave as directors, or to devote sufficient time to their directorial responsibilities. The reward system leads them to focus upon short-term departmental objectives, and to adopt a departmental perspective rather than that of the company as a whole.

- Managers often expect 'their directors' to have a longer term perspective. When the priorities, and the role model behaviour, of members of the board depart from such expectations, or those derived from the vision, goals and values of the company, managers can become disillusioned.[10]
- In many companies there is a degree of confusion concerning the respective horizon and focus of the manager and the director. For example, we saw in Chapter 4 how arenas of conflict can arise between directors and managers, and how managers who 'buy in' to building long-term relationships with customers can feel betrayed and duped by the unexplained 'short-termism' of a board.[10, 16]
- The departmental approach does not focus upon the key management and business processes that generate value for customers, as these tend to be cross-functional. The directors may have little or no incentive even to identify these cross-functional processes, and the problems and delays that arise at the 'cross-over points' between departments remain hidden.
- Directors themselves can become confused and dissatisfied when so little attempt appears to be made to link performance in the boardroom with the contributions sought from directors, or the criteria that are used (see Chapter 8) when new appointments to the board are made. As one interviewee stated: 'Given my expectations, it took the wind out of my sails to learn that it was "business as usual". I have a fancier job title, but I expected and wanted more. The promotion has increased my dissatisfaction.'

What can be learned from the criteria that do not appear to be used to assess directorial effectiveness? For example, leadership was not mentioned by any of the respondents to the 'chairman' survey.[16] Those interviewed tended either to take the view that 'all managers need to lead their teams', or to stress that within both the board and the company generally the 'leadership role' was undertaken by the chief executive officer.

CEOs themselves believe they require leadership skills, and the charisma to influence and inspire.[17] Again there are undesirable consequences:

- Rather than being *primus inter pares*, many CEOs appear to have acquired an unhealthy degree of dominance over their boardroom colleagues. This can blunt the independence and objectivity of directors, and lead to the crawling, boot-licking and toadying that is so widespread within corporate bureaucracies.
- Individual directors may not 'buy in' and 'share' key objectives of the board. Initiatives such as quality programmes may prosper as long as they have the patronage of a particular CEO. When vision, goals, values and objectives are not agreed and shared by the board as a team, the

lack of unity and group commitment can undermine attempts at corporate transformation and lead to disillusionment.[18]

The individual and the team

In Chapter 10 we saw that in a survey of directors, undertaken by
Adaptation Ltd for the IOD,[19] 'teamwork' emerged as the number one
boardroom issue. Over three-quarters of the participants were chairmen
or chairmen and chief executive officers of their companies. Is their concern with 'teamwork' reflected in the performance criteria applied to the
boardroom?

It would appear that director assessment criteria are not being used *per
se* to influence behaviour in the boardroom. Among the responses to the
'chairman' survey[16] concerning the measurement of directorial contributions, there was not a single reference to being a 'team player' or contributing to the board as a team.

Those interviewed consider that corporate performance results from
the contribution of the 'board as a team' rather than the efforts of individual
directors. According to one interviewee: 'I didn't mention teamwork, as I
assume all those appointed to the board are team players. Otherwise, they
wouldn't be there. It is for the chairman and the board as a whole to
commit to operating as a team. One director alone can't be responsible
for that.'

Those interviewed also expressed the view that the evaluation of the
effectiveness of individual directors is more difficult than assessing the
performance of the board as a team. This is why departmental performance
rather than boardroom performance is used to assess directors.

One chairman and chief executive officer explained:

> There are responsibilities the whole board has as a team, and there are particular
> responsibilities that are allocated to each director. I measure myself in terms of
> the company as a whole, and each director on their departmental performance.
> This is the most practical way of doing it, but it does encourage them to 'back
> off' when overall performance is bad. They say their 'bit' is OK, and leave me
> to 'carry the can'.

Assessment and board membership

In earlier chapters of this book it has been suggested that the chairman
should assume responsibility for ensuring that a board is both effective
and constituted of directors who are individually competent. Particular
aspects of the role of the chairman in improving board performance are

Undertake an annual review of the function and purpose of the board
Ensure that various accountabilities are understood and discharged
Ensure an annual review of corporate vision, values, goals and
objectives occurs
Ensure that vision, goals, values and objectives are shared
Review individual and collective roles and responsibilities
Review size, composition, operation and effectiveness
Review information and support requirements
Assess effectiveness and contribution of all directors
Ensure that all new directors are aware of their legal duties and
responsibilities
Build unity while encouraging individual contributions
Establish, build and sustain relationship with CEO

Example 11.1 The role of the chairman in improving board effectiveness

listed in Example 11.1. One of the responsibilities of the chairman in this example is to review the size, composition, operation and effectiveness of the board. This could be done on an annual basis and linked to an assessment of directorial contributions. However, the 'chairman' survey[16] suggests that the lack of formal assessment in many boardrooms would not allow this to be done.

In the case of many boards, it is difficult to envisage non-departmental performance related circumstances that would terminate board membership, beyond failure to 'fit in' or be a team player. In practice, few people appear to lose a 'seat on the board' as a result of a formal appraisal process. Board membership generally appears to end because of disagreement over a major change of policy, expiry of a term of office, retirement, a personality clash, or rationalization following a takeover, rather than inadequate individual performance in the boardroom.

The owner-director can be particularly difficult to remove, while in the case of many smaller companies co-directors may be 'friends'. With a board consisting of only two or three members, or composed of owner-directors, there may not be an effective mechanism for the termination of a directorship in the event of inadequate performance other than by voluntary resignation. In such situations, directorial self-awareness, and an ability and willingness to be frank in the assessment of one's own boardroom performance, may be of some importance to the prospects of a company.

Improving board effectiveness

Are there particular areas that one should focus upon when assessing

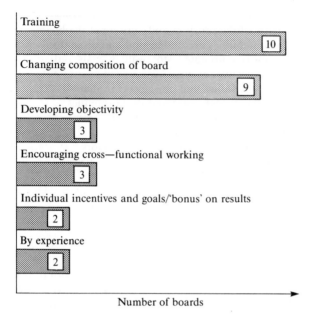

Figure 11.3 Suggested ways of improving the effectiveness of the board (mentioned by more than one respondent)

board effectiveness? Reference has already been made to the importance of teamwork. In Chapter 10 we considered the views of the participants in the survey of chairmen[16] concerning the 'top ten' ways of ensuring teamwork in the boardroom (Figure 10.3).

Some further clues are suggested by the areas which chairmen feel should be improved. The 'top ten' ways suggested by the 'chairman' survey[16] respondents of improving the effectiveness of their boards are given in Figure 11.3. The responses suggest widespread dissatisfaction with board performance. Three-quarters of the respondents believe that the effectiveness of their companies' boards could be improved, although there is little agreement on what needs to be done to improve board effectiveness. Many of the responses were general rather than specific.

The participants in the 'chairman' survey[16] were asked to identify areas of deficiency in relation to their particular boards. A number of responses hint at the inherent dangers of board members behaving as managers rather than directors. The fatalistic tone of some replies suggests that confusion concerning the distinct responsibilities of the director is regarded as an inevitable fact of boardroom life, rather than as a matter to be addressed.

About a fifth of the respondents mentioned a role for training to improve some aspects of board performance, and a similar number referred in varying ways to the importance of standing back and remaining detached from day-to-day pressures, and developing a degree of objectivity.

11.6 Identifying and addressing development needs

In an earlier Adaptation Ltd survey for the IOD[19] respondents attached some importance to assessing the development needs of directors, and the setting of development objectives. In the 'chairman' survey[16] some concern was expressed as to how this might be done:

- Participants were not convinced of the applicability of general 'definitions' of what constitutes a competent director to the situation and circumstances of their own particular company.
- There was some questioning of the objectivity and motives of private consultancies that offer development services, since it was thought that they would promote those things they were good at, rather than what might be needed by a particular board. It was also thought that many of their packages concerned management skills rather than direction competences.
- Participants were also not convinced of the director development credentials of the major business schools. There is some suspicion that existing management programmes are being 're-packaged' to appeal to more senior audiences.
- Few companies appear to operate an effective 'induction' process for newly appointed directors. Unlike the effort devoted to briefing and inducting new members of staff, directors are required to 'pick things up' as they go along.
- It is not clear that directors are motivated to become more competent. Only two respondents mentioned a financial reward or bonus as an incentive for improved performance.
- Other than the case of bringing new directors into the boardroom, only two respondents suggested that 'action should be taken' against individual directors as a result of their inadequate performance. In all other cases, what was being suggested in terms of action, activity, process or structure would impact upon the board as a whole.
- In most cases it was felt that the key areas of deficiency related to the board as a whole rather than to particular directors. Interviewees were not convinced that individual development activity *per se* would have a significant impact upon group performance.
- Several interviewees acknowledged that they were not devoting sufficient time to tackling the barriers to director development they had

identified. It would appear that in many companies there is not the commitment to action that is needed if a significant improvement in directorial performance is to be achieved.

Some of the respondents in the 'chairman' survey[16] appear to be operating under self-imposed constraints. In theory, the board should have greater freedom to alter its structure and mode of operation than perhaps any other group within a company. In certain cases, interviewees referred to a board's structure or framework as if it was something imposed and over which they had little control.

11.7 Accountability and performance

We saw in Chapter 3 that in return for the privilege of limited liability, companies and their boards assume certain obligations. Directors are accountable as stewards and trustees, and they may have entered into contractual commitments with a range of external stakeholders. However, many board members appear to view their main duty to their company in terms of accountability to themselves.[16] During the course of the 'chairman' survey this was particularly evident in the case of owner-directors or private companies with sympathetic shareholders. A number of chairmen mentioned the lack of any third party to whom they needed to explain their actions.[16]

To keep boards on their toes, both internal and external action may be required:

- Internally, it is desirable that the directors regularly review their performance as a board. In some cases chairmen are endeavouring to undertake such reviews.
- Externally, the shareholders could do more to ensure that the boards of those companies in which they invest are competent. A significant institutional investor could legitimately enquire as to what, if anything, is done by a board to monitor and improve its own effectiveness.
- Similarly, major companies assessing potential suppliers or business partners could devote more effort to the assessment of the calibre of their boards. The effectiveness of a board could be a key determinant of the potential of a company to sustain a longer term relationship.

There is little evidence that the lending teams of most major financial institutions are equipped to assess board effectiveness. Too many banks, and other suppliers of loan finance, encourage companies to borrow in 'good times', and subsequently put up their charges or even close them down in 'bad times' without at any stage evaluating the composition and effectiveness of their boards. Investigations of directors of smaller companies usually focus on their assets – for example, houses upon which loans can be secured – rather than their directorial competence.

Improving board performance assessment

There was little active experimentation among participants in the 'chairman' survey[16] with new ways of assessing board performance:

- One possibility would be 'peer review' by one or more members of the board of a non-competing company. Perhaps boards could form consortia of those willing to 'audit' and assess each other's effectiveness as boards. As one chief executive officer put it: 'To explain yourself you need to know yourself and, by the same token, by the exercise of explaining yourself you get to know what you do, and don't, know about yourself and your organization.'
- To encourage comparison with the imaginative, rather than the typical, a board could make use of 'benchmarking' to seek out and evaluate examples of board structure or operation that could be relevant to the situation and circumstances of the company.[20]
- Many boards have a parochial view of 'what is possible', and are very reluctant to depart from what is considered 'traditional practice'. An international benchmarking process could uncover wide variations of practice. The board of a US company could find itself evaluating the merits of a 'two-tier' board in Europe, or a board with 40 or 50 members in Japan.
- A board could invite one or more 'outside' people to sit in on certain board meetings, on an ad hoc basis, for particular items of business. These could include reviews of the performance of the board. Such individuals could contribute when invited to do so by the chairman, and the minutes could make clear that they are 'in attendance'. In the interest of continuity, not to mention the legal duties and responsibilities of directors, it is desirable for directors to be in a majority, while the directors alone should vote at such meetings.

Pressure of business should not be used as an excuse to defer consideration of board effectiveness. An annual performance review could be built into the board calendar as an item of core business, while the review process itself could be regarded as one of the key processes of the board.

Given that directors have only a limited amount of time, it is important that this is used to maximum effect. Wherever possible, general updating and more routine matters should be considered outside the boardroom.

Periodic informal briefings and inputs from relevant authorities could be arranged for a board apart from its formal meetings.

11.8 The role of non-executive directors

Reference has already been made (e.g. in Chapter 5) to the advantage to be gained from the independence and objectivity of the good non-executive director. The overwhelming majority of listed UK companies appear to have established an 'audit committee', and a 'remuneration committee' with a preponderance of non-executive directors.[21] A committee of non-executive directors could be established to review the performance of executive directors and the effectiveness of the board. However, many chairmen and CEOs of companies in general appear reluctant to submit themselves and their colleagues to independent scrutiny. Less than one in ten participants in the 'chairman' survey[16] mentioned non-executive directors as a 'resource' for improving board effectiveness.

Given the relatively small size of some of the boards covered by the 'chairman' survey sample, and the limited number of non-executive directors, there was a tendency for interviewees to stress the extent to which non-executive directors could be integrated into the team, rather than brought in as an independent check. Particular questions raised by sceptical interviewees include:

> On what basis would they [non-executive directors] evaluate performance? If we asked them to do it, I suspect they would be very subjective.

> Would you invite someone in to keep an eye upon you, when how you are doing depends upon the viewpoint?

> Customers should decide at the end of the day. They have a choice. The executive and the non-executive directors are paid and involved. Is someone who is responsible and shares responsibility really independent?

> What is there at the end of the day to evaluate? Shouldn't the accounts say it all? I want the members of the board to concentrate upon achieving corporate objectives. I don't want them playing the part of being good directors in order to get a good review.

'Marketing' the value of non-executive directors as an independent 'watch-dog' or 'check' on the CEO and executive directors has little appeal for many of those interviewed. Such a role could, it was thought, undermine the desire for a collective approach and common understanding. Many potential users of non-executive directors would be more attracted by references to the value of bringing complementary skills and perspective to a particular board, or the opportunity to learn from a director with a very different background.

In April 1992, a significant example of 'muscle-flexing' by non-executive directors did occur when the chairman of the board of General Motors was replaced as chairman of the company's executive committee by a non-executive director.[22] The board also replaced the group president of the company.

As far as annual reports and accounts are concerned, it is not clear that the presence of non-executive directors upon the boards of public companies has resulted in more open and realistic financial reporting to stakeholders. A UK study has suggested that financial reporting which consistently makes use of the most favourable interpretation and treatment can and does sometimes conceal a significant deterioration in underlying corporate performance.[23]

'Steve' Shirley, founder-director of FI Group plc, believes that among directors: 'Integrity is essential and those who question what it means surely do not have it.' Integrity demands honest reporting, and a board should be assessed in terms of how truthful it is prepared to be when confronted by an unwelcome reality. Richard Masterman, chairman of Key Organics Ltd and of the Professional Development Committee of the IOD, reminds us that: 'Truth, trust and openness do not just happen.'[24]

11.9 Summary

In this chapter we have seen that the performance of a board needs to be considered in the context of the nature, situation and circumstances of a company. What constitutes directorial effectiveness depends upon the perspective of the evaluator, and the evaluation criteria that are employed. In practice, many directors are assessed according to managerial rather than directorial criteria. Few boards systematically assess their performance as a board.

11.10 Checklist

1. Does the board of your company regularly assess its own effectiveness?
2. Could the process used to evaluate the effectiveness of the board of your company be improved?
3. Does the board operate as a board, or as an executive management team?
4. How effective is the board at implementing strategy, or 'making it happen'?
5. Does the board add value in proportion to its cost?

6. Do you think the effectiveness of the board of your company could be improved?
7. What main areas or aspects need to be improved; and how do you believe this improvement could be achieved?
8. Is the quality of the contributions of individual members of the board regularly assessed?
9. How is the effectiveness of individual members of the board evaluated?
10. Do the assessment criteria that are used focus on their contributions as directors or as functional managers?
11. Could the process used to evaluate the effectiveness of individual members of the board of your company/organization be improved?
12. Who is responsible, and who in your view should be responsible, for ensuring that the members of the board of your company are competent, and the board itself is effective?
13. What is standing in the way of better directorial and board performance?
14. Does the board have a 'vital few' programme of actions to ensure that the major barriers to the achievement of corporate vision, goals, values and objectives are overcome?
15. Does the board have the will to confront what is new, daunting and unfamiliar?
16. Given the capability, performance and commitment of the board, is it likely that the vision, goals, values and objectives of the company will be achieved?
17. Do you think your effectiveness in your current directorial (or other) role could be improved?

Notes and references

1. Crystal, G. S., 'Do directors earn their keep?', *Fortune International*, 6 May 1991, 56–8.
2. Companies House, *Annual Report 1991–92*, HMSO, 1992; and Jack, A., 'Agency has surplus of £1.56m', *Financial Times*, 4 August 1992, p. 8.
3. Pearce, J. A. and Zahra, S. A., 'The relative power of CEOs and boards of directors' associations with corporate performance', *Strategic Management Journal*, **12** (2), February 1991, 135–53.
4. Zahra, S. A. and Pearce, J. A., 'Determinants of board directors' strategic involvement', *European Management Journal*, **8** (2), June 1990, 164–73.
5. Boyd, B., 'Corporate linkages and organisational environment, a test of the resource dependence model', *Strategic Management Journal*, **11** (6), October 1990, 419–30.
6. Alkafaji, A. F., 'Effective boards of direction', *Industrial Management and Data Systems*, **90** (4), 1990, 18–26.
7. Seashore, S. E., Lawler, E. E., Mirvis, P. H. and Camman, C., *Assessing Organisational Change*, Wiley, 1982.
8. Parker, H., *Letters to a New Chairman*, Director Publications, 1990.

9. Coulson-Thomas, C., *Developing Directors: Building an effective boardroom team*, McGraw-Hill, 1993.
10. Coulson-Thomas, C., *Transforming the Company: Bridging the gap between management myth and corporate reality*, Kogan Page, 1992.
11. Rudd, R., 'Institutional concern over a top banker's dual role', Company News: UK, *Financial Times*, 6 August 1992, p. 19.
12. Coulson-Thomas, C., *Public Relations is Your Business: A guide for every manager*, Business Books, 1981, pp. 59–66.
13. Demb, A. and Neubauer, F-F., *The Corporate Board: Confronting the paradoxes*, Oxford University Press, 1992.
14. Mace, M. L., *Directors: Myth and Reality*, Division of Research, Graduate School of Business Administration, Harvard University, 1971; and Coulson-Thomas, C., 'Strategic vision or strategic con?: Rhetoric or reality?', *Long Range Planning*, **25** (1), 1992, 81–9.
15. Mintzberg, H., *The Nature of Managerial Work*, Harper & Row, 1973 and 1980.
16. Coulson-Thomas, C. and Wakelam, A., *The Effective Board: Current practice, myths and realities*. An IOD discussion document, 1991.
17. Steiner, G. A., Kunin, H. and Kunin, E., 'The new class of chief executive officer', in B. Taylor, *Strategic Planning: The chief executive and the board*, Pergamon Press, 1988.
18. Coulson-Thomas, C. and Coe, T., *The Flat Organisation: Philosophy and practice*, BIM, 1991.
19. Coulson-Thomas, C., *Professional Development of and for the Board*. A questionnaire and interview survey undertaken by Adaptation Ltd of company chairmen. A summary has been published by the IOD, February 1990.
20. Camp, R. C., 'Benchmarking', *The Search for Industry Best Practices that Lead to Superior Performance*, Quality Press, 1989.
21. Korn/Ferry, *Boards of Directors Study UK 1992*, Korn/Ferry International, 1992.
22. Dickson, M., 'GM coup promotes ex-chief of Procter & Gamble' and 'Impatient GM board flexes its muscles', *Financial Times*, 8 April 1992, pp. 1 and 20, and p. 21.
23. Smith, T., *Accounting for Growth: Stripping the camouflage from company accounts*, Century Business, 1992.
24. Masterman, R., *Resumé of Comments on Creating an Effective Board*, Institute of Personnel Management 1991 National Conference, October 1991, p. 2.

12
The next steps

A shared vision and sustained commitment in the boardroom is vital if outcomes are to match expectations. There is little point creating an excellent strategy which is not implemented. (PETER MORGAN, director general, Institute of Directors.)

So what are the next steps for a group of directors intent upon creating excellence in the boardroom? We have seen, at a number of points in the course of this book, that achieving an effective board composed of competent directors is no easy task, and requires continuing commitment and vigilance. Single solutions, fads and panaceas should be avoided.[1]

What is to be done must reflect the nature, situation and circumstances of the company and any particular deficiencies that have been identified. The context in which the board operates, and the development challenges and opportunities a company faces, are likely to be in a continual state of flux. A corporation needs to renew itself in order to survive.[2] The board is a living and evolving community, as members grow, adjust to each other, and come and go.

Some actions could be directed at individual members of the board, while other initiatives may concern the board as a whole. Scepticism, caution, uncertainty and a degree of suspicion, if not cynicism, have been encountered during the course of the surveys upon which this book draws (Appendix 2). What is proposed needs to be perceived by busy people as both practical and relevant. Consider the following interview comments:

At this moment in time I must distinguish between a great many things that would be nice to do, and those which are really essential. However, I would take a look at something that focused on a real problem that we have.

Fundamental corporate changes do not just happen. The board must ensure that the management team has all that it needs to turn words into deeds.

There is only one board. You don't experiment, test or prototype on the board. . . . I have to be really convinced that it is all worth while.

Colleagues are all too aware of slickness and hype. . . . Breaking in, or how to begin is the issue. I suspect that when we start, people will want more. The first step is a critical one.

My preference would be for something that benefited both us as a board and the company. The benefit to the company is important. . . . We don't want to appear as self-serving.

Chairmen are not naive, far from it. Almost all of the chairmen one encounters are interested in 'real benefits', rather than the 'cosmetics', of director development or board improvement. Many of those interviewed tended to 'sit up' when the conversation shifted to how the board might become more effective at overcoming some of the many obstacles to corporate transformation that were being encountered.

12.1 Pressures for change

So what are the pressures for change? Reference was made in Chapter 1 to various criticisms of directors and boards, and the 'corporate governance' debate that is occurring on both sides of the Atlantic. But there are other trends and challenges which, as we saw in Chapter 2, are leading to a review of corporate organization and have consequences for boards.

Survival in the global marketplace is one place to start. Allen Sykes, a former managing director of Consolidated Gold Fields, has suggested a link between the pattern of corporate financing and corporate governance[3]:

- In such English-speaking countries as the US, UK, Australia, Canada and New Zealand a relatively greater dependence upon equity finance tends to result in passive or short-term oriented investors and self-perpetuating boards; while
- in 'continental Europe' and Japan, there is more emphasis upon loan finance, with lending banks taking a longer term view and being more prepared to intervene actively in the field of corporate management.

Internationalizing companies are becoming more aware of alternative 'models' and their advantages and disadvantages, while 'domestic' companies may be competing with enterprises led by boards with different perspectives and approaches. The need for flexibility, speed and 'implementation' is bringing a sense of urgency into boardrooms. They are becoming less cosy, as corporate survival can no longer be assumed.

Greater cooperation between corporate management and 'external' influences, and more focused pressure from outside forces, have been identified as possible catalysts of greater board effectiveness.[4] Where such goads, or irritants depending upon perceptions, are absent the board must provide its own motivation for change, and individual boards are likely to vary in their commitment to action.

12.2 Back to basics: the company director and the board

Where should one begin? Before a programme of 'next steps' can be drawn up, areas in which action is needed must be identified. These will vary from board to board, reflecting the situation and circumstances of each company. One approach would be to consider the various issues raised in this book, perhaps using Appendix 1 as a checklist to form an initial overview. This could assist the identification of those areas that might need to be addressed. The following are some examples of matters raised in particular chapters:

1. For many companies, the motivation to action results from an awareness and understanding of the challenges and opportunities facing a business and the board (Chapter 2). In many cases, incremental change is of itself not enough. If the board is the heart, soul and will of the company, then the initial drive and the sustained impetus for significant change must emanate from the boardroom.

2. The role and function of the board need to be understood by the board, and all directors should be aware of their legal duties and responsibilities (Chapter 3). The core role of the board in determining, monitoring and reviewing objectives and strategy, and the consequent need for strategic awareness and general business understanding should not be overlooked. The distinct requirements of boardroom roles such as that of chairman also need to be understood.

3. Calling people directors does not necessarily make them act like directors. The members of the board need to understand the distinction between direction and management (Chapter 4) and what characterizes the competent director (Chapter 6) and the effective board (Chapter 7).

4. Before 'rushing in' to 'general solutions', the nature, situation and circumstances of the company, and the development needs of the business should be understood. These factors will determine the type, size and composition of the board (Chapter 5). As one chairman put it: 'You need to get the membership right before you start thinking about development needs. Otherwise you may develop inappropriate people.'

5. The competent director needs legal, financial and other relevant knowledge, a range of personal skills and competences, and an awareness of issues and matters concerning directors and boards (Chapter 6).

6. Any attempt to define direction competences should acknowledge and reflect the general diversity of company types and board challenges, and the particular corporate climate, culture and context. A too tight and detailed definition of competences could inhibit flexibility.

Certain requirements may need to be adapted or refined as a business evolves.

7. Similar considerations apply to 'model' board structures (Chapter 7). These, too, should be considered cautiously, as what is most appropriate will depend upon the context, development challenge and particular combination of personalities sitting around the boardroom table.

8. Criteria need to be established for the selection of directors (Chapter 8). In many companies there does not appear to be a generally accepted statement of the qualities that are sought in members of the board. Neither is there a transparent route and 'development path' to the boardroom.

9. The development needs of individual directors, and of boards as teams, are not being fully addressed (Chapters 9 and 10). For example, there are many more company directors than qualified accountants, and yet, in spite of their legal duties and responsibilities, the resources being devoted to the training of directors is but a small fraction of that devoted to the professional development of the accountants who support them.

10. The training efforts of most professional bodies are almost entirely devoted to initial qualification and professional updating, with little, if any, serious attempt being made to equip their 'members' for the boardroom.

11. Both formal and informal development activities and learning opportunities need to be considered (Chapter 9). Directors, and particularly chairmen and CEOs, can benefit from networks of those to whom they can turn for advice concerning boardroom matters, and to obtain some insight, balance and perspective on key board and business issues.

12. The members of the board need to work together effectively as a team (Chapter 10). A minimal amount of imagination is devoted to innovation in the way the board itself functions.

13. A board could consider how the use of IT might enable them to operate in new ways. For example, a 'directors' network' could enable members of the board 'team' to discuss issues without the need to physically 'get together'. In far too many companies, the quality of catering in the executive or directors' dining room is more likely to be a matter of boardroom debate than 'board processes'.

14. Both individual effectiveness and team performance in the boardroom should be evaluated and assessed (Chapter 11). A chairman ought to understand how to evaluate directorial contributions and development needs, and set development objectives.

15. A board that is unable to 'implement' cannot be considered excellent. Barriers to the achievement of board objectives need to be identified and overcome (the present chapter). Ultimately, effectiveness derives not from the formulation of plans and statements, but the insight and commitment to ensure that they are put into effect.

Which of the above areas is most relevant will depend upon the particular company. A chairman might be happy with an existing board, but concerned about where the next generation of directors is to come from. 'Succession' is a concern of many chairmen.[5] Another chairman may have been happy in the past with his or her board, but might now face the prospect of coping with a major international expansion. The globalization of a market can give rise to a need to internationalize a board.[6]

12.3 The role of the chairman

Reference was made in Chapter 11 to the important role of the chairman in monitoring and evaluating director and board performance. The chairman of the board should assume responsibility for ensuring that individual board members are competent, and that the board as a whole is effective. The person who chairs board meetings is generally the individual who is best able to assess the directorial (as opposed to 'managerial') contributions of those who are seated around the boardroom table.

Because director development can be such an onerous responsibility, it is generally desirable that separate individuals hold the appointments of chairman and chief executive officer. The CEO should be free to concentrate upon running the executive team and delivering the 'business results'. In many companies director development does not occur simply because it is regarded as the responsibility of a busy CEO who does not have the time to focus upon it.

The chairman should act as catalyst in (a) causing the development needs of the board to be assessed and (b) ensuring that appropriate action is taken to tackle any deficiencies that emerge. As well as encouraging the use of formal learning where appropriate, a chairman could conduct boardroom discussions in such a way as to create opportunities for informal learning. A chairman should ensure that all directors are equipped and motivated to learn from their experience.

What else should the chairman do? We have seen throughout this book that there are many aspects of creating an effective board. Each chairman will have his or her own priorities according to the context. The following are among the many questions that could be asked by a new chairman:

1. When was the size and composition of the board last reviewed?

Particular attention may need to be given to the appointment of non-executive directors, and whether the search for candidates for executive director appointments might be extended beyond the senior management team.

2. A chairman should not flinch from changing the composition of the board if new attitudes, perspectives, approaches and qualities are required. The achievement of change may require the support of those who are not fettered by attachments, loyalties, associations and commitments to the past.[7] At the same time, a game of musical chairs should not be played in order to give the appearance of action.

3. Is the role of the non-executive director understood, or could better use be made of the non-executive directors? In promoting the desirability of non-executive directors, stress should be laid upon the value of bringing complementary skills, and a broader and more independent perspective, to a particular group.

4. Is there an 'induction' programme for all new appointees to the board? The chairman must ensure that, on appointment to the board, all directors are made aware of what they are expected to contribute, and of their legal and fiduciary duties and responsibilities.

5. Do the existing board members understand the role of the board, and their accountabilities, duties and responsibilities? When new appointments to the board are registered, the individuals concerned could be required to sign a declaration to the effect that they have examined and understand their legal duties and responsibilities as directors.

6. How effectively does the board operate as a team? The chairman should monitor the effectiveness of the board on an ongoing basis, and at least once a year the board itself should be invited to carry out a self-assessment of its effectiveness. To ensure objectivity, the board could seek external assistance in facilitating such a review.

7. It is particularly important that a board does not fall victim to collective self-deception and 'groupthink'. A board must be energetic at, and honest when, rooting out obstacles and barriers, including its own deficiencies, if these are to be tackled.

8. What does each of the directors contribute to the work of the board? The chairman should assess the personal effectiveness of all directors in the boardroom at least once a year. In the case of boards that have them, the chairman could seek the views of the non-executive directors when assessing the executive directors.

9. How often does the board undertake a fundamental review of whether there are alternative modes of operation that might be more appropriate in certain circumstances? For example, a company could make use of 'director networks' to ensure that directors are 'in touch'

to the extent necessary to allow them to discharge their accountabilities, duties and responsibilities.

10. How appropriate is the director development activity that is undertaken? For example, is a clear distinction made between 'direction' and 'management' by those who supply the company with director development services? As far as formal development is concerned, directors tend to have a preference for short courses that are participative and offered in a modular form.[5, 9]

11. Does the company publicly acknowledge its commitment to the development of individual directors and the boardroom team? An appropriate item could be included in the chairman's report. Those investing in companies should question the existence of, or the adequacy of, director development.

The board should benchmark itself against, and learn from, other boards. Sir John Harvey-Jones has pointed out that 'unless a board continuously criticizes the way it is working, is clear as to what it should be seeking to achieve, and its members . . . learn from each other, it is extraordinarily difficult for it to improve its performance'.[10]

Changes that occur as a result of posing questions such as those above should be considered, rather than introduced as a consequence of a panic reaction to a crisis situation. What is concluded in the 'heat of the moment' may not be appropriate for the 'long haul'.[11] It is often counter-productive, and generally unwise, to tinker with boards, treating directors as if they are pawns on a chessboard.

12.4 The strategic dimension

In two of the surveys that have been cited in this book,[12, 13] strategic awareness and understanding emerge as the priority director development requirements. The prominence given to strategic awareness is consistent with the essence of the distinction between direction and management, which we considered in Chapter 4. There we reviewed survey evidence which stressed the requirement for directors to look ahead, and with the perspective of the 'company as a whole'.[5]

Senge[14] has argued that in order to bring about fundamental change it is necessary to adopt a holistic perspective and understand how various elements and relevant factors are interrelated. The competent board needs to understand the interrelationships between strategy, structure, people, process and technology.[15] An integrated overview is needed in order to bring about significant organizational change.

While people at various levels may be involved and may participate in the strategy process, the board is expected to give a lead in the determination and implementation of strategy.[16] We saw in Chapter 3 how this activity relates to a central function of the board.

Interviews suggest that many chairmen of larger companies believe their boards should become more actively involved in driving change through the corporate organization. Excellence at crafting strategy is often matched with indifferent implementation, and gaps between aspiration/achievement and rhetoric/reality appear to be widespread.[17]

The strategy of a company should be matched to the ability of the board and management team to deliver.[17] If the capability to implement is lacking, the right strategy can lead to frustration (Figure 12.1). However, the implementation of the wrong strategy can lead to 'termination'. On the other hand, some boards have been saved from the consequences of their own collective errors of judgement by a failure to implement.[17]

Assembling the vision, capability and sense of purpose to turn aspiration into achievement should be regarded as equal to or greater than strategy formulation in terms of importance. Without implementation, the most perceptive and intuitive strategy will remain as 'words on paper'.

12.5 The board and corporate transformation

In Chapter 2 we considered the extent to which many companies are having to undergo a process of transformation in order to cope with the challenges and opportunities of a turbulent business environment. Reference has been made at a number of points in the book to the need for the board (a) to articulate the need for significant change and (b) to 'make it happen'. To do this 'helps' and 'hinders' must be identified, and obstacles and barriers overcome.

Many companies are using the quest for total quality as a 'catalyst of corporate transformation'. The creation of a quality culture is a reasonable enough aspiration.[18] Cultural and other changes need to occur if bureaucratic organizations are to make the transition to more flexible and responsive forms that are better able to tap the potential of their people and deliver value to customers.[19, 20] However, there is a widespread phenomenon of a considerable gap between corporate aspiration and the reality of achievement. Why, when the desire for corporate transformation among directors is so widespread, is so little progress being made? Why is a consensus in the boardroom on the need to change so rarely matched by an awareness of how to bring it about?[21, 22]

In Chapters 7 and 10 we identified the need for clear vision and strategy as the key change requirement. In a growing number of companies, cards containing mission statements have been distributed, and staff have been

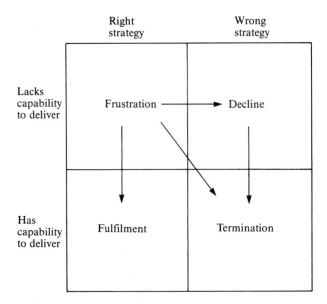

Figure 12.1 Strategy and capability[33]

'quality trained'. But where are the results in terms of changes of attitudes and behaviour? The particular and important case of quality is examined in the author's 'companion' book on developing directors,[23] but there is a general problem of failure to implement corporate programmes that needs to be addressed.[17]

Have exercises to formulate visions and missions not been accompanied by implementation strategies that could bring them about? In general, people are working hard, but decisions in the boardroom have not always been followed by management actions that have delivered tangible benefits for customers. Why are large investments in information technology and training so often reducing rather than increasing management productivity?

Corporate transformation is taking longer to achieve than many boards envisaged. There is frustration in the boardroom:

- Often the 'shelf life' of a corporate requirement is less than the time it might take to bring it about. This phenomenon can result in an 'action stalemate'.
- Reorganizations that involve termination payments and penalties on unexpired leases, etc., can be 'horrendously expensive'. As one interviewee stated: 'You spend money to lose money.'
- People readily pick up and use new words, but thinking through what they mean, and changing attitudes and behaviour takes time. 'Hearts

and minds' are difficult to reach. Many have grown cold and become cynical.

- In a growing number of organizations there is disenchantment and dis-illusion, as a result of a wide gulf between expectation and achievement.[21]
- Those with an interest in the status quo will resist change. A board should assume that there will be those who will resist the achievement of plans and policies that are perceived as inimical to their interests.[24]

In Chapter 4 we considered the arenas of conflict that exist in many companies as a result of different horizons and perspectives. Have efforts to articulate and share visions and missions been counter-productive, or is it too soon to judge?

The results of recent surveys[21, 22, 25] highlight the need for both clear vision and sustained top management commitment. They reveal that, in spite of good intentions in the boardroom, many managers are not being equipped with the skills to bring about corporate transformation and build a quality culture. They suggest that two new areas of focus are required in corporate boardrooms:

1. Key management and business processes, particularly those that cross departments and functions, need to be identified and re-engineered.
2. Attitudes and approaches, and tools and techniques, that have trans-formed management performance in 'benchmark' companies should be more widely adopted.

There is also a need for a more holistic approach, as only a minority of major companies appear to have 'a formal management of change programme'.[25] Only about one in six have 'a formal management of change programme' linked to a systems strategy.[25]

Companies with change programmes appear to be putting too much emphasis upon restructuring, and are devoting insufficient attention to attitudes, behaviour, values and processes. Changing the corporate culture is regarded by Schein[26] as a key element of the leadership provided by the board and senior management team.

Those intent upon corporate transformation should not underestimate the extent to which a corporate bureaucracy may 'fight back'. According to Tom Peters: 'Good intentions and brilliant proposals will be dead-ended, delayed, sabotaged, massaged to death, or revised beyond recognition or usefulness by the overlayered structures at most large and all too many small firms.'[27]

12.6 How to make it happen

The failure of many companies to turn aspiration into achievement often

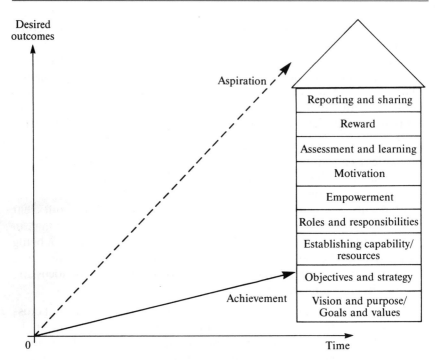

Figure 12.2   Assembling the building blocks[33]

results from gaps or missing elements in the corporate transformation strategy that is adopted. What is needed to bridge the gap between rhetoric and reality is to ensure that all the change elements that make up the transformation jigsaw puzzle, or the necessary building blocks, are in place[17] (Figure 12.2). The individual change elements that are needed will vary from company to company. However, in all cases they will need to be put in place, and in a logical order, if the board is to build upon firm foundations.

Thus the vision, goals and values need to be agreed and shared before measurable objectives are established. Objectives need to be determined before roles and responsibilities relating to their achievement can be allocated. What represents value to customers, and business objectives, will underlie process re-engineering; and how people are empowered, equipped, and rewarded will depend upon what they need to do to deliver value to customers and meet business objectives.

The lure of the fast result, blandishments and hype should be avoided. For those companies such as Xerox that are willing to confront reality, it is possible to bring about a significant change of attitudes and behaviour.[17, 28] In such companies a combination of appropriate change elements are assembled and applied to overcome obstacles and barriers to change, diversity and learning are encouraged, and there is a focus upon reality and the customer.[17]

12.7 The credibility challenge

Many boards appear to face a 'credibility challenge'. The 'gap' between vision and conduct, and rhetoric and reality, which appears to have emerged[21, 22, 25] suggests a widespread 'lack of top management commitment'. *The Flat Organisation* report,[21] the *Communicating for Change* survey[25] and other evidence[17] reveal much cause for concern. For example:

- There is widespread awareness of the need to transform organizations. Boards sense, and many can articulate, what is required. However, commitment to, and the desire for, significant change is rarely matched by the use of approaches and processes that might bring it about.
- The change elements that are necessary for successful transformation are not being assembled. Boards are not thinking through the implications and requirements. Many are 'clutching at straws', and adopting simplistic and partial approaches that are doomed to fail because key change elements are missing.
- Tactical adjustments, and simple or 'cosmetic' changes are occurring. Day-to-day priorities can and sometimes do alter overnight. However, fundamental changes at the level of the 'roots' of an organization are rare. Attitudes and values are difficult to shift, and the adoption of an altered approach or perspective usually takes much longer. Some boards are changing direction before 'the results have time to come through'.
- 'Short-termism' can sap the managerial spirit. The short-term actions of many boards, in response to economic recession, are not always consistent with either a company's vision or the building of long-term relationships with its customers. Many boards are oblivious to the disillusion caused by the gaps between their words and their subsequent actions and conduct.
- While CEOs and members of boards stress the need for delegation and the importance of improving the quality of management, individual managers are not being equipped to handle the new demands that are being placed upon them. Too many boards are using the language of empowerment while persisting in a command and control approach.

In the case of quality programmes, the board itself is seen as a major constraint. The *Quality: The Next Steps* survey[22] reveals that the main barrier, by a large margin, in terms of 'very significant' replies is 'top management commitment'. Over nine out of ten respondents consider this to be a very significant barrier to the successful implementation of a quality process. Many of those interviewed 'pointed a finger' at the board, citing directors who were not thought to be 'serious' about quality, or who do not 'really believe in it', or are 'not doing it'. Directors acknowledged that some of their colleagues were 'not good ambassadors', or 'role models'. One director of quality referred to director colleagues as 'passengers on the quality journey, who would "get off at the first stop" if they were able to do so'.

The implementation of quality, and the 'benchmark' experience of Rank Xerox, are considered in some detail in the author's companion books on developing directors[23] and corporate transformation[17].

Many boards find it very difficult to cope with fundamental challenges. In order to bring about a significant change of attitudes and perspective in the boardroom it may be necessary to change the directorial team, and CEOs are particularly vulnerable when significant gaps between aspiration and achievement are visible.[29] Hence there is sometimes a desire to conceal reality. A board should be rewarded rather than penalized for openness and honesty in reporting performance gaps, providing 'root causes' are identified, corrective action plans are put in place, and learning occurs.

12.8 Understanding where you are

In a turbulent and challenging market and corporate environment in which discontinuities abound, there is considerable scope for misperception and misunderstanding.[30] A board should confront rather than avoid reality. In some corporate organizations, concealment and deception abound, and effort and persistence may be required to find the 'root causes'.

Many companies are striving to become flatter and more flexible without first identifying those activities that really add value for customers. Responsibilities are given to managers, and other employees, who are not equipped to cope with them.[21] Problems are not anticipated, and likely barriers are not identified and removed. As a result, many corporate change initiatives are built upon foundations of sand. It is little wonder that such wide and visible gaps emerge between rhetoric and reality.

Before initiating a demanding transformation, or total quality programme, a board should undertake a comprehensive 'corporate health check' in order to (a) understand the current situation in terms of both the need for, and potential for, change; and (b) identify change constraints and how they might be overcome. Some boards will need the help of trained facilitators to guide structured review sessions, and detailed frameworks for such an exercise exist.[31]

On the completion of a 'corporate health check' review process, the members of a board should understand 'where they are'. Gaps, barriers and deficiencies should have been identified. Among other 'health check' outputs, the board should be provided with an action programme and timetable that is tailored to the particular situation and circumstances of the company.

The carrying out of a systematic analysis, and the development of an action programme should allow a board to proceed with greater awareness and confidence. Downside risks should be reduced, and the prospects for success improved. In particular:

- The directors should share an agreed understanding of the current situation and practical suggestions concerning the way ahead. A greater degree of unity might result from the consensus achieved.
- The action programme should detail the next steps to be taken, including the techniques and tools that could be used to overcome implementation barriers. It should be designed to shape thought, change attitudes and behaviour, and achieve differentiation in the marketplace.
- The action programme suggested should be capable of implementation, and the timetable should be realistic. It ought to be within the capability of the company, and, in the case of a total quality initiative, should lead not only to the achievement of a recognized quality standard, but beyond.

The members of an effective board ought to have the perspective to see the broad picture and to assemble all the 'pieces of the puzzle'. However, 'role model' or 'benchmark' boards are scarce:

- Most companies are 'missing some pieces'. Their boards are generally looking for them in the wrong places.
- Within corporate organizations there are obstacles and barriers, frequently unrecognized, that are preventing the 'breakthroughs' that could lead from rhetoric to reality.

A board needs to ensure that an honest assessment has been made of the situation or context within which change needs to occur. Particular attention should be devoted to determining which pieces of the transformation 'jig saw' are missing. Throwing more people and resources into the transformation task may increase frustration if key obstacles are not removed or if key enablers are not put in place. As we have seen, the right strategy needs to be matched by the capability to deliver (see Figure 12.1).

12.9 The board and key management and business processes

The 'corporate governance' debate is focused very much upon accountability to shareholders and 'control' matters such as the use of non-executive directors, and 'audit' and 'remuneration' committees. To 'restore the balance', let us conclude with the identification and delivery of what represents value to customers, and an emerging focus upon processes that could have profound consequences for the responsibilities of the executive director.

The 'delivery' of corporate objectives, including the achievement of total quality targets, can depend critically upon certain vital management and business processes.[17, 32] Many boards do not even know what they are, let alone exercise any reponsibilities towards them. Identifying and documenting them may be a crucial 'next step'.

Of especial importance are those key cross-functional and inter-organizational processes that add value for customers.[17] Their role in bridging the gap between 'customer requirement' and 'customer satisfaction', and their potential for shortening it, is illustrated in Figure 12.3.

Too often, investments in training and information technology are made upon a departmental basis (Figure 12.3). They are applied to 'visible' and departmental activities, and frequently miss the 'hidden' delays and other problems at the cross-over points that fall between the 'stools of functional responsibility'[17]:

- While the major source of a delay is caused by the 'interface' between departments, no amount of departmental 'investment' of resources may 'speed things up'. The 'real' obstacle to improved performance may remain undetected.
- When adjacent departments 'invest' in incompatible training, or technology from different 'proprietory' sources, the 'interface' problems, and a tendency to 'departmental introversion', may actually increase. This gives rise to the common phenomenon of expenditure on training, and particularly technology, actually *reducing* management productivity.

The key to improving 'white-collar' productivity and the 'quality of management' is to focus investment in both training and technology upon the cross-functional processes that 'deliver' customer satisfaction and remove customer dissatisfaction. The board should ensure that a horizontal rather than a vertical approach is adopted (Figure 12.3):

- The key cross-functional processes should be 'owned', preferably by a member of the board.
- They should be supported by the account management process; and employees should be equipped and empowered to harness corporate

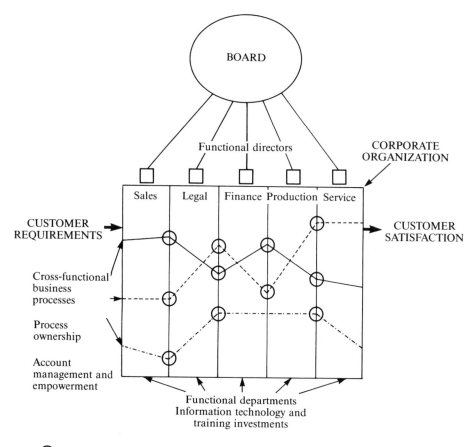

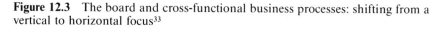

Figure 12.3   The board and cross-functional business processes: shifting from a vertical to horizontal focus[33]

resources, irrespective of function, location and nationality, in order to satisfy a customer.
– Use should be made of appropriate tools and approaches to ensure that processes are re-engineered to meet changing customer requirements.

A board that is intent upon making significant improvements in management productivity should pay particular attention to the document process. The flow of documents across and through the corporate organization is often the 'vehicle' that 'makes it happen' for the customer. Most companies spend only the equivalent of a small proportion of their information technology budget upon supporting key cross-functional flows of documents.

The outcome of a 'focus upon process' could be the allocation of process responsibilities to executive board members. Eventually, process responsibilities could replace departmental responsibilities in the boardroom. This would help to lift the 'curse of professionalism' from many boardrooms[17] and enable more executive directors to develop a cross-functional perspective.

Responsibilities for inter-organizational processes could extend the perspective of the board to embrace the full network of supply chain relationships. As a consequence, the growth and development of the board would be more likely to match the changing requirements for the effective direction of the evolving network organization.

Above all, the process approach encourages a focus upon 'the customer'. The director and the board should never forget that 'the customer', and not the boardroom, is the source of all value.

12.10 Summary

In this chapter we have examined possible 'next steps'. Actions and initiatives should reflect the nature, situation, circumstances and business development needs of the company. In particular, they should tackle priority deficiencies and obstacles to the achievement of corporate vision, goals, values and objectives.

For a large number of boards, the challenge is not so much determining what needs to be done, as 'making it happen'. However competent the directors and effective the board, the capability that has been established must be kept up to date. In particular, the management and business processes of a company need to be kept continually under review to ensure that they focus upon whatever constitutes value for customers.

Most boards face the daunting challenge of turning aspiration into achievement, and in the context of a turbulent and demanding business environment. The key to success is to ensure that: (a) the board is united, committed, and focused; (b) 'every element of the corporate transformation jigsaw puzzle is in place'; and (c) the 'vital few' actions are initiated to tackle the major barriers to the attainment of a shared corporate vision.

12.11 Checklist

1. Who in your company is responsible for ensuring that it has an effective board made up of competent directors?
2. Has the board accepted a commitment to, and agreed a programme of, ongoing learning and development?

3. Does such a programme adequately reflect the particular situation and circumstances of the company, and the nature of the business it is in?
4. Is there a shared and compelling vision that is rooted in the customer?
5. Does the development programme reflect the vision, goals, values and objectives of the company, and its business development needs?
6. Have all the key areas of deficiency or need been addressed; and is there sufficient stress upon the need to 'make it happen'?
7. Where such a programme does not exist, who is to act as a catalyst for its creation?
8. What are the main barriers, obstacles or 'hinders' to director and board development, and what is being done to overcome them?
9. Is there sustained 'top management' commitment to corporate renewal and transformation; and do the directors and senior executives exude role model behaviour ?
10. Have all the change elements been assembled to bring about a successful corporate transformation?
11. Is the board motivated, and the company 'run', according to customer-related objectives? Is performance measured in terms of its impact upon the customer; and are corporate processes and procedures focused on the customer?
12. Are people involved, empowered and committed; and is reward strategy consistent with corporate goals and objectives?
13. Have the key cross-functional management and business processes that add value for customers been identified, re-engineered, as appropriate, in order to focus more clearly upon customer requirements, and have responsibilities for them been allocated in the boardroom?

Notes and references

1. Prahalad, C. K., 'Developing strategic capability: An agenda for top management', *Human Resource Management*, **22** (3), Fall 1983, 237–54.
2. Waterman, R. H., *The Renewal Factor*, Bantam, 1987.
3. Sykes, A., 'Corporate governance, bigger carrots and sticks', *Financial Times*, 31 October 1990, p. 19.
4. Mills, G., 'Who controls the board?', *Long Range Planning*, **22** (3), 1989, 125–32; and Dobrzynski, J. H. *et al.*, 'Taking charge', *International Business Week*, 3 July 1989, pp. 36–43.
5. Coulson-Thomas, C., *Professional Development of and for the Board*. A questionnaire and interview survey undertaken by Adaptation Ltd of company chairmen. A summary has been published by the IOD, February 1990.
6. Coulson-Thomas, C., *Creating the Global Company: Successful internationalization*, McGraw-Hill, 1992.

7. Hambrick, D. and Mason, P., 'Upper echelons: The organisation as a reflection of its top management', *Academy of Management Review*, **9** (2), 1984, 193–206.
8. Janis, I. L., *Victims of Groupthink*, Houghton-Mifflin, 1972.
9. Wakelam, A., *The Training & Development of Company Directors*. A report on a questionnaire survey undertaken by the Centre for Management Studies, University of Exeter for the Training Agency, December 1989.
10. Harvey-Jones, Sir J., *Making it Happen*, Collins, 1988, p. 162.
11. Allison, G., *Essence of Decision*, Little Brown, 1971.
12. Coulson-Thomas, C. and Wakelam, A., *The Effective Board: Current practice, myths and realities*. An IOD discussion document, 1991.
13. Coulson-Thomas, C., *The Role and Function of the Personnel Director*. An interim Adaptation Ltd survey carried out in conjunction with the Research Group of the Institute of Personnel Management, 1991.
14. Senge, P., *The Fifth Discipline: The art and practice of the learning organisation*, Doubleday/Currency, 1990.
15. Benjamin, R. I. and Scott Morton, M., 'Information technology, integration, and organisational change', *Interfaces*, **18**, May–June 1988, 86–98.
16. Houlden, B., *Understanding Company Strategy: An introduction to thinking and acting strategically*, Blackwell, 1991; and Davies, A., *Strategic Leadership: Making corporate plans work*, Woodhead-Faulkner, 1991.
17. Coulson-Thomas, C., *Transforming the Company: Bridging the gap between management myth and corporate reality*, Kogan Page, 1992.
18. Coulson-Thomas, C. and Brown, R., *Beyond Quality: Managing the relationship with the customer*, BIM, Corby, 1990.
19. Coulson-Thomas, C. and Brown, R., *The Responsive Organisation: People management, the challenge of the 1990s*, BIM, 1989.
20. Kanter, R. M., *When Giants Learn to Dance*, Simon & Schuster, 1989.
21. Coulson-Thomas, C. and Coe, T., *The Flat Organisation: Philosophy and practice*, BIM, 1991.
22. Coulson-Thomas, C. and Coulson-Thomas, S., *Quality: The Next Steps*. An Adaptation Ltd survey for ODI, Adaptation Ltd, 1991; executive summary available from ODI Europe, 1991.
23. Coulson-Thomas, C., *Developing Directors: Building an effective boardroom team*, McGraw-Hill, 1993.
24. Bennis, W., Benne, R. and Chin, R. (eds), *The Planning of Change*, Holt, Rinehart and Winston, 1970.
25. Coulson-Thomas, C. and Coulson-Thomas, S., *Communicating for Change*. An Adaptation Ltd survey for Granada Business Services, Adaptation Ltd, 1991.
26. Schein, E. H., *Organisational Culture and Leadership*, Jossey-Bass, 1985.
27. Peters, T., *Thriving on Chaos*, Alfred A. Knopf, 1987.
28. Jacobson, G. and Hillkirk, J., *Xerox, American Samurai: The behind-the-scenes story of how a corporate giant beat the Japanese at their own game*, Macmillan, 1986.
29. Tushman, M. L., Newman, W. H. and Nadler, D. A., 'Executive leadership and organisational evolution: Managing incremental and discontinuous change', in R. Kilman and T. J. Covey (eds), *Corporate Transformation*, Jossey-Bass, 1988.
30. Jervis, R., *Perception and Misperception in International Politics*, Princeton University Press, 1976.
31. Adaptation/Rank Xerox, *The Business Excellence Health Check*. A six category

'corporate health check' of 41 items, Adaptation Ltd and Rank Xerox (UK) Ltd, 1992.

32. Bartram, P., *Re-inventing the Company: The use of IT to re-engineer corporate processes*, Business Intelligence, 1992; and Woolfe, R., *The Role of Information Technology in Transforming the Business*, Butler Cox Foundation, 1991.

33. Figures 12.1–12.3 are taken from Coulson-Thomas, C., *Transforming the Company: Bridging the gap between management myth and corporate reality*, Kogan Page, 1992. This book takes a more extensive look at a range of myths and misunderstandings; gaps between aspiration and achievement, and rhetoric and reality; and the role of the board in the successful implementation of corporate transformation.

Appendix 1: Forming an overview

Director and board effectiveness checklist

This book raises many issues and questions that could be drawn upon to form an overview of director and board effectiveness. The following checklist represents an illustrative list of questions:

Challenges facing business and boards (from Chapters 1 and 2)

- How committed are members of the board to the company and its stakeholders?
- Has the board defined the essence and purpose of the company, and to what extent is this distinctive?
- Does the board understand the changing nature of the business and market environment?
- Does the board operate an effective issue monitoring and management process?
- Does the board fully understand the requirements, aspirations and perspective of customers and employees?
- How well equipped is the board for the challenge of corporate transformation?
- How effective is the board at establishing and sustaining relationships with stakeholders and other interested parties?

Role and function of the board (from Chapter 3)

- How does the board see its primary role, and priority functions?
- To whom does the board consider it is accountable, and for what?
- How effectively does the board arbitrate between the interests of various stakeholders?

- Does the board regularly review its accountabilities and responsibilities?
- Do all the directors understand their legal duties and responsibilities?
- Has the board articulated a compelling corporate vision and clear goals, values and objectives?
- Are members of the board able to distinguish between the roles of owners, directors and managers?
- Has the chairman assumed responsibility for the development of competent directors and an effective board?

Distinction between direction and management (from Chapter 4)

- Is there a shared understanding in the boardroom of the essence of direction?
- Do all members of the board understand the distinction between direction and management?
- Do the executive directors devote sufficient attention to the 'direction' aspects of their role?
- Within the company, is there actual or potential conflict between the focus and horizons of directors and those of managers?
- Are there problems of awareness, attitude, perspective, communication, or understanding in the relationships between directors and managers?
- How smooth and effective is the transition from manager to director?

Type, size and composition of boards (from Chapter 5)

- Is the nature of the board appropriate to the situation and circumstances of the company?
- Has the evolution of the board matched the development of the company's business?
- How appropriate is the size and composition of the board in relation to the vision, goals, values and objectives of the company?
- Does the board regularly review its composition?
- Should the membership of the board include (further) non-executive and facilitating directors?
- Are the necessary processes in place to ensure that the board secures access to the various inputs of information and expertise that it requires?

The competent director (from Chapter 6)

- Does the board regularly review what constitutes a competent director in relation to the situation and circumstances of the company?

- Has the board identified, grouped and prioritized its key competence requirements?
- How complementary are the qualities of the existing members of the boardroom team?
- Do all the directors understand the contribution they are expected to make to the work of the board?
- How aware are the directors of ethical issues and considerations?

DIRECTOR KNOWLEDGE AND SKILL REQUIREMENTS

- Are the various factors which influence skill requirements understood?
- Are members of the board aware of the legal, financial and other knowledge, and of the personal skills and competences, they should possess?
- To what extent do members of the board have a directorial perspective?
- How many of the directors are aware of, and understand, key boardroom issues?
- How strong are the facilitating and corporate transformation, or the 'making it happen', skills of members of the board?
- Do the directors understand, and is the board focused upon, the key management and business processes that add value for customers?

The effective board (from Chapter 7)

- Are the priorities of the board appropriate to the situation and context of the company?
- Does the perspective of the board extend to supply chain relationships?
- Does the board operate as a board, or as a 'management committee'?
- How effective is the board in terms of how it conducts its business?
- Is the board a 'learning board', and is the boardroom a learning environment?
- Does the board regularly and systematically review its own effectiveness?
- Have the main barriers to board effectiveness been identified, and is appropriate action being taken to overcome them?
- Has the board allocated responsibilities, and established actions, in respect of the key management and business processes that add value for customers?
- Does the board have a view on the key issues, and the various options, concerning corporate governance?

Selection and appointment of directors (from Chapter 8)

- Are the prevailing routes to the boardroom appropriate to the situation, circumstances and context of the company?
- How open, transparent and accessible are the prevailing routes to the boardroom?
- Has the board determined and made explicit the qualities that it is seeking in new members?
- Has the board established and agreed the criteria and process to be used to select additional members?
- In particular, is full account taken of the qualities and contributions of the existing members when new appointments are made to the board?
- Do those with directorial prospects and potential understand (a) the qualities that are sought in directors and (b) the selection process?
- Have the development implications of both the qualities that are sought, and the selection process that is used, been thought through?
- Should the pool of 'potential director' candidates and the 'directorial development arena' be widened?
- Is there a director development programme to meet the directorial quality, knowledge and skill requirements that have been identified and are sought?
- How adequate is the process of director selection?
- What advice is available to the individual with directorial ambitions?

Developing directors (from Chapter 9)

- Is there a comprehensive induction programme for new members of the board?
- Are all directors (both existing and new) made aware of their legal duties and responsibilities?
- Is the need for director development matched by appropriate action?
- Are obstacles to director development identified and overcome?
- How positive are the attitudes of members of the board towards director development, and does it have its champions within the boardroom?
- How effective is the informal preparation for the boardroom that is undertaken?
- Are members of the board actively participating in directors' networks?
- Is the role and contribution of formal development understood?
- How do members of the board keep their directorial skills and awareness up to date?
- Does the board have access to appropriate sources of director development advice?

– Does the board make appropriate and effective use of relevant sources of director development services?
– Does the development activity that is undertaken reflect the development preferences of members of the board?
– Are the special development requirements of particular and future directors understood and met?
– Is director development integrated into, and complementary to, overall development activity, and does the board encourage formal and informal learning throughout the organization?

Building the boardroom team (from Chapter 10)

– What are the main barriers to board performance?
– How might board performance be improved?
– How effectively do the members of the board work together as a team?
– Does the board actively learn from its own activities and discussions?
– Are learning opportunities within the boardroom identified, and is full opportunity taken of them?

Evaluating performance (from Chapter 11)

– Has the board established standards of excellence in terms of attitudes, behaviour, and processes to which the company should aspire?
– Have measurable outputs been agreed in respect of each objective of the board, and are these monitored and corrective action taken as appropriate?
– Does the board establish criteria for distinguishing between effective and inadequate performance in respect of: (a) the contributions of individual directors; and (b) the work of the board as a team?
– Is the effectiveness of the board evaluated at least once a year?
– Is full use made of the relative objectivity of non-executive directors when boardroom performance and board effectiveness are evaluated?
– Does the board regularly monitor the operation of, and re-engineer as appropriate, key board, management and business processes?
– Are periodic board document audits undertaken, i.e. does the board (and its membership) receive information in a form that is conducive of understanding?
– Does the chairman regularly assess the directorial contribution of each member of the board?
– Are deficiencies identified and tackled by appropriate development activities?
– How open, receptive and willing to learn is the board?

– Does the board actively learn, on a best practice basis, from the experiences of non-competing 'benchmark' boards and companies?

The next steps (from Chapter 12)

– Are all the elements in place to allow the vision, goals, values and objectives of the company to be achieved?
– Which elements are missing, i.e. what are the main barriers and obstacles?
– Have all the key cross-functional management and business processes been identified and documented?
– Has the board identified and prioritized the 'vital few' next steps that need to be taken to ensure that the vision, goals, values and objectives of the company are achieved?
– What do the various stakeholders, and, particularly, the owners, customers, employees and business partners, think of the board?

And, finally:

The overall assessment (from Chapters 1 to 12)

– How effective is the board in terms of its function, accountabilities and responsibilities?
– How competent are the members of the board in their directorial roles?
– Has the board established, communicated and shared (a) a compelling and distinctive vision and (b) clear and challenging goals, values, and objectives?
– Do the members of the board act as learning role models?
– Is working and learning integrated within the boardroom, and in the company generally?
– Does director development activity meet the 'needs of the business'?
– Is the board, as a team, equipped to 'make it happen'?
– Are the key processes and enablers in place to turn rhetoric into reality, and aspiration into achievement?
– Overall, is the board a 'help' or a 'hinder', an enabler or a burden?

Appendix 2:
Source surveys

'Director and board' surveys

The following selection of reports from an ongoing programme of investigations of directorial and boardroom practice represent the prime source of background evidence used in the preparation of this book:

Coulson-Thomas, C. (1990), *Professional Development of and for the Board*. An Adaptation Ltd survey for the Institute of Directors. A summary published by the IOD, London.

Coulson-Thomas, C. (1990), *Developing IT Directors*. An interim Adaptation Ltd report to the Department of Computing Science, Surrey University.

Coulson-Thomas, C. and Wakelam, A. (1990), *Developing Directors*. A survey, funded by the Training Agency, undertaken by Adaptation Ltd with the Centre for Management Studies, University of Exeter.

Coulson-Thomas, C. (1991), *The Role and Development of the Personnel Director*. An interim Adaptation Ltd survey undertaken in conjunction with the Institute of Personnel Management (IPM) Research Group, IPM, Wimbledon.

Coulson-Thomas, C. and Wakelam, A. (1991), *The Effective Board: Current practice, myths and realities*. An Institute of Directors discussion document, IOD, London.

Coulson-Thomas, C. (1992), *Development Needs of NHS Authority and Board Members*. An Adaptation Ltd report prepared on behalf of the NHS Training Directorate, London.

Boardroom issue surveys

The following selection of reports have also been drawn upon in order to understand the interrelationship between directorial responsibilities; board strategy, objectives, policies and issues; and the market and corporate context:

Coulson-Thomas, C. (1988), *The New Professionals*, BIM, Corby.

Coulson-Thomas, C. and Brown, R. (1989), *The Responsive Organisation: People management, the challenge of the 1990s*, BIM, Corby.

Coulson-Thomas, C. (1989), *Too Old at 40?*, BIM, Corby.

Coulson-Thomas, C. and Brown, R. (1990), *Beyond Quality: Managing the relationship with the customer*, BIM, Corby.

Coulson-Thomas, C. (1990), *Human Resource Development for International Operation*. An Adaptation Ltd survey sponsored by Surrey European Management School, Adaptation, London.

Coulson-Thomas, C. (1990), *The Role and Status of Project Management*. An Adaptation Ltd survey for the Association of Project Managers, Adaptation, London.

Coulson-Thomas, C. and Coulson-Thomas, S. (1990), *Managing the Relationship with the Environment*. An Adaptation Ltd survey sponsored by Rank Xerox (UK) Ltd, Adaptation, London.

Coulson-Thomas, C. and Coulson-Thomas, S. (1990), *Implementing a Telecommuting Programme: A Rank Xerox guide for those considering the implementation of a telecommuting programme*, Adaptation, London.

Coulson-Thomas, C. and Coulson-Thomas, S. (1991), *Quality: The Next Steps*. An Adaptation Ltd survey sponsored by ODI International, Adaptation and (Executive Summary) ODI International, London.

Coulson-Thomas, C. and Coulson-Thomas, S. (1991), *Communicating for Change*. An Adaptation Ltd survey sponsored by Granada Business Services, Adaptation, London.

Coulson-Thomas, C. and Coe, T. (1991), *The Flat Organisation: Philosophy and practice* (the initial questionnaire survey was entitled: *Managing the Flat Organisation*), BIM, Corby.

Coulson-Thomas, C. (1993), *Harnessing the Potential of Groups*. An Adaptation Ltd survey sponsored by Lotus Development, Adaptation, London.

Related books

Some of the issues raised in *Creating Excellence in the Boardroom* are considered in greater detail in the following books, which also draw, in part, upon the above research programme:

Coulson-Thomas, C. (1992), *Creating the Global Company: Successful internationalization*, McGraw-Hill, Maidenhead.

Coulson-Thomas, C. (1992), *Transforming the Company: Bridging the gap between management myth and corporate reality*, Kogan Page, London.

Coulson-Thomas, C. (1993), *Developing Directors: Building an effective boardroom team*, McGraw-Hill, Maidenhead.

Further information

Further information on any of the surveys referred to in this appendix can be obtained from Adaptation Ltd, Rathgar House, 237 Baring Road, Grove Park, London SE12 OBE, England. Tel: 081-857 5907.

Details of the BIM publications cited, and of other related BIM surveys and reports, can be obtained from the Publications Department, Institute of Management, Management House, Cottingham Road, Corby, Northants, NN17 1TT, England. Tel: 0536 204222.

Details of director development courses, workshops and seminars of the IOD, and related publications, can be obtained from the Centre for Director Development, Institute of Directors, 116 Pall Mall, London SW1Y 5ED, England. Tel: 071-839 1233.

Bibliography

3i's, *Corporate strategies and the FD*, 3i's sixth plc UK survey, Financial Director, February 1992: 24–5.

3i's, *The FD and corporate governance*, 3i's seventh plc UK survey, Financial Director, April 1992: 23–4.

The Association of British Insurers (ABI), *The Responsibilities of Institutional Shareholders*, ABI, March 1991.

Adair, J., *Effective Teambuilding*, Gower, 1986.

Alkhafaji, A. F., 'Effective Boards of Directors', *Industrial Management and Data Systems*, Vol. 90, No. 4, 1990: 18–26.

Allison, G., *Essence of Decision*, Little Brown, 1971.

Ansoff, H. I., *Corporate Strategy*, McGraw-Hill, 1965.

Ansoff, H. I., *Implanting Strategic Management*, Prentice-Hall, 1984 and 1990.

Aram, J. D. and Cowen, S. S., 'Information Requirements of Corporate Directors: The Role of the Board in the Process of Management', Final Report to the National Association of Accountants, April 1983.

Argyris, C. and Schon, D. A., *Organisational Learning: A theory of action perspective*, Addison-Wesley, 1978.

Argyris, C., *Strategy, Change and Defensive Routines*, Pitman, 1985.

Bachrach, P., and Baratz, M., 'Two Faces of Power', *American Political Science Review*, Vol. 56, 1962, 947–52.

Bacon, J., 'Membership and the Organization of Corporate Boards, Research', Report No. 886, Conference Board, 1986.

Baker, J. C., *Directors and Their Functions*, Harvard University School of Business Administration, 1945.

Bartram, P., *Re-inventing the Company, the use of IT to re-engineer corporate processes*, Business Intelligence, 1992.

Bartram, P., and Coulson-Thomas, C., *The Complete Spokesperson, a workbook for managers who meet the media*, Kogan Page, 1991.

Bavly, D., 'What is The Board of Directors Good For?', in B. Taylor (ed.), *Strategic Planning, the Chief Executive and the Board*, Pergamon Press, 1988: 35–41.

Beer, M. and Walton, E., 'Developing the Competitive Organisation, Interventions and Strategies', *American Psychologist*, Vol. 45, No. 2, February 1990: 154–61.

Beevor, J. G., *The Effective Board: a Chairman's View*, BIM, 1975.

Belbin, R., *Management Teams*, Heinemann Educational Books, 1981.

Benjamin, R. I. and Scott Morton, M., 'Information Technology, Integration, and Organisational Change', *Interfaces*, Vol. 18, May–June 1988: 86–98.

Bennis, W., *On Becoming a Leader*, Hutchinson Business Books, 1990.

Bennis, W., Benne, R. and Chin, R. (eds), *The Planning of Change*, Holt, Rinehart and Winston, 1970.

Bennis, W. and Nanus, B., *Leaders: The Strategies for Taking Charge*, Harper & Row, 1985.

Boone, L. and Johnson, J., 'Profiles of the 801 men and one woman at the top', *Business Horizons*, February 1980, 47–52.

Boyd, B., 'Corporate linkages and organisational environment, a test of the resource dependence model', *Strategic Management Journal*, Vol. 11, No. 6, October 1990: 419–30.

Burns, T. and Stalker, G. M., *The Management of Innovation*, Tavistock, 1961.

Brunsson, N., *The Organisation of Hypocrisy*, John Wiley, 1991.

Cadbury, Sir A., *Company Chairman*, Director Books, 1990.

Camp, R. C., *Benchmarking: The Search for Industry Best Practices that Lead to Superior Performance*, Quality Press, 1989.

Campbell, A. and Yeung, S., 'Do You Need a Mission Statement?', *Economist* Special Report No. 1208, 1990.

Carr, A. Z., 'Can an Executive Afford a Conscience?', *Harvard Business Review*, July–August 1970: 58–74.

Chandler, A. D., *Strategy and Structure: Chapters in the History of the American Industrial Enterprise*, The MIT Press, 1962.

Charkham, J. P., 'Effective Boards', The Institute of Chartered Accountants in England and Wales, 1986.

Committee on The Financial Aspects of Corporate Governance (Chairman, Sir Adrian Cadbury), Draft Report issued for public comment, 27 May 1992, Committee on The Financial Aspects of Corporate Governance, 1992.

Coopers & Lybrand Deloitte, *Becoming a Director?: What you need to know*, Coopers & Lybrand Deloitte, 1991.

Copeman, G., *The Chief Executive*, Leviathan House, 1971.

Copeman, G., *The Managing Director*, Business Books, 2nd edn 1982.

Coulson-Thomas, C., 'Career Paths to the Boardroom', *International Journal of Career Management*, Vol. 2, No. 3, 1990: 26–32.

Coulson-Thomas, C., 'Company Directors, the myths and the realities', *Administrator*, May 1991: 4–6.

Coulson-Thomas, C., *Creating the Global Company: Successful internationalization*, McGraw-Hill, 1992.

Coulson-Thomas, C., 'Customers, Marketing and the Network Organisation', *Journal of Marketing Management*, 1991, 7, 237–55.

Coulson-Thomas, C., 'Developing Competent Directors and Effective Boards', *Journal of Management Development*, Vol. 11, No. 1, 1992: 39–49.

Coulson-Thomas, C., 'Developing Directors', *European Management Journal*, Vol. 8, No. 4, December 1990: 488–99.

Coulson-Thomas, C., *Developing Directors: Building an Effective Boardroom Team*, McGraw-Hill, 1993.

Coulson-Thomas, C., 'Developing IT Directors', an Adaptation Ltd report to the Department of Computing Science, Surrey University, 1990.

Coulson-Thomas, C., 'Development Needs of NHS Authority and Board Members', an Adaptation Ltd report prepared on behalf of the NHS Training Directorate, July 1992.

Coulson-Thomas, C., 'Directors and IT, and IT Directors', *European Journal of Information Systems*, Vol. 1, No. 1, 1991: 45–53.

Coulson-Thomas, C., 'From personnel professional to successful personnel director: developing competent directors and effective boards', seminar paper prepared for the 1991 Annual Conference of the IPM, Harrogate, 24 October 1991.

Coulson-Thomas, C., 'Human Resource Development for International Operation', a survey sponsored by Surrey European Management School, Adaptation Ltd, 1990.

Coulson-Thomas, C., 'IT directors and IT strategy', *Journal of Information Technology*, **6**, 1991: 192–203.

Coulson-Thomas, C., 'Preparation for the Boardroom' *Training & Development*, Vol. 8, No. 12, December 1990: 18.

Coulson-Thomas, C., 'Professional Development of and for the Board', a questionnaire and interview survey undertaken by Adaptation Ltd of company chairmen. A summary has been published by the Institute of Directors, 1990.

Coulson-Thomas, C., *Public Relations is Your Business, a guide for every manager*, Business Books, 1981.

Coulson-Thomas, C., 'Quality: Where Do We Go from Here?', *International Journal of Quality and Reliability Management*, Vol. 9, No. 1, 1992: 38–55.

Coulson-Thomas, C., 'Strategic Vision or Strategic Con?: Rhetoric or Reality?', *Long Range Planning*, Vol. 25, No. 1, 1992: 81–9.

Coulson-Thomas, C., 'The Competent Director', *Corporate Administrator*, July 1990: 12–14.

Coulson-Thomas, C., 'The Role and Development of the Personnel Director', an Adaptation Ltd interim survey undertaken in conjunction with the Institute of Personnel Management (IPM) Research Group, IPM, Wimbledon 1991.

Coulson-Thomas, C., 'The Role and Status of Project Management', an Adaptation Ltd survey and report for the Association of Project Managers, 1990.

Coulson-Thomas, C., *Too Old at 40?*, BIM, 1989.

Coulson-Thomas, C., *Transforming the Company: Bridging the Gap Between Management Myth and Corporate Reality*, Kogan Page, 1992.

Coulson-Thomas, C., 'What the Personnel Director Can Bring to the Boardroom Table', *Personnel Management*, October 1991: 36–9.

Coulson-Thomas, C. and S., 'Communicating for Change', an Adaptation Ltd survey for Granada Business Services, 1991.

Coulson-Thomas, C. and S., 'Managing the Relationship with the Environment', an Adaptation Ltd sponsored by Rank Xerox (UK) Ltd, 1990.

Coulson-Thomas, C. and S., 'Quality: The Next Steps', an Adaptation Ltd survey for ODI, 1991. An executive summary has been published by ODI Europe, 1991.

Coulson-Thomas, C. and Brown, R., 'Beyond Quality: Managing the Relationship with the Customer', BIM, 1990.

Coulson-Thomas, C. and Brown, R., *The Responsive Organisation: People Management, the Challenge of the 1990s*, BIM, 1989.

Coulson-Thomas, C. and Coe, T., 'The Flat Organisation: Philosophy and Practice', BIM, 1991.

Coulson-Thomas, C. and Didacticus Video Productions Ltd, 'The Change Makers, Vision & Communication', booklet to accompany integrated audio and video tape training programme by Sir John Harvey-Jones. Available from Video Arts, 1991.

Coulson-Thomas, C. and Wakelam, A., 'Developing Directors'. A survey, funded by the Training Agency, undertaken by Adaptation Ltd with the Centre for

Management Studies, University of Exeter, 1990.

Coulson-Thomas, C. and Wakelam, A., 'The Effective Board, Current Practice, Myths and Realities', an IOD discussion document, 1991.

Crystal, G., 'Do directors earn their keep?', *Fortune International*, May 1991: 56–8.

Crystal, G., *In Search of Excess, the Overcompensation of American Executives*, Norton, 1992.

Davies, A., *Strategic Leadership: Making Corporate Plans Work*, Woodhead-Faulkner, 1991.

Demb, A. and Neubauer, F.-F., 'How Can the Board Add Value?', *European Management Journal*, Vol. 8, No. 2, 1990: 156–60.

Demb, A. and Neubauer, F.-F., 'Subsidiary Company Boards Reconsidered', *European Management Journal*, Vol. 8, No. 4, 1990: 480–7.

Demb, A. and Neubauer, F.-F., 'The boards mandate mediating corporate lifespace', *European Management Journal*, Vol. 7, No. 3, 1989: 273–82.

Demb, A. and Neubauer, F.-F., *The Corporate Board: Confronting the Paradoxes*, Oxford University Press, 1992.

Department of Trade and Industry, *Companies in 1990-91*, HMSO, October 1991.

Dobrzynski, J. H. *et al*, 'Taking Charge', *International Business Week*, 3 July 1989: 36–43.

Drucker, P. F., *The Age of Discontinuity*, Heinemann, 1989.

Drucker, P. F., 'The bored board', in *Towards The Next Economics and Other Essays*, Heinemann, 1981.

Drucker, P. F., *Management: Tasks, Responsibilities, Practices*, Heinemann, 1974.

Drucker, P. F., *The New Realities*, Heinemann, 1989.

Dyer, W. G., *Team Building, Alternatives and Issues*, Addison-Wesley, 1977.

Elliot, J., *Training Needs and Corporate Strategy*, IMS Report No. 164, Institute of Manpower Studies, 1989.

Farmer, A. F., 'Accountability and the board of directors', *Chartered Institute of Building Society Journal*, May 1983: 52 and 53.

Fearnley, H., 'Window dressing or watchdogs', *Financial Weekly*, No. 536, 10 August 1989: 16–18.

Federation of Small Businesses, 'The Penalties of Being in Business', December 1990.

Garratt, B., *Creating a Learning Organisation: a Guide to Leadership, Learning and Development*, Director Books, 1990.

Goold, M. and Campbell, A., 'Non-executive director's role in strategy', *Long Range Planning*, Vol. 23, No. 6, 1990: 118–19.

Gordon, R. A., *Business Leadership in the Large Corporation*, Brookings Institution, 1945.

Greanias, G. C. and Windsor, D., *The Changing Boardroom*, Gulf, 1982.

Gupta, L. C., *Corporate Boards and Nominee Directors*, Oxford University Press, 1989.

Hambrick, D. C., 'The Top Management Team: Key to Strategic Success', *California Management Review*, Vol. 30, 1987: 88–108.

Hambrick, D. and Mason, P., 'Upper Echelons: The Organisation as a Reflection of Its Top Management', *Academy of Management Review* 1984, Vol. 9, No. 2: 193–206.

Handy, C., *The Age of Unreason*, Business Books, 1989.

Harper, J., 'Developing Competent Directors', paper presented at Institute of Personnel Management Annual Conference, Harrogate 1991.

Harvey-Jones, Sir J., *Making it Happen*, Collins, 1988, and 2nd edn, Fontana, 1989.

Heidrick & Struggles Inc, *The Changing Board*, Heidrick & Struggles, 1987.

Heller, R., *The New Naked Manager*, Weidenfeld & Nicolson, 1985.

Henke, J. W., 'Involving the Board of Directors in Strategic Planning', *Journal of Business Strategy*, Vol. 7, No. 2: 87–95.

Hills, R. M., 'Ethical Perspectives on Business and Society', in Yerachmiel Kugel and Gladys W. Gruenberg, *Ethical Perspectives on Business and Society*, Lexington Books, 1977.

Holton, V. and Rabbetts, J., 'Powder in the Boardroom', Report of a Survey of Women on the Boards of Top UK Companies, Ashridge Research Group, Ashridge Management College, 1989.

Horovitz, J. H., 'Strategic Control: a New Task for Top Management', *International Studies of Management and Organisation*, Vol. III, No. 4, 1979: 96–112.

Howe, E. and McRae, S., *Women on the board*, Policy Studies Institute, 1991.

Houlden, B., *Understanding Company Strategy, an Introduction to Thinking and Acting Strategically*, Blackwell, 1991.

Houston, W. and Lewis, N., *The Independent Director: Handbook and guide to corporate governance*, Butterworth Heinemann, 1992.

Iacocca, L., *Iacocca, an Autobiography*, Sidgwick & Jackson, 1988.

Institutional Shareholders Committee (ISC), *The Role and Duties of Directors, a Statement of Best Practice*, ISC, 18 April 1991.

Institute of Chartered Secretaries and Administrators, *Good Boardroom Practice: a Code for Directors & Company Secretaries*, The Institute of Chartered Secretaries and Administrators, February 1991.

Institute of Directors, 'Guidelines to Boardroom Practice, Companies in Financial Difficulties', *Direct Line*, No. 94, January 1991.

Institute of Directors, *Guidelines for Directors*, Director Publications, 4th edition, May 1991.

Institute of Directors, *Women's Participation in the Workforce*, Director Publications, 1992.

Jacobson, G. and Hillkirk, J., *Xerox, American Samurai: the behind-the-scenes story of how a corporate giant beat the Japanese at their own game*, Macmillan, 1986.

Janis, I. L., *Victims of Groupthink*, Houghton-Mifflin, 1972.

Jenkins, B., 'Companies in need of a code', *Boardroom Agenda*, No. 1, February 1992: 18–19.

Jervis, R., *Perception and Misperception in International Politics*, Princeton University Press, 1976.

Johnson, C., *Revolutionary Change*, Little, Brown and Company, 1966.

Kakabadse, A., *The Wealth Creators: Top People, Top Teams & Executive Best Practice*, Kogan Page, 1991.

Kanter, R. M., *When Giants Learn to Dance*, Simon & Schuster, 1989.

Kaye, D., *Gamechange: the impact of information technology on corporate strategies and structures, a boardroom agenda*, Heinemann Professional, 1989.

Kelly, J., 'Baptism of apathy', *Infomatics*, March 1989: 55, 56, 58, 60.

Kenward, M., 'Should the boffins come on board?', *Director*, July 1991: 56–9.

Kester, C. W., *Japanese Takeover: the global contest for corporate control*, Harvard Business School Press, 1991.

Kilmann, R. and Covey, T. J. (eds), *Corporate Transformation*, Jossey-Bass, 1988.

Koontz, H, *The Board of Directors and Effective Management*, McGraw-Hill, 1967.

Korn/Ferry, 'Boards of Directors Study UK', Korn/Ferry International, 1989–92.

Lawrence, P. R. and Dyer, D., *Renewing American Industry*, The Free Press, 1983.

Lawrence, P. R. and Lorsch, J. W., *Organisation and Environment*, Richard D. Irwin, 1967.

Lindon-Travers, K., *Non-executive Directors: a guide to their Role, Responsibilities and Appointment*, Director Books, 1990.

Lorsch, J. and MacIver, E., *Pawns or Potentates: the Reality of America's Corporate Boards*, Harvard Business School Press, 1989.

Loose, P. and Yelland, J., *Company Director: His Functions, Powers and Duties*, 6th edn, Jordans, 1987.

Mace, M. L., 'Directors: Myth and Reality', Division of Research, Harvard Graduate School of Business Administration, 1971.

McDougal, W. J., 'Corporate Boards in Canada', Research report, University of Western Ontario, 1968.

McDougal, W. J. (ed.), *The Effective Director*, University of Western Ontario, 1969.

Mills, G., *On the Board*, Gower/Institute of Directors, 1981.

Mills, G., 'Who Controls the Board?', *Long Range Planning*, Vol. 22, No. 3, 1989: 125–32.

Mintzberg, H., *Mintzberg on Management*, The Free Press, 1989.

Mintzberg, H., *The Nature of Managerial Work*, Harper & Row, 1973 and 1980.

Monks Partnership, 'Disclosing Board Earnings in Company Annual Reports', Monks Partnership, 1992.

Monks, R. and Minow, N., *Power and Responsibility*, Harper Business Books, 1991.

MORI, 'Shareholder Value Analysis Survey', Coopers & Lybrand Deloitte, 1991.

Mueller, R. K., *The Incomplete Board*, Lexington, 1981.

Mueller, R. K., *Directors and Officers Guide to Advisory Boards*, Quorum Books, 1990.

Mumford, A., Honey, P. and Robinson, G., *Director's Development Guidebook – Making Experience Count*, Institute of Directors and Department of Employment, September 1990.

Mumford, A., Robinson, G. and Stradling, D., *Developing Directors: the Learning Process*, Manpower Services Commission, 1987.

Norburn, D. and Schurz, F., 'The British Boardroom: Time for a Revolution?', in B. Taylor, *Strategic Planning, the Chief Executive and the Board*, Pergamon Press, 1988: 43–51.

Ohmae, K., *The Mind of the Strategist*, McGraw-Hill, 1982.

Pascale, R. T., *Managing On the Edge*, Simon & Schuster, 1990.

Pearce, J. and Zahra, S., 'The relative power of CEOs and boards of directors associations with corporate performance', *Strategic Management Journal*, Vol. 12, No. 2, February 1991.

Peters, T., 'Thriving on Chaos', Alfred A. Knopf, 1987.

Pettigrew, A. M. and Whipp, R., *Managing Change for Competitive Success*, Blackwell, 1991.

Pitt, W., 'How many routes to the top?', *Director*, June 1991: 45–50.

Popper, K., *The Poverty of Historicism*, Routledge & Kegan Paul, 2nd edition, 1960.

Porter, M. E., *Competitive Strategy: Techniques for Analysing Industries and Competitors*, The Free Press, 1980.

Porter, M. E., *Competitive Advantage*, The Free Press, 1985.

Prahalad, C. K., 'Developing Strategic Capability: An Agenda for Top Management', *Human Resource Management*, Fall 1983, **22**, (3): 237–54.

PRO NED, 'Research into the role of the non-executive director', PRO NED, July 1992.

Redwood, J., 'Corporate Governance', Department of Trade and Industry Press Notice P/90/722, 7 December 1990.

Revans, R. W., *Action Learning*, Blond & Briggs, 1979.

Rock, S. (ed.), *Family Firms*, Director Books, 1991.

Ryan, C. L., *Company Directors: Liabilities, rights and duties*, 3rd edn, CCH Editions, 1990.

Sadler, P., *Designing Organisations: The foundation for excellence*, Mercury Books, 1991.

Sadler, P., 'On shaping the balance of power', *Director*, March 1992: 25.

Sadler, P., 'The painful path to competence', *Director*, September 1991: 23.

Schein, E. H., *Organisational Culture and Leadership*, Jossey-Bass, 1985.

Schonberger, R. J., *Building a Chain of Customers*, The Free Press & Business Books, 1990.

Schmidheiny, S. and the Business Council for Sustainable Development, *Changing Course*, MIT Press, 1992.

Senge, P., *The Fifth Discipline: the Art and Practice of the Learning Organisation*, Doubleday/Currency, 1990.

Slatter, S., *Corporate Recovery, Successful Turnaround Strategies and their Implementation*, Penguin Books, 1984 & 1987.

Steiner, G. A. and Kunin, H. and E., 'The New Class of Chief Executive Officer', in B. Taylor (ed.), *Strategic Planning, the Chief Executive and the Board*, Pergamon Press, 1988.

Sullivan, T. and Bottomley, P., *Boards of Directors Study UK*, Korn/Ferry International, 1991.

Syrett, M. and Hogg, C., *Frontiers of Leadership*, Blackwell, 1992.

Taylor, B. (ed.), *Strategic Planning, the Chief Executive and the Board*, Pergamon Press, 1988.

Taylor, B. and Tricker, R. I., (eds), *The Director's Manual*, Director Books, 1990.

Tricker, R. I., *Corporate Governance: practices, procedures and powers in British companies and their Boards of Directors*, Gower, 1984.

Tricker, R. I., 'Should the chairman also be the CEO?', *Accountancy*, 99, February 1987: 109–10.

Tricker, R. I., *The Independent Director, a study of the non-executive director and of the audit committee*, Tolley Publishing Company, 1978.

Tushman, M., Newman, W. and Nadler, D., 'Executive Leadership and Organisational Evolution, Managing Incremental and Discontinuous Change', in R. Kilmann and T. J. Covey (eds), *Corporate Transformation*, Jossey-Bass, 1988: 102–30.

Vance, S. C., *Board of Directors: Structure and performance*, University of Oregon Press, 1964.

Vancil, R., *Passing the Baton: Managing the Process of CEO succession*, Harvard Business School Press, 1987.

Van Ham, K. and Williams, R., 'The quest for quality at Philips', in B. Taylor (ed.), *Strategic Planning, the Chief Executive and the Board*, Pergamon Press, 1988: 93–8.

Van Sinderen, A. W., 'The Board Looks at Itself', *Directors & Boards*, Winter 1985: 20–3.

Wakelam, A., 'The Training & Development of Company Directors', Report for the Training Agency, Centre for Management Studies, University of Exeter, October, 1989.

Waterman, R. H., *The Renewal Factor*, Bantam Books, 1987.

Webley, S., *Business Ethics and Company Codes*, Institute of Business Ethics, 1992.

Weisbach, M. S., 'Outside directors and CEO turnover', *Journal of Financial Economics*, Vol. 20, 1988: 431–60.

Whiteley, R. C., *The Customer-Driven Company: Moving from talk to action*, Business Books, 1991.

Woolfe, R., *The Role of Information Technology in Transforming the Business*, Butler Cox Foundation, 1991.

Wright, D., *Rights & Duties of Directors*, Butterworths, 1991.

Zahra, S. A., 'Increasing the Board's Involvement in Strategy', *Long Range Planning*, Vol. 23, No. 6, 1990: 109–17.

Zahra, S. A. and Pearce, J. A., 'Determinants of Board Directors' Strategic Involvement', *European Management Journal*, Vol. 8, No. 2, 1990: 164–73.

Index

induction programme, 207
motivated teamwork training, 240–
    241
opportunities for teamwork, 229–230
Thompson, D., 11, 222
Training, 286
Tricker, R., 35, 44, 143

Unitary board, relationships between
    executive and non-executive

directors, 226

Values, 45–46, 80–81, 124–125, 231,
    282
Vision, 230, 241–245, 282

Wakelam, Alan, 54, 60, 92, 93, 96, 97,
    107, 167, 194, 195, 200, 258
Winding-up, 51
Wolfson, Sir Brian, 86